C Programming in the MVS Environment

C Programming in the MVS Environment

V. Mitra Gopaul
and
Walter Falby

VNR VAN NOSTRAND REINHOLD
New York

Copyright © 1992 by Van Nostrand Reinhold

Library of Congress Catalog Card Number 91-45495
ISBN 0-442-00628-4

All rights reserved. No part of this work covered by the copyright hereon may be reproduced or used in any form or by any means—graphic, electronic, or mechanical, including photocopying, recording, taping, or information storage and retrieval systems—without written permission of the publisher.

Manufactured in the United States of America

Published by Van Nostrand Reinhold
115 Fifth Avenue
New York, New York 10003

Chapman and Hall
2–6 Boundary Row
London, SE 1 8HN

Thomas Nelson Australia
102 Dodds Street
South Melbourne 3205
Victoria, Australia

Nelson Canada
1120 Birchmount Road
Scarborough, Ontario M1K 5G4, Canada

Library of Congress Cataloging-in-Publication Data

Gopaul, V. Mitra
  C programming in the MVS environment / by V. Mitra Gopaul and Walter Falby.
    p.   cm.
  ISBN 0-442-00628-4
  1. C (Computer program language) 2. MVS (Computer file)
  I. Falby, Walter F. II. Title.
  QA76.73.C15G665 1992
  005.2'22—dc20   91-45495
                                                           CIP

To my uncle, Vinod Gungah, who helped and encouraged me when it was really needed. I will always remember the brief but quality time we spent while on this physical plane before he moved on to the spiritual world.

V.M.G.

Laura
    My partner in life, in everything

W.F.

Trademark

IBM, OS/2, and OS/400 are registered trademarks of IBM Corporation.
MVS/XA, MVS/ESA, MVS/DFP, CICS/ESA, IMS/ESA, DATABASE 2, System Application Architecture, SAA, GDDM, DB2, and PC-DOS are trademarks of IBM Corporation.
UNIX is a registered trademark of AT&T.
VAX is trademark of Digital Equipment Corporation.
SAS/C is a registered trademark of SAS Institute Inc.

Disclaimer

The authors and publishers of this book shall not be liable for any loss or damage caused or alleged to be caused by relying on the information and programs contained in this book.

Contents

Preface xix

Introducing C 1
WHY C? 1
SAA 3
ENVIRONMENTAL ISSUES 3

Chapter 1 **Getting Started** 5
1.1 PROGRAM ORGANIZATION 5
1.2 ELEMENTS OF C 6
   1.2.1 Characters and Tokens 6
   1.2.2 Trigraphs 7
   1.2.3 Escape Sequences 7
   1.2.4 Comments 8
   1.2.5 Identifiers 9
   1.2.6 Language Keywords 9
   1.2.7 Constants 10
     Integer 10
     Floating-point 11
     Character 11
     String 11
     Enumeration 11
1.3 PREPARING A C PROGRAM 11
1.4 COMPILE, LINK-EDIT, AND EXECUTE A PROGRAM 14
   1.4.1 Batch 14
   1.4.2 Interactive 16
1.5 TESTING AND DEBUGGING 16

Chapter 2 Data Declarations 17

    2.1 DATA TYPES 18
        2.1.1 Characters 19
        2.1.2 Floating-Point Variables 21
        2.1.3 Integers 21
        2.1.4 Void Type 23
        2.1.5 Arrays 23
        2.1.6 Enumerations 28
        2.1.7 Pointers 29
        2.1.8 Structures 30
        2.1.9 Unions 33
        2.1.10 Typedef-name 35
    2.2 STORAGE SPECIFIER 37
        2.2.1 Class-Specifier `auto` 37
        2.2.2 Class-Specifier `static` 37
        2.2.3 Class-Specifier `extern` 39
        2.2.4 Class-Specifier `register` 41
    2.3 DECLARATORS 42
    2.4 INITIALIZERS 43

Chapter 3 Expressions and Operators 44

    3.1 PRECEDENCE AND ASSOCIATIVITY 45
    3.2 LVALUE EXPRESSION 46
    3.3 CONSTANT EXPRESSION 46
    3.4 PRIMARY EXPRESSION 48
        3.4.1 Parenthesized Expression ( ) 48
        3.4.2 Function Call ( ) 48
        3.4.3 Array Element Specification [ ] 49
        3.4.4 Structure and Union Specifications (. or ->) 49
    3.5 UNARY OPERATORS 49
        3.5.1 Increment ++ 50
        3.5.2 Decrement — 51
        3.5.3 Unary Plus + 51
        3.5.4 Unary Minus - 51
        3.5.5 Logical Negation ! 52
        3.5.6 Bitwise Negation ~ 52
        3.5.7 Address & 53
        3.5.8 Indirection * 53
        3.5.9 Cast 53
        3.5.10 sizeof 53
    3.6 BINARY OPERATORS 54
        3.6.1 Multiplication * 54
        3.6.2 Division / 55
        3.6.3 Remainder % 55
        3.6.4 Addition + 55

3.6.5 Subtraction - 56
3.6.6 Bitwise Left and Right Shift << >> 56
3.6.7 Relational < > <= >= 57
3.6.8 Equality = = != 57
3.6.9 Bitwise AND & 57
3.6.10 Bitwise Exclusive OR ¬ 58
3.6.11 Bitwise Inclusive OR | 58
3.6.12 Logical AND && 59
3.6.13 Logical OR || 59
3.7 CONDITIONAL OPERATOR ?: 59
3.8 ASSIGNMENT OPERATOR = 60
3.8.1 Simple Assignment 61
3.8.2 Compound Assignment 61
3.9 COMMA OPERATOR , 62
3.10 CONVERSIONS 62
3.10.1 Arithmetic Conversions 63
3.10.2 Type Conversions 63
3.10.3 Function Conversions 63
3.10.4 Assignment Conversions 63

Chapter 4 **Control Flow 64**

4.1 LABEL 65
4.2 IF STATEMENT 65
4.2.1 Nested if 67
4.2.2 If-else-if Ladder 68
4.3 SWITCH STATEMENT 69
4.4. FOR STATEMENT 72
4.5 WHILE STATEMENT 75
4.6 DO/WHILE STATEMENT 76
4.7 BREAK STATEMENT 77
4.8. CONTINUE 78
4.9 GOTO STATEMENT 79

Chapter 5 **Why Function? 81**

5.1 main( ) 81
5.2 FUNCTION DEFINITION 83
5.3 FUNCTION PROTOTYPE 88
5.4 CALLING FUNCTIONS AND PASSING VALUES 89
5.5 RETURN STATEMENT 91
5.6 RECURSION 92

Chapter 6 **Input and Output 94**

6.1 STREAMS AND FILES 95
6.1.1 Streams 95
6.1.1.1 Text Stream 95

6.1.1.2 ASA files   96
6.1.1.3 Binary Stream   96
6.1.2 Files   96
6.2 FILE ACCESS FUNCTIONS   97
6.2.1 Open File   97
6.2.2 Close File   101
6.2.3 Read and Write File   102
6.2.4 Memory File   103
6.3 OPERATIONS ON FILE   104
6.3.1 Delete a File   104
6.3.2 Rename a File   105
6.3.3 Temporary File   105
6.4 FORMATTED INPUT AND OUTPUT   105
6.4.1 Standard I/O Streams   105
6.4.2 File I/O   106
6.5 UNFORMATTED INPUT AND OUTPUT   108

Chapter 7   Pointers   110

7.1 DYNAMIC MEMORY ALLOCATION   111
7.1.1 Functions   111
void *calloc (size_t n, size_t size);   111
void *malloc(size_t size);   111
void *realloc(void *ptr, size_t size);   111
void free(void* ptr);   112
7.1.2 Heap Storage   112
7.1.3 Memory File   112
main( )   113
MFILE *mf_ist(int row, int col)   113
int mf_rls(MFILE *mfptr)   113
int mf_read(MFILE *mfptr, char *fptr)   114
UCHAR *mf_getrp(MFILE *mfptr, row)   114
7.2 POINTER ARITHMETIC   118
7.2.1 Increment and Addition   118
7.2.2 Decrement and Subtraction   120
7.2.3 Comparison and Assignment   122
7.3 POINTERS AND FUNCTIONS   123
7.3.1 Pointers as Function Arguments   123
7.3.2 Function Returning Pointers   124
7.3.3 Pointer to a Function   125
7.4 POINTER AND STRING   127
7.5 ARRAYS OF POINTERS   128

Chapter 8   Preprocessor Directives   130

8.1 #include   130
8.2 #define AND #undef   133

8.3 MACROS   134
    8.3.1 Predifined Macros   135
    8.3.2 Macros in ctype.h   136
8.4 CONDITIONAL COMPILATION   136
    8.4.1 #if, #else, and #endif   137
    8.4.2 #elif   139
    8.4.3 #ifdef   140
    8.4.4 #ifndef   140
8.5 #PRAGMA   141
8.6 NULL DIRECTIVE   141
8.7 #OPERATOR   141
8.8 ##OPERATOR   142
8.9 LINE CONTROL   142
8.10 #ERROR   143

Chapter 9   Pitfalls in C Programming   144

9.1 HAZARDS OF USING POINTERS   144
    9.1.1 Uninitialized Pointer   144
    9.1.2 Pointer and Array   146
    9.1.3 Pointer and String   146
9.2 ARRAY INDEXING   147
9.3 STRING AND CHARACTERS   147
9.4 PASSING ADDRESS   148
9.5 CASE SENSITIVE   148
9.6 = is not = =   149
9.7 & and | not && or || 150
9.8 WHAT HAPPENED TO ELSE?   150
9.9 ADDRESSING MODE   152

Chapter 10   Compilers and Compiling   153

10.1 THE COMPILERS   153
    10.1.1 Run-time Libraries   154
    10.1.2 Waterloo C by WATCOM Products Inc.   154
    10.1.3 C/370 by IBM Corp.   155
    10.1.4. C for System/370 by Whitesmiths, Ltd.   156
    10.1.5 SAS/C by SAS Institute Inc.   156
10.2 COMPILING   158
    10.2.1 Compiling under TSO   158
    10.2.2 Compiling with JCL   159

Chapter 11   Preparing Your Programs for Execution   160

11.1 LINKAGE EDITOR   160
11.2 LINKING   161
    11.2.1 Linking under TSO   161
    11.2.2 Linking with JCL   162

EXEC statement   163
SYSPRINT DD statement   163
SYSLMOD DD statement   163
SYSUT1 DD statement   163
SYSLIN DD statement   163
11.3 PROGRAM ATTRIBUTES   164
11.3.1 Addressing and Residency Modes   164
11.3.2 Not Editable Attribute   165
11.3.3 Reusability Attribute   165
11.3.3.1 Reenterable Attribute   165
11.3.3.2 Serially Reusable Attribute   165
11.4 AUTOMATIC MODULE REPLACEMENT   165

Chapter 12 Executing Your Programs   1

12.1 RUN-TIME OPTIONS   1
HEAP(size,increment,location,status)   1
ISAINC(size)   168
ISASIZE(size)   168
REPORT   168
SPIE   168
STAE   168
12.4.1 *freopen* Function   169
12.4.2 Redirection Symbols   170
12.4.3 Data Definition (DD) Name Association   170
12.5.1 *signal* Function   171
12.5.2 *raise* Function   172
12.5.3 Examples   172

Chapter 13 MVS Files   173

13.1 NON-VSAM FILES   173
13.1.1 Record Formats   174
13.1.1.1 Fixed-Length Records   174
13.1.1.2 Variable-Length Records   174
13.1.1.3 Undefined Records   174
13.2 VSAM FILES   174
13.2.1 KSDS   175
13.2.2 ESDS   175
13.2.3 RRDS   175
13.2.4 Alternate Index   175
13.2.5 Selecting a File Type   176
13.3 VSAM FILE FUNCTIONS   176
13.3.1 File Access   176
13.3.1.1 Access Mode   176
13.3.1.2 Access Direction   177
13.3.1.3 Record Format   177

13.3.1.4 OPEN Example   177
13.3.2 File Positioning   177
13.3.3 Direct I/O   178
13.4 FILE CREATION   179
  13.4.1 Non-VSAM File Creation   179
    13.4.1.1 Batch File Creation   179
    13.4.1.2 TSO File Creation   180
  13.4.2 VSAM File Creation   180
    13.4.2.1 Using AMS Commands   180
    13.4.2.2 Using JCL   181
13.5 FILE ALLOCATION   182
  13.5.1 JCL File Allocation   182
  13.5.2 Dynamic Allocation   182
  13.5.3. TSO ALLOCATE Command   183
13.6 EXAMPLES   183
  13.6.1 Fixed-Length File   183
  13.6.2 Variable-Length File   185
  13.6.3 VSAM File Processing   186

Chapter 14 Interlanguage Communication   191

14.1 EXCHANGING DATA   191
14.2 THE *linkage* PRAGMA   192
14.3 C AND 370 ASSEMBLER   192
  14.3.1 Registers at Routine Entry   192
  14.3.2 Registers at Routine Exit   193
  14.3.3 Managing the C Environment   193
  14.3.4 Compatible Data Types   193
  14.3.5 Examples   193
  14.3.6 Special Considerations and Limitations   196
14.4 C AND COBOL   196
  14.4.1 Creating the COBOL Environment   196
  14.4.2 Compatible Data Types   197
  14.4.3 COBOL to C   197
  14.5.1 Creating the PL/I Environment   200
  14.5.2 Compatible Data Types   200
  14.5.3 Special Considerations and Limitations   200
14.6 C and FORTRAN   200
  14.6.1 Creating the FORTRAN Environment   201
  14.6.2 Compatible Data Types   201
  14.6.3 Special Considerations and Limitations   202

Chapter 15 Advanced Programming Techniques   203

15.1 REENTRANCY   203
15.2 MULTITASKING   205
  15.2.1 Storage Allocation   206

15.2.2 Input/Output 207
15.2.3 Passing Data 207
15.2.4 Exceptional Condition Handling 207
15.2.5 Redirecting Standard Streams 207
15.2.6 Subtask Load Module 208
15.2.7 Special Considerations and Limitations 208
15.2.8 MTF Functions 209
  15.2.8.1 Task Attach 209
  15.2.8.2 Task Scheduling 209
  15.2.8.3 Task Synchronization 210
  15.2.8.4 Task Detach 210
15.2.9 Example 210
15.3 DYNAMIC FILE ALLOCATION 213
15.3.1 Allocate/Acquire a File 214
15.3.2 Unallocate/Release a File 214
15.3.3 Concatenation 214
15.3.4 Deconcatenation 215
15.3.5 File Information Retrieval 215
15.3.6 Example 215

Chapter 16 C and Database and Data Communication Products 218

16.1 C AND CICS 218
  16.1.1 EXED CICS ADDRESS Command 219
  16.1.2 Exception Handling 219
  16.1.3 Storage Management 220
  16.1.4 File Access 220
  16.1.5 Unavailable C Functions 221
  16.1.6 Program Termination 221
  16.1.7 Preparing C Programs for CICS Execution 222
  16.1.8 Run-time Options 222
  16.1.9 Accessing CICS Resources and Facilities 222
  16.1.10 Special Considerations and Limitations 223
16.2 C AND IMS 223
  16.2.1 Accessing IMS Facilities 223
  16.2.2 Extended Addressing 224
  16.2.3 Exception Handling 224
  16.2.4 Program Termination 225
  16.2.5 Run-time Options 225
  16.2.6 Special Considerations and Limitations 225
16.3 C AND DATABASE 2 226
  16.3.1 DB2 Access 226
  16.3.2 Preparing C Programs to Access DB2 226

Chapter 17 Full-Screen Application Development 227

17.1 IBM PRODUCTS 228

            17.1.1 Customer Information Control System (CICS)   228
            17.1.2 Information Management System (IMS)   230
            17.1.3 Graphical Data Display Manager (GDDM)   234
            17.1.4 Interactive System Productivity Facility (ISPF)   234
        17.2 FULL-SCREEN APPLICATIONS USING
            WATERLOO C   237
        17.3 FULL-SCREEN APPLICATIONS USING SAS/C   239

Chapter 18   Databases   240

   18.1 IMS/DB   240
       18.1.1 Database Types   242
       18.1.2 Accessing an IMS Database   242
   18.2 DATABASE 2   243
       18.2.1 Accessing DB2   243
       18.2.2 Example   243

Chapter 19   Library Function Summary   246

   19.2 CHARACTER HANDLING   #include <ctype.h>   247
   19.3 ERRORS   #include <errno.h>   248
   19.4 FLOATING-POINT LIMITS   #include <float.h>   248
   19.5 INTEGER LIMITS   #include <limits.h>   248
   19.6 LOCALIZATION   #include <locale.h>   249
   19.7 MATHEMATICS   #include <math.h>   249
   19.8 NONLOCAL JUMP   #include <setjmp.h>   251
   19.9 SIGNAL HANDLING   #include <signal.h>   251
   19.10 VARIABLE ARGUMENTS   #include <stdarg.h>   252
   19.11 COMMON DEFINITIONS   #include <stddef.h>   252
   19.12 INPUT/OUTPUT   #include <stdio.h>   252
   19.13 GENERAL UTILITIES   #include <stdlib.h>   254
   19.14 STRING AND MEMORY   #include <string.h>   256
   19.15 TIME AND DATE   #include <time.h>   257

Chapter 20   Run-time Library Functions   259

Glossary   309

Bibliography   315

Index   319

Preface

C Programming in the MVS Environment explores the benefits of using a powerful and elegant language in a unique environment. Keeping in mind the difficulty in learning a language like C and the complexity of MVS, we have delved into all the key areas to make this book useful in many programming situations. There is no doubt that productive programming requires a sound understanding of the language you use and its possible interfaces to the operating system, as well as of software products. In this book we cover all the linkages with step-by-step descriptions, enhanced by complete and useful programs.

ABOUT THIS BOOK

Our goals in writing this book are to provide a description of the C language and tell how it fits into the MVS environment for two distinct groups of computer professionals. One group is made up of programmers who already know C, but are unfamiliar with the MVS operating system. The other is composed of programmers who are comfortable navigating within MVS, but have little or no experience with C.

To get the most from this book you must have certain skills and knowledge. If you are comfortable using C, you are ready for the discussion on C in the MVS environment. You will learn many different ways to use the language system and application software development. You will learn about program execution, file access, interlanguage communications, and how to program in C to access a variety of commonly used software products that run under MVS. But, if you are not proficient in C, we also provide a comprehensive discussion of the C language, which will prepare you for software development specific to the operating system.

If you have used other languages, such as COBOL, PL/I, and assembly language, to develop applications for MVS, the chapters on interlanguage communication and advanced programming techniques will be of particular interest to you.

HOW THIS BOOK IS ORGANIZED

This book consists of three parts, a glossary of terms, and a bibliography. Part I describes the C language. In chapter 0 we introduce the C language, for those of you who are not familiar with it. Very briefly, it is an appreciation of the language. In Chapter 1 you will begin programming in MVS environment, after learning a few essential aspects, such as program organization and elements of C. Chapter 2 is very important; it shows you how data is declared, named, and manipulated. In chapter 3 you will learn how expressions with C operators are evaluated. Chapter 4 will show you the control-flow—the heart of the language—and how it is used in many situations. In chapter 5 we discuss functions, the building blocks of C programs. In chapter 6 you will learn the unique concept of I/O and how it works in the MVS operating system. In chapter 7 you will acquire a sound understanding of pointers, which can add flexibility and power to programming and is essential for avoiding disastrous programming errors. Chapter 8 describes the preprocessor directives. Chapter 9 makes you aware some of the traps and pitfalls that programmers fall into.

In Part II we describe how C fits into the MVS environment. Chapter 10 discusses a number of different compilers and shows you how to compile a C program, using IBM C/370 (version 1.2) compiler. Chapters 11 and 12 describe how to create an executable version of your program, as well as how to run it. Also, in Chapter 12, we discuss redirecting standard streams and error handling. In Chapter 13 we look at files and how to access them. Chapter 14 describes how to use C in combination with a number of commonly used programming languages in the MVS environment. Chapter 15 describes programming techniques that previously have been available only to 370 assembly language programmers. The remaining chapters delve into the C interface, which is available in a number of MVS software products, such as Customer Information Control System (CICS), Information Management System (IMS), and interactive SPF. Also, we describe how to develop full screen applications and access databases.

Part III is a reference section for all library functions defined according to the ANSI standard. Chapter 19 is a quick reference. Chapter 20 discusses in detail all the functions in alphabetical order.

The glossary provides definitions for acronyms and terms that are used in this book. The bibliography lists the many manuscripts and texts that we referenced during our research.

Acknowledgement

We are very grateful to Dianne Littwin and the staff at VNR for giving us the opportunity to work together to produce this book and for their efforts to make it valuable.

Many thanks to Mel Goldberg, Shanaz Mangru, and Ken Deering for their constructive comments, ideas, and suggestions. Our appreciation goes to Susan Reid and Colin Pryce for their eagerness to help us find material during the research of this book.

Finally, we are deeply grateful to our families (Mitra's wife Gaye, daughter Laila, and son Sanjiv, and Walter's wife Laura and daughter Jordan) for their unfailing support and encouragement throughout this project; also for their understanding when we took time away from them.

C Programming in the
MVS Environment

Introduction

Introducing C

WHY C?

C was developed in Bell Laboratories in 1972 as a general-purpose programming language, and it was first used for the UNIX operating system. Since then it has gained acceptance in a wide variety of systems, including MVS, VM/CMS, PC-DOS, OS/2, and VAX/VMS, as both a system and application language.

In the late 1980s, C developed into a mature, viable, and useful language. The American National Standards Institution (ANSI) adopted C and formulated its standard like other widely used languages, such as COBOL and Fortran. The ANSI C standard was published in December 1989 in the document # X3J11/88-090. This gave the industry (software vendors and developers) a framework to produce and use standard C compilers.

Under ANSI, the language has been extended and clarified. However, there are many applications available that have been written with compilers that don't have the ANSI C enhancements and its rigidity of standards. These programs are called "traditional C." Many compilers do tolerate the old ways unless it is in conflict with the new. In this book we follow the ANSI C standards.

As a programming tool, C offers numerous benefits: efficiency, versatility, maintainability, modularity, and portability.

Efficiency. Generally, C programs are more efficient than other high-level languages, such as COBOL Fortran, and PL/I. A good optimizer, that comes with the compiler, can go even further to produce tighter code; in some cases the efficiency is the same as or closer to assembler programs.

Versatility. C language is considered to be one level higher than assembler and just below COBOL, Fortran, and PL/I. With C, it is quite easy to do any kind of programming: system, communication, and application. For example, you can easily interface with existing programs written in any language, thus tying many languages together. With the same flexibility you can access any database: IMS, DB2, or Oracle. With C programs you can interface to software such as CICS, GDDM, ISPF, TCP/IP, and VTAM.

Maintainability. As a high-level language, C is easier to maintain than assembler. The modular approach to software development makes changes and enhancements much easier tasks to accomplish.

Modularity. Although the C language itself has a powerful data declaration method, flexible data operators, and modern control flow, it still allows you to "add" instructions by using functions. In other words, you can develop and maintain your own libraries for specific or general purposes.

Portability. C is different than most high-level languages in that it does not have verbs that are hardware dependent. Memory management and all I/O operations, such as files, keyboards, and displays, are done by C library functions. These functions work the same in any hardware or software environment. Therefore, it is relatively easy to move programs from one platform to another with little or no change. Also, the preprocessor allows conditional compilation for different target machines. Since portability is a viable option to consider in software development, a further discusion of the subject is done in the next section.

The concept of program portability has been around for many decades, although it is thought to have surfaced with C language. In the early 1960s, COBOL programs had been moved from one machine to another successfully.

Although programs written in many languages have been ported from one system to another, C seems to be the choice language for many reasons. Portability itself is a vast subject and in no way can we discuss it here. Obviously, in this section we will only touch upon some of the key issues, in case you have to port programs from MVS to another environment, or vice-versa.

Portability is the degree to which a program can be moved from one computer environment to another. In general terms, portability can have many different scenarios. Some of them are:

- Moving from one operating system to another (OS/2 to MVS, VM/CMS to MVS, or UNIX to MVS).
- Moving from one version of an operating system to another (MVS/XA to MVS/ESA).
- Moving to a higher version of the compiler.

Porting is not simply making a program work in a target machine. It also should use reasonable resources and CPU time. If a program is written with portability in mind and conforms to ANSI C, portability can be less complicated and more satisfying.

The main reason to consider portability is economics. The expenses of software development and maintainance far outweighs the cost of hardware. This reality makes portability a viable consideration. First, there is a huge economic incentive to lengthen the life of a software, going beyond many generations of hardware. Secondly, there are demands for successful products on one system to run on many other platforms, such as micro, mini, and mainframe computers. Finally, there is a strong desire in IS departments to develop software on a cheaper, more responsive PC environment for mainframe or mini computers.

The flexibility available in C language is often misleading. Its powerful instructions, which allow programmers to do anything, tend to frustrate many newcomers. C is a terse language that allows programmers to produce cryptic code that is unreadable and difficult to debug and maintain. Also, when you make mistakes, it is unforgiving, especially in the areas of memory addressing (pointers) and operator usage. One learns very quickly that productive C programming demands deciphine, a necessary skill for becoming a mature, experienced developer.

SAA

The Systems Application Architecture (SAA), introduced on March 17, 1987, is IBM's strategy to allow applications to be portable among its three platforms: OS/2, OS/400, and mainframe. SAA is not a product, but a set of guidelines, principles, and facilities that enable architects and developers of software to produce complex programs that can achieve a high level of interconnectivity and portability among the three IBM platforms. SAA is a concept encompassing many operating systems, languages, and products; therefore, it is beyond the scope of this book to describe its many aspects. Here, it suffices to say that the main thrust of SAA is to provide consistency and connectivity in the following areas of software developments:

- Common User Access (CUA).
- Common Programming Interface (CPI).
- Common Communications Support (CCP).
- Common Applications by making use of CUA, CPI, and CCP.

ENVIRONMENTAL ISSUES

In designing software with portability in mind, there are many issues to consider. The specifics of each task depends on the environment you are dealing with. The following describes some of the issues to keep in mind.

Operating systems. MVS is a multi-user and multi tasking system. It executes programs both in batch and online modes. Other systems may not have all these facilities. For example, PC-DOS is a single-user, single-task operating system, allowing both batch and online processing. OS/2 is a multi tasking system able to do tasks in batch and online. When transplanting programs, the impact of these environmental differences have to be appraised. Even small tasks, such as getting time and date, can be a major factor; the smallest slice of time can affect the logic of a program.

File access. As mentioned earlier, C language does not have verbs or statements for file I/O. C programmers rely on C library functions to manage data files. Although file operations such as open, close, write, and read behave functionally the same way in any system, there are a few environmental concerns that must not be overlooked.

In MVS, the common files used for data are sequential file, partitioned data set (PDS), and VSAM. The first two employ sequential access and are record based, while VSAM allows both sequential and random access methods. Although it is possible to dynamically allocate and deallocate files from a program, it is not a common practice.

In the PC and OS/2 environments, files are byte streams and are not record based. Their naming conventions are different than MVS. Also, they are dynamically created and allocated. Unlike MVS, they maintain a structure of file directory.

Database. In MVS environment, databases such as IMS and DB2 are accessed by functions that come with the compiler. These functions are not yet part of ANSI C; therefore, these databases are not available in other systems. In PC there are numerous databases used, each providing library functions to maintain the databases.

Processing speed. The speed at which your program is executed is definitely different from one system to another. The speed of executing in CRAY, ES/9000, and 80386 varies tremendously and, if part of the code depends on the speed of the CPU, you have a problem. Let's say you have an empty loop for n times, to calculate the lapse of 10 seconds. The "10-second" loop will vary from one system to another.

Data representation. The data representation is also an implementation dependent. The *sizeof(int)* in MVS is 4 bytes. The same expression will yield 2 in PC or OS/2 and 16 on an AS/400.

User interfaces. In MVS the common user interfaces facilities are CICS, GDDM, and ISPF dialog manager. Other systems do not have such facilities.

Other interfaces. A software may call for interfaces to equipment, such as printers, plotters, scanners, FAX, and modems. You have to consider how such devices are connected in both the host and target environments.

1

Getting Started

The best way to learn C or any other language is by writing programs. Running your program successfully is perhaps one of the first and basic hurdles you have to overcome. To make this initial, important experience as least frustrating as possible, this chapter is a tutorial on how to prepare, compile, and run a program.

This chapter is simple in essence. At this stage you don't want to be overwhelmed by details. It provides a framework for beginners and experienced programmers to develop their own programs. Of course, the rest of the book deals with C programming in the MVS environment in more detail. We assume that you are familiar with ISPF editor, TSO, CLIST, and batch mode of MVS.

Before starting, we will dwell on two essentials. One is the library—organization that tells where different C programs files are located. Secondly, we describe the elements of C language.

After this orientation of the language, we will show all the steps to:

- Prepare a program.
- Compile a program.
- Link-edit and execute a program.

We will give examples of how to accomplish the last two steps in both batch and interactive modes. All these steps will be done using IBM C/370 (version 1.2) compiler, ISPF, and MVS utilities.

1.1 PROGRAM ORGANIZATION

This section briefly describes different types of file libraries required during software development.

Source library. A source library is where you keep the source code of all the programs. Usually, it is a partitioned data set (PDS), each member containing part or whole program. In either case, it must have all the necessary parts, such as preprocessor directives, data declarations, and functions, to make a compilation step complete. As a user, you create and maintain the source library.

Object library. After a successful compilation is done, an object module is produced by the compiler. This module is used in the link-edit phase to create an executable program. The object module can be stored in a PDS member, sequential dataset, or temporary file. As a user, during the compilation step you specify the destination of the object module. The user creates and maintains this library.

Load library. The load library is a PDS, each member containing an executable program after it has been compiled and link-edited. You run a program from the load library. It is the user's responsibility to allocate and maintain this library.

Include library. An include file contains the part of a program that can be incorporated into one or more programs during compilation. There are two kinds of include files: system and user. A system include library has all the include files that come with the C compiler. It is placed in a special PDS that is accessible during the compilation of programs. The name of this library may differ from one installation to another. The user library contains include members written by the programmer. The system include library is created and maintained by the system staff, while the user include library is managed by programmers. Generally, an include file contains preprocessor directives, data declarations, function prototypes, and macros.

Run-time library. A run-time library contains all the executable functions for the system and standard C library. It is required during both compilation and run-time.

1.2 ELEMENTS OF C

Before you can start writing C programs, you must know the basic elements of C.

1.2.1 Characters and Tokens

A program is made up of a sequence of characters. The following is a list of characters that are recognized by the C language:

- Lower and upper case letters
  a b c d e f g h i j k l m n o p q r s t u v w x y z
  A B C D E F G H I J K L M N O P Q R S T U V W X Y Z
- Decimal digits
  0 1 2 3 4 5 6 7 8 9
- Graphic characters
  ! " # % & ' ( ) * + , - . / : @ $
  ; < = > ? [\ ] _ { } ~ ¬ |
- Space characters.

- Control sequence characters, for horizontal tab, vertical tab, form feed, and end-of-string.

A sequence of these characters is called a token. Many tokens, separated by spaces and placed according to C language rules, make a program.

1.2.2 Trigraphs

Some of the characters used in C language are not available in all keyboards. Such characters can be represented by a sequence of three characters, called a *trigraph*. The trigraph is entered in your program where such characters are needed. The following is a list of all the trigraph sequences:

??=	#
??(	[
??)	]
??<	{
??>	}
??/	\
??'	^
??!	|
??-	~

1.2.3 Escape Sequences

The following lists nongraphic characters, which are represented by a sequence of two characters called escape sequence. The first character is always a backslash '\', followed by a control character.

Escape Sequence	Character Represented
\a	Alert
\b	Backspace
\f	New page
\n	New line
\r	Carriage return
\t	Horizontal tab
\v	Vertical tab
\\	Backslash
\'	Single quotation
\"	Double quotation
\0	Null character (end-of-string)

1.2.4 Comments

To document your program, *comments* can be placed anywhere. A comment must start with characters /* and end with characters */—for example:

```
/*This is a comment */
```

A comment can occupy more than one line. The compiler treats comments as white spaces; they are ignored. The comment characters cannot be used in a nested manner. Nested comment:

```
/* /* This is a wrong comment */ */
```

will be flagged as errors by the complier. The next program shows how comments can be used in various ways. For example, the first comment occupies three lines. The next one is on one line. The last three comments are on the same line as the C statements.

```
/***********************************************
This program is to illustrate comments
***********************************************/
/* include directive */
#include <stdio.h>
/*define directives */
#define NUM_OF_CHERRIES    10
#define NUM_OF_GRAPES       9
/*variable declarations */
static int a, b;
/*function prototype */
void swap( int *xp, int *yp );
main()
{
    /* initialize variables */
    a = NUM_OF_CHERRIES;
    b = NUM_OF_GRAPES;
    printf( "a = %d, b = %d\n", a, b);
    /* call function swap()*/
    swap( &a, &b );
    /* print swapped values */
    printf( "a = %d, b= %d\n", a, b );
}
/* swap() exchanges the values of two integer
variables. The inputs are two integer pointers */
```

```
void swap( int *xp, int *yp )
{
int temp;
/* save data of xp */     temp = *xp;
*xp = *yp;    /* copy data of yp to xp*/
*yp = temp;   /* copy data of temp to xp*/
}
```

1.2.5 Identifiers

Identifiers are names given to functions, data objects, and labels. An identifier is a token made of a sequence of letters, digits, and underscores (_). An identifier must be chosen with care so that it will contribute to readability and documentation, and also removes any confusion. There are some limitations on the length and significance of identifiers.

Identifier	Significance
Internal data object names	31 characters
Internal function names	31 characters
External data object names	8 characters
External function names	8 characters

All internal names are case sensitive. In other words, the compiler recognizes the difference between upper case and lower case characters. In external names, upper and lower case characters are treated the same.

You should avoid using an underscore (_) as the first character of an identifier. Although there is no rule against an identifier beginning with an underscore, the system names used by the compiler start with an underscore. If you have a name in your program that is the same as a system name, it will cause unpredictable behavior.

1.2.6 Language Keywords

The C language has many reserved words that have special meanings in the context of programming. These keywords should not be used in any other way nor redefined.

Keywords

auto	break	case	char	const	continue
default	do	double	else	enum	extern
float	for	goto	if	int	long
register	return	short	signed	sizeof	static
struct	switch	typedef	union	unsigned	void
volatile	while				

When programming, you should also keep in mind names that have been used for system calls and library functions. These names are not C language reserved words, but using them out of context may result in unpredictable results.

1.2.7 Constants

A constant is a data object that does not change during the execution of a program. There are five types of constants:

> Integer
>
> Floating-point
>
> Character
>
> String
>
> Enumeration

Integer

There are three kinds of integer constants: decimal, octal, and hexadecimal.

A *decimal* constant can have any of the digits between 0 and 9, although such a constant cannot start with 0 for reasons explained later. The following are decimal constants:

-10

+29612

50

5

An *octal* constant must begin with 0 and can have any digit between 0 and 7.—for example:

-010

+07777

00000

057

05

A *hexadecimal* constant must have 0x as its first two characters, followed by a hexadecimal number. A hexadecimal number can be any digit between 0 and 9 and any character from A to F.—for example:

0×FF

0×123B

0×11

0×5

Floating-point

A floating-point constant is made up of an integer, decimal point, fraction, and exponent. The integral and fractional parts consist of decimal digits. The following are examples of *float* constants:

1.0

3.1415

6.887e4

0.7e-5

Character

A *character* constant is a character enclosed in single quotes, such as 'a', '+', and 'z'. Any character represented by the escape sequence is also treated as a character constant. Some of the escape sequence characters are '\0', '\n', and '\f'.

String

A *string* constant is a series of characters that are enclosed by double quotes. In this case, the compiler always appends a NULL character ('\0') after the last character of the string. Some examples of the string constants are:

"New World Order"

" "   /* NULL string */

"   " /* a string of blanks */

Enumeration

In a definition of an enumeration, a set of identifiers are given an integer value. The identifier is an enumeration constant. The following example shows the definition of enumerations and the values represented by each identifier:

```
enum furniture { chair, table, sofa } ;
                  0      1      2
enum fruit { mango = 5, pineapple, banana } ;
                5           6         7
```

1.3 PREPARING A C PROGRAM

In this section we assume that you are familiar with ISPF and MVS data set naming conventions. First, we will prepare a program called MYPROG, using

ISPF editor (option 2). Then we can save it in a PDS member called C.TEST.SOURCE(MYPROG). Next is a listing of the program, followed by a description of its different parts. This program as your first attempt in C programming may seem overwhelming. Put simply, it swaps the contents of two variables and prints them before and after the exchange. Read the description carefully, and every line of this code will become logically clear.

```c
/***************************************************************
This program swaps the contents of two variables
***************************************************************/

/* include file stdio.h*/
#include <stdio.h>

/* define constants */
#define NUM_OF_CHERRIES    10
#define NUM_OF_GRAPES       9

/* variable declarations */
static int a, b;

/* function prototype */
void swap ( int *xp, int *yp );

main()
{
 /* initialize variables */
 a = NUM_OF_CHERRIES;
 b = NUM_OF_GRAPES;
 printf( "a = %d, b = %d\n", a, b );
 /* call function swap()*/
 swap( &a, &b );
 /* print swapped values */
 printf( "a = %d, b = %d\n", a, b );
}

/* swap() exchanges the values of two integer
   variables. The inputs are two integer pointers */

void swap( int *xp, int *yp )
{
int temp;
temp = *xp;    /* save data of xp in temp */
*xp = *yp;     /* copy data of yp to xp */
*yp = temp;    /* copy data of temp to yp */
}
```

1

This comment briefly describes the program that is enclosed between /* and */.

2 `#include <stdio.h>`

This preprocessor directive is replaced by the content of include file *stdio.h*. This include file is required because we use `printf` function.

3
```
#define NUM_OF_CHERRIES    10
#define NUM_OF_GRAPES       9
```

Next, we define two constants:
NUM_OF_CHERRIES as 10
and
   NUM_OF_GRAPES as 9.

4

In this area of the program, we declare two variables, a and b, as integers, with the statement

`static int a, b;`

Also, we declare the `swap` function with the statement

`void swap( int *xp, int *yp );`

5 `main()`
`{`

Every program must have only one `main` function. The parentheses indicate to the compiler that the identifier `main` is a function. The character { is the start of the body of the function.

6

In the body of the `main` function, there are several statements, but they can be put into two categories. First, the variables a and b are initialized with previously defined constants.

`a = NUM_OF_CHERRIES;`

`b = NUM_OF_GRAPES;`

Secondly, three function are called:

`printf( "a = %d, b = %d\n", a, b );`

The `printf` function displays the value of a and b before the swap. The statement

`swap( &a, &b );`

invokes `swap` function, with pointers of a and b as arguments. The statement

`printf( "a = %d, b = %d\n", a, b );`

displays the value of *a* and *b* after the values are swapped.

⑦ `}`

Finally, we terminate the `main` function with character }.

⑧ `void swap (int *xp, int *yp)`

This statement is the definition of a function and tells us several things. The keyword `void` means that the function returns no value. The identifier `swap` is the function name. Within the parantheses, two parameters are included, each as a pointer to an integer.

⑨ `int temp;`

This statement defines the local variable `temp` as an integer data type.

⑩

This section is the body of the *swap* function. It saves the data of `xp` in `temp`, moves data of `xp` to `yp`, and then restores data `xp` into `yp`.

The output of this program is:

```
a=10, b=9
a=9, b=10
```

1.4 COMPILE, LINK-EDIT, AND EXECUTE A PROGRAM

This section shows how to produce an executable program from a source program. Before a program is ready to run, it must be compiled and link-edited without any error. We will show these two steps, using MYPROG program, prepared previously, as an example. These tasks can be achieved in both batch and interactive modes. Also, we will demonstrate how to execute the program. If you are familiar with the IBM C/370 compiler in MVS environment, perhaps you may want to skip over this section.

1.4.1 Batch

Under MVS, Job Control Language (JCL) is the means to direct the operating system to execute any program in batch mode. The following JCL is prepared to do the following two steps:

1. Compile and link-edit the MYPROG program.
2. Execute the MYPROG program.

```
//MYPROG    JOB (accounting info), 'MYPROG'         ① 
//*
```

```
//* COMPILE AND LINK-EDIT STEP
//*
//COMPLINK   EXEC PROC=EDCCL,
//   INFILE='TEST.C.SOURCE(MYPROG)',
//   OUTFILE='TEST.C.LOAD',
//   NAME='MYPROG'
//*
//* RUN MYPROG
//*
//RUN    EXEC PGM=MYPROG
//STEPLIB     DD DSN=TEST.C.LOAD,DISP=SHR
//SYSPRINT    DD DSN=TEST.C.SYSPRINT, DISP=SHR
```

1

This JOB statement defines a batch job called MYPROG. It also identifies the start of a job. The accounting information, necessary to submit a JCL, is acquired from your IS department.

2

This step is called COMPLINK. It calls a catalogued procedure named EDCCL, which is a JCL subroutine. This procedure compiles and link-edits a source program, invoked by the EXEC statement

```
//COMPLINK    EXEC PROC=EDCCL,
```

The input is identified by the parameter INFILE in the line

```
//           INFILE='TEST.C.SOURCE(MYPROG)',
```

The output library is a PDS, identified by the parameter OUTFILE in the line

```
//           OUTFILE='TEXT.C.LOAD',
```

The parameter NAME in the line

```
//           NAME='MYPROG'
```

indicates the member of the output PDS.

3

To run the MYPROG program, we use the EXEC statement again:

```
//RUN   EXEC PGM=MYPROG
```

The DD statement

```
//STEPLIB     DD DSN=TEST.C.LOAD,DISP=SHR
```

informs the operating system of the library where MYPROG program is to be found, namely

TEST.C.LOAD.

The next statement

```
//SYSPRINT    DD DSN=TEST.C.SYSPRINT,DISP=SHR
```

informs the system that the output of the program should go to
TEST.C.SYSPRINT.

1.4.2 Interactive

A program can be compiled interactively under MVS/TSO. In this section we will go through three distinct steps:

1. Compile
2. Link-edit
3. Execution

In the first two steps we will use IBM-supplied CLIST programs. CLIST is a command language for TSO.

Compile. To compile our example MYPROG, we use the CLIST command CC:

```
CC 'TEST.C.SOURCE(MYPROG)'
OBJ ('''TEST.C.OBJ(MYPROG)''')
```

The parameter

TEST.C.SOURCE(MYPROG)

is the source file. The object created from this compilation is placed in

TEST.C.OBJ(MYPROG).

Link-edit. The link-edit step is accomplished by CLIST command CMOD by entering the command

```
CMOD OBJ('''TEST.C.OBJ(MYPROG)''')
LOAD('''TEST.C.LOAD(MYPROG)''')
```

Run. To run the MYPROG program, type

CALL 'TEST.C.LOAD(MYPROG)'

The result

$$a = 10, b = 9$$
$$a = 9, b = 10$$

will be displayed on the screen.

1.5 TESTING AND DEBUGGING

INSPECT for C is a facility you can use to test and debug your program. It also helps you analyze your code by allowing you to examine, monitor, and control a C program. You can use INSPECT interactively, or commands can be issued in batch mode.

2

Data Declarations

In C, variables must first be declared before they are used. In this chapter we will discuss data declarations, which serve two purposes. First, a declaration of variable instructs the compiler to reserve a specific amount of memory space associated with an identifier (or name). Second, a program is able to manipulate the variable, which is already declared as a data object.

To illustrate these two aspects of data declaration, let's look at a simple example.

```
/* to illustrate data declaration */
#include <stdio.h>
main()
{
    int x, y, z; /* data declaration of
        variables x, y, z */
    x = 10, y = 20; /* initialize x with
        value 10 and y with 20 */
    z = x + y; /* add variables x and y and
        place the result in variable z */
    /* print the value of z */
    printf( "x + y = %d \n", z );
}
```

The statement

```
int x, y, z ;
```

tells the compiler to reserve memory space for three variables and to give them the names x, y, and z. The keyword int (discussed in the next section) indicates that each variable must be large enough to hold an integer value. In the next statement,

```
x = 10, y = 20;
```

the program uses the two variables x and y by assigning values 10 and 20, respectively. This is an instruction to the compiler to place values in the memory space already reserved. Next, we have the expression

```
z = x + y ;
```

Again, this statement instructs the compiler to calculate x + y and to place the result in memory occupied by variable z. Finally, we print the result value z, using `printf` function.

There are many aspects to data declaration. They are data types, storage class, duration, scope, and initialization. We will discuss all these aspects in the rest of this chapter. A sound understanding of these facets of variables will allow you to use data objects to their fullest.

The general form of a declaration is:

```
storage-specifier type-specifier variable-list;
```

The *storage-specifier* is a way of telling the compiler how to store the variables that follows. The *type-specifier* describes the type of the data object. The *variable-list* associates a name to the data object, which can be used in a program. Next, we will discuss the various data types available in C language.

2.1 DATA TYPES

The *type-specifier* describes the kind of data the variable will have. There are several data types, and they can be grouped into two categories: scalar and complex. The scalar data types are:

> Characters
>
> Floating-point numbers
>
> Integers
>
> Pointer
>
> Enumeration

From these data types, you can build more complex data arrangements, such as:

> Arrays
>
> Structures
>
> Unions

This section describes how to use variables with all these data types, and also shows how to define your own data type names derived from the basic types.

2.1.1 Characters

C has three kinds of character data types. They are char, unsigned char, and signed char. The difference between these different types of characters are the ranges of values that each can hold. The following shows the different types, storage size, and range in MVS environment using IBM C/370 compiler.

Type	Size	Range
char	1 byte	0 to 255
unsigned char	1 byte	0 to 255
signed char	1 byte	-128 to 127

A character variable can also be used like an integer variable. If it is declared as signed, the high-order bit determines whether the value is negative or positive. If the character variable has an unsigned data type, the compiler treats all values as positive.

A variable with any of these character data types will hold a single character. A char variable is initialized with a character constant, which is formed by enclosing a character with a pair of *single* quotes (not to be confused with double quotes, which is used for enclosing string constants and will be discussed later). In the following statement, for example, variable char_var is initialized to character 'w':

```
char char_var = 'w' ;
```

You can also initialize a character variable with a non-printable character constant. In the following example, the variable newline is defined as char data type and set to initial value '\n' (new line):

```
char newline = '\n';
```

A list of all nongraphic characters is found in Section 1.2.3 of Chapter 1.

In the next example, the variable number_of_books is declared as unsigned char, and its initial value is set to 20:

```
unsigned char number_of_books = 20 ;
```

The type-specifier *char* can also be used to declare an array of characters. In the following example, the variable *city* is declared as a character array, and each element of the array is initialized with a character ('N', 'e', 'w', etc.). The statement

```
for( i = 0; i< 8; ++i )
    printf( "%c", city[i] );
```

loops eight times, starting with i = 0 to i = 7, and prints each element of the array city. (A detailed discussion of the for-loop is found in Chapter 4.)

```
/************************************************************
This program illustrates an array of characters
************************************************************/

#include <stdio.h>

static char city[] = { 'N', 'e', 'w', ' ', 'Y', 'o', 'r', 'k' };

main()
{
    int i;

    for ( i = 0; i < 8; ++i)
    printf( "%c" city[i] );
    printf( "\n" );
}
```

The output is:

    New York

The statement

    printf("\n");

prints a new line after printing all the elements of the array city.

Since C does not have a string data type, the char specifier is used for a string variable. In fact, a string is made of individual characters and terminated with a NULL character ('\0'). In the following example, the variable city is declared as an array of characters and initialized with a string constant, rather than setting individual cells to a character constant as in the previous example. This time, double quotes are used; the compiler automatically adds a NULL character after the last character of the string. In contrast, the string is printed using the format specifier "%s", which prints the string. In the previous example, we printed individual character of the array city.

```
/********************************************************
This program illustrates string
********************************************************/

#include <stdio.h>

static char city[] = "New York";

main()
{
    printf( "%s\n", city );
}
```

The output is:

    New York

2.1.2 Floating-Point Variables

A floating-point variable is declared with three different data type specifiers: float, double, and long double. You need one of these data types if a variable is to have a fractional component or if it contains very large numbers. Variables defined with float, double, and long double differ only in the range of values that they can hold. The following table lists the type, storage size, and range of each floating-point specifier in MVS:

Type	Size	Range
float	fullword	5.397605E-79 to 7.237005E+75
double	doubleword	1.7E-308 to 1.7E+308
long double	doubleword	1.7E-308 to 1.75E+308

In the following example, the variable float_var is declared as float, double_var as double, and long_var as long double. Each is initialized with a floating-point number and then printed with printf function.

```
/*****************************************************************
This program illustrates floating-point variables
*****************************************************************/
#include <stdio.h>

main()
{
    float float_var = 441.22 ;
    double double_var = 9.44E+11 ;
    long double long_var = 8.55E+55 ;

    printf( "float variable = %f \n", float_var );
    printf( "double variable = %E \n", double_var );
    printf( "double long variable = %E \n", long_var );
}
```

The output is:

```
float variable = 411.22
double variable = 9.440000E+11
double long variable = 8.550000E+55
```

2.1.3 Integers

Variables holding integer values can be declared with six different data type specifiers. They are:

> short or short int
>
> int or signed int
>
> long or long int

unsigned short or unsigned short int

unsigned or unsigned int

unsigned long or unsigned long int

The following table lists the type, storage size, and range of each integer data types.

Type	Bit Size	Range
short	halfword	-32768 to 32767
int	fullword	-2147483648 to 2147483647
long	fullword	-2147483648 to 2147483647
unsigned short	halfword	0 to 65535
unsigned int	fullword	0 to 4294967295
unsigned long	fullword	0 to 4294967295

In the following example, the variable short_num is declared as an array of integers with short data type. The elements of the array are initialized to values: -127, 0, 10, and 128. Variable i is declared with int specifier, while variable unsigned_num is declared with unsigned specifier with initial value of 65000. And variable long_num is defined with long specifier with the initial value set to -80000.

```
 1  /************************************************
 2  This program illustrates integer variables
 3  ************************************************/
 4
 5  #include <stdio.h>
 6
 7  main()
 8  {
 9      short    short_num[] = { -127, 0, 10, 128 } ;
10      int      i ;

11      unsigned    unsigned_num = 65000 ;
12      long        long_num = -80000 ;
13
14      for ( i = 0 ; i < 4 ; ++i )
15      printf( "short integer number = %d \n",
16                  short_num[i]);
17      printf( "unsigned integer = %d \n", unsigned_num);
18      printf( "long integer = %ld \n", long_num);
19  }
```

The output is:

```
short integer number = -127
short integer number = 0
short integer number = 10
```

```
short integer number = 128
unsigned integer = 65000
long integer = -80000
```

In this program, lines 14 through 15 index array `short_num` and print each element of the array. Integer variable *i* is the index. Line 17 prints `unsigned int` variable `unsigned_num`, and line 18 prints `long` variable `long_num`.

2.1.4 Void Type

Variables can be declared to hold no value with specifier `void`. The `void` data type is mainly used to declare functions that do not return a value. (Returns of a function are described in Chapter 5.)

2.1.5 Arrays

An array is made of two or more data objects occupying contiguous memory space. The data type of all the data objects in an array is the same. Each data object is called an element, which is accessed by an index. All the elements are referenced by the same identifier, found in the array declaration. An array can have one or more dimensions.

A single dimension array declaration has the following general form:

```
storage-specifier type-specifier variable-name [size];
```

The *storage-specifier* denotes whether an array is a local or a global variable (discussed in Section 2.2). The *type-specifier* establishes the data type of all the elements of the array. The *variable-name* is the identifier of the array and all its elements. The *size* indicates to the compiler the number of elements that the array will hold.

In the following example, the variable `number` is declared as an array of four integers. Each element of this one-dimension is set to an initial value, namely -127, 0, 10, and 128.

```
int number[4] = { -127, 0, 10, 128 } ;
```

The values of each element of `number` looks like this:

Element	Value
number[0]	-127
number[1]	0
number[2]	10
number[3]	128

Note that the first index of an array is 0. The following program prints the index and value of each element of `number` array.

```
/***********************************************************
This program illustrates integer array
***********************************************************/
#include <stdio.h>
    static int     number[4] = { -127, 0, 10, 128 } ;
main()
{
    int i;
    for ( i = 0 ; i < 4 ; ++i )
      printf( "Index is %d, value is = %d \n",
                         i, number[i] );
}
```

The output is:

```
Index is 0, value is -127
Index is 1, value is 0
Index is 2, value is 10
Index is 3, value is 128
```

Arrays can be of any data type. We just saw an example of an integer array. Arrays can also have data types of float and char. In C, the most common arrays are that of characters. Since C does not have a string data type, an array of characters is a string. The end of the string is indicated by a '\0' (NULL) value.

A character array can be initialized in two ways: with character constants or with string constants. As discussed earlier, the character constants are enclosed in single quotes and separated by commas, and the character constant list is enclosed in braces. The string constant is enclosed in double quotes and optionally enclosed in braces. In the following statements, character arrays are declared and initialized: array month1 with characters; array month2 with a string with double quotes and braces; and array month3 with string enclosed with double quote only:

```
static char month1[] = { 'F', 'e', 'b' } ;
static char month2[] = { "Feb" } ;
static char month3[3] = "Feb" ;
```

If you omit the dimension of the array and set a string constant as an initial value, as was done for variable month2, the compiler terminates the array with a character constant '\0' (NULL). But for variable month3, only 3 bytes are allocated and initialized. The following table shows how the compiler initializes elements of these three arrays.

Element	Value	Element	Value	Element	Value
month1[0]	F	month2[0]	F	month3[0]	F
month1[1]	e	month2[1]	e	month3[1]	e
month1[2]	b	month2[3]	b	month3[2]	b
		month2[4]	\0		

The declaration of a multidimensional array has the following general form:

```
Storage-specifier type-specifier variable-name [size1]
[size2]…[sizen];
```

It is similar to the one-dimension array declaration except that there are multiple size values.

The following declaration of an array variable `points` has two dimensions, containing 12 elements; all elements all elements are integer data type:

```
int points[3][4];
```

The compiler always finds contiguous space for an array of any dimension. For the sake of convenience, let's look at this two-dimension array as a rectangular form with rows and columns. Therefore, the array `points[3][4]` has 3 rows and 4 columns. It can be arranged as follows:

	column 1	column 2	column 3	column 4
row 1	points[0][0]	points[0][1]	points[0][2]	points[0][3]
row 2	points[1][0]	points[1][1]	points[1][2]	points[1][3]
row 3	points[2][0]	points[2][1]	points[2][2]	points[2][3]

This two-dimension array can be accessed in many ways. One way is to use indices i and j for row and column, respectively. Each element of `points[3][4]` can be represented by the expression

```
points[j][i] where 0 < j < 3 and 0 < i < 4.
```

Another way of accessing an array is with a pointer. The expression `points[j][i]` is equivalent to

```
*(points[j] + i)
```

or

```
(*(points + j))[i]
```

where * is an indirection operator. For more information on indirection operator, refer to Chapter 3. Pointers are discussed in details in Chapter 7.

Next, we initialize each element of the array `points` in the following way:

```
int points[3][4] = {
                    1,2,4,8,
                    2,4,8,16,
                    3,6,12,24
                   };
```

In the following program, we use the information about arrays that we have learned so far. First, we declare and initialize array `points`. In the body of the `main` function, there are two for-loops.

```
/****************************************************************
This program illustrates a multi-dimension array variable
****************************************************************/
#include<stdio.h>

static points[3][4] = {
                        1,2,4,8,
                        2,4,8,16,
                        3,6,12,24
                      };
main()
{
int i,j;
        for ( j = 0; j < 3; j++ )
          for ( i = 0 ; i < 4 ; i++ )
            printf( "points[%d][%d] = % d\n",
                j, i, points [j][i] );
}
```

The output is:

```
points[0][0] =  1
points[0][1] =  2
points[0][2] =  4
points[0][3] =  8
points[1][0] =  2
points[1][1] =  4
points[1][2] =  8
points[1][3] = 16
points[2][0] =  3
points[2][1] =  6
points[2][2] = 12
points[2][3] = 24
```

The outer loop

```
for ( j = 0; j < 3; j++ )
```

indexes the row with j. The inner loop

```
for ( i = 0 ; i < 4 ; i++ )
    printf( "points[%d][%d] = % d\n",
        j, i, points[j][i] );
```

indexes the column with j and prints the value of each element `points[j][i]`.
There are several ways of initializing an array, and the following two are equivalent:

```
int points[3][4] = { 1,2,4,8,2,4,8,16,3,6,12,24 };

int points[2][4] = {1,2,4,8},{2,4,8,16},{3,6,12,24}};
```

In the first example, there is no inner braces, therefore, each element starting from `points[0][0]` until `points[2][3]` is given a value from the given list. Note that the initialization is done by rows starting from the first. If there are not enough values between the braces to fill all the elements, the remaining ones are set to zero values.

In the second declaration, there are two points to note: the first bracket pair is empty, and the initial values are grouped into threes with inner-brace pairs. In this case, the compiler decides upon the first size, namely the number of rows, by the number of inner brace pairs, which is 3. The number of columns must be explicitly given.

Now, let's consider the following declaration and initialization:

```
int points [][4] = {{1,2},{2,4},{3,6}};
```

The second size 4 is given explicitly. The first size is decided by the number of inner-brace pairs,which is 3. With each brace pair, only two values are given, used to set the first two elements of a row, while the next two elements are set to zero. The values of array will look as follows:

```
points[0][0] = 1

points[0][1] = 2

points[0][2] = 0

points[0][3] = 0

points[1][0] = 2

points[1][1] = 4

points[1][2] = 0

points[1][3] = 0

points[2][0] = 3

points[2][1] = 6

points[2][2] = 0

points[2][3] = 0
```

Finally, if you want to initialize all elements by a single value, place the value between braces—for example,

```
int points[3][4] = {0};
```

2.1.6 Enumerations

An *enumeration* is a data type you choose to have represent a set of integer values. After defining an enumeration, you can declare a variable, using that enumeration data type. Such a declaration specifies all the valid values of that data type. The general definition form is:

```
enum identifier { enum1, enum2, ... } variable-list ;
```

The keyword *enum* defines an enumeration data type. The *identifier* is the name you give to such a data type. The list of enumerators (*enum1, enum2*, etc.) gives the data type a set of constant integer values. The *variable-list* is an option to declare variables of the enumeration data type.

The following statements declare an enumeration called coins and declare a variable money of that data type:

```
enum coins ( penny, nickel, dime );

coins money;
```

In C it is allowed to have an "unnamed" identifier in an enumeration declaration; however, in such a case you must include a *variable-list*. Consider, for example, the declaration

```
enum ( chair, table, sofa ) furniture;
```

where furniture is a variable of enumeration data type, which has no name.

In the following program, flag is defined as an enumeration data type. The variable sw is declared to be of enumeration data type flag and initialized to off, one of the enumerators. The next statement

```
if ( sw == off )
    printf( "The switch is off\n" );
```

tests whether variable sw is enumerator *off*; if it is true, the printf function is executed. Next, variable sw is assigned the value represented by enumerator on. Again, testing sw, which is on, printf function is called.

```
/***********************************************
This program illustrates enumeration.
***********************************************/
#include <stdio.h>

main()
{
    enum flag { on, off } sw = off ;

    if ( sw == off )
      printf ( "The switch is off\n" );

    sw = on ;

    if ( sw == on )
```

```
        printf ( "The switch is on\n" );
}
```

The output is:

```
The switch is off
The switch is on
```

The main point about enumeration is that each enumerator is a symbol representing an integer value. There are three ways of assigning the values. First, the default is that the compiler sets the value of the first enumerator to 0, the second enumerator to 1, the third to 2, and so on. For example, the declaration

```
enum fruit { orange, peach, apple, mango };
```

will assign 0 to orange, 1 to peach, 2 to apple, and 3 to mango.

Second, you can explicitly give an enumerator a value by placing an equal sign (=) and an integer after the enumerator. In the declaration

```
enum fruit { orange = 5, peach, apple, mango };
```

orange has value 5 and peach, apple, and mango will have 6, 7, and 8, respectively.

Third, an unassigned enumerator will always have one value greater than the previous one. Of course, if it is the first unassigned enumerator, its value is always zero. For example, the definition

```
enum coins { penny, nickel, dime=10, quarter };
```

gives the value 10 to enumerator dime. Each symbol will have the following value:

penny	0
nickel	1
dime	10
quarter	11

2.1.7 Pointers

One of the strongest features of C language is its flexibility in handling pointers. Here, pointers are addresses to data objects. Therefore, it is important to understand pointers and use them correctly to write effective and successful C programs. In this section we will briefly touch upon this crucial subject just enough to give you an idea of this data type. In Chapter 7 we will provide an in-depth discussion on pointers and their various uses. In Chapter 9 we show how to recognize and avoid programming pitfalls when using them.

A variable declared as a *pointer* is used to store a memory address of a data object. The general form of a *pointer* declaration is:

type-specifier **variable-list;*

The *type-specifier* can be any data type. The *variable-list* consists of one or more variables of the data type.

2.1.8 Structures

A structure is a collection of variables or data objects. It is a convenient way to keep and manage related data. Unlike array—requiring all elements to have the same data type—the variables of a structure can be of different data types. Each data object of a structure is called a *member* (also known as *field* or *element*).

The general form of declaring a structure is:

```
struct identifier    {
                     type-specifier variable-name;
                     type-specifier variable-name;
                        •
                        •
                        •
                     } variable-list;
```

The keyword `struct`, placed at the beginning, is used to declare a structure. The *identifier* is the name you give to the structure. For each member, you have to include a *type-specifier* and *variable-name*. Also, you can include a *variable-list*, containing one or more variables as part of the structure declaration. The *identifier* and *variable-list* are optional; however, you cannot omit both of them. In a structure declaration, the compiler does not allocate any memory space unless a variable-list is included.

Generally, you would use a structure to group logical elements that are related to each other. In the following declaration of a structure `employee`, there are seven fields, each with different data characteristics, but all part of an employee record. Each element is a variable, declared with a data type and an identifier, and terminated with a semi-colon (;). The variables `temp_employee` and `perm_employee` are also part of the structure `employee` declaration. The variable `retired_employee` is declared as the same structure data type, but on a separate statement.

```
struct employee      {
                     char name[30];
                     int street_num;
                     char street[40];
                     char city[20];
                     char prov [3];
                     char postal_code[6];
                     unsigned long int salary;
                     } temp_employee, perm_employee;
struct employee retired_employee;
```

The name of each field must be unique within a structure, but you can use the same member name in more than one structure. Also, you cannot declare a structure to have itself as a member. But it is allowed to include a member as being a pointer to the structure. For example, in the following structure address, a member next_rec is a pointer to the structure address:

```
struct address      {
                    int street_num;
                    char *street;
                    char *city;
                    char *state;
                    l unsigned long zip; struct address *next_rec;
                    };
```

You can initialize all or some members of the structure during the declaration. For example, the next program shows a declaration of the structure address and the variable new_address. Each member of the variable new_address is set to a value or string constant with the statement

```
struct address new_address =
    { 1233, "Belle View Lane", "New York", "NY", 10003 };
```

Next, using the printf function, the program prints each element of the structure. The general forms to access a field are:

```
structure_variable.member_name
```

```
pointer_to_structure_variable->member_name
```

```
/*********************************************************
This program illustrates structure variable
*********************************************************/

#include <stdio.h>

struct address      {
            int street_num;
            char *street;
            char *city;
            char *state;
            unsigned long zip;
            };
struct address new_address =
    { 1233, "Belle View Lane", "New York", "NY", 10003 };
main()
{
    printf( "%d %s\n",          new_address.street_num,
                                new_address.street );
    printf( "%s, %s %ld\n",     new_address.city,
                                new_address.state,
                                new_address.zip );
}
```

The output is:

```
1233 Belle View Lane
New York, NY 10003
```

Unlike many other high-level computer languages, C provides a built-in facility to store and access information as bits within a byte.

To do so, you declare a member of a structure as integer with a specific length of bits. Such a member is called a *bitfield*. There are many reasons why you would want to use bits as fields of data. Some of them are:

1. Bits can be *Boolean* variables, especially when storage is limited.
2. To interface with devices that encode information in bit strings.
3. To access any bit within a byte.

Although these operations can be achieved with the bitwise operators of C, bitfield adds structure, efficiency, and readability to your programs.

Bitfield is declared as a special kind of structure. The data type of the elements can only be `int`, `unsigned`, or `signed`. The declaration of each bitfield contains a type-specifier, a variable-name, and a colon (:), and is followed by the length of the field. The general form of a bitfield structure is:

```
struct identifier   {
                    type-specifier variable-name : length;
                    type-specifier variable-name : length;
                        •
                        •
                        •
                    } variable-list;
```

If length is 0, it causes the next field to be aligned on the next integer boundary. A structure variable with bitfield elements cannot be an array, nor can you declare a pointer to bitfield.

The following program declares a structure called `flags` and a variable `comm`. The structure has seven elements, but the storage of `comm` requires only four integers. Each element occupies memory as follows:

	Member	Storage
Integer 1		
	active	2 bits
	ready	1 bit
	error	1 bit
Integer 2		
	counter	integer
Integer 3		
	receive	10 bits
Integer 4		
	xmit	10 bits

Since the fourth element `counter` requires a full integer for storage, the compiler gives the first three elements a full integer, although they occupy only 4 bits. Now, the fifth and seventh elements get one integer each because they are separated by the sixth element, which has length zero. Note that to access a structure member you need the structure name and member name separated by a dot (.)—for example, `comm.error`.

```
/********************************************************
This program illustrates bitfield variables
********************************************************/

#include<stdio.h>

struct flags {
            unsigned active : 2 ;
            unsigned ready : 1  ;
            unsigned error : 1  ;
            int counter ;
            unsigned receive : 10 ;
            unsigned 0 ;
            unsigned xmit : 10    ;
            } comm ;

main()
{

    comm.error = 0;
    comm.ready =1;
    comm.receive = 999;

    if ( comm.error )
      printf( "Error\n" );
    else if ( comm.ready )
      printf( "Received data is %d \n", comm.receive );
}
```

The output is:

```
Received data is 999
```

2.1.9 Unions

A *union* provides a way of having two or more variables share storage. A union declaration is similar to that of a structure, with elements having different data types. In a structure, each element has its own memory space; in a union, all elements occupy the same memory location. The general form of a union declaration is:

```
union identifier    {

               type-specifier variable-name;

               type-specifier variable-name;

                        •

                        •

                        •

               } variable-list;
```

The keyword to declare a union is union, placed at the beginning. The identifier is the name you give to the union. For each member, you have to include a type-specifier and variable-name, giving it the data type and name, respectively. You can also include a *variable-list*, containing one or more variables as part of the union declaration. The identifier and variable-list are optional; however, you cannot omit both of them.

In the following example, the identifier wt_code is declared as a union type. One member weight is a type short int and the other code is type char. In the next statement, the union variable *convert* is declared as type wt_code. The compiler allocates enough memory to hold the largest member; therefore, 2 bytes are allocated to the variable covert. In this case, short int type requires 2 bytes, and char occupies only 1 byte. These 2 bytes are allocated to the variable convert.

```
union wt_code {
          short int weight ;
          char code ;
          };
union wt_code convert ;
```

Now, let's look at how both members weight and code share the same storage. The variable weight takes a half word (2 bytes), of which the first byte is also used by variable code.

<— weight —>	
byte 0	byte 1
< -code->	

In the following program, the union profile and the variable employee are declared in the same statement. The union profile has four elements. The first three variables are name, birthday, and age, and their basic data types are char and int. The fourth element is a union variable convert. The compiler gives the variable employee 20 bytes of storage and all its member share the same memory location.

```
/************************************************
This program illustrates union variables
************************************************/
#include <stdio.h>
union wt_code {
            int weight ;
            char code ;
            };
union profile {
            char name[20];
            char birthday[9];
            int age;
            union wt_code convert ;
            } employee = "John Smith" ;
main()
{
  printf( "Name is %s.\n", employee.name );
  employee.age = 30 ;
  printf ( "Age is %d.\n", employee.age );
}
```

The output is:

```
Name is John Smith.
Age is 30.
```

The variable employee is initialized with a string constant "John Smith". Only the values of the first member of a union variable may be initialized.

To access a union member, use the same notation as that used to access a member of a structure. The three statements in the body of the above program illustrate how to access union members. The first one prints the field *name*; the second assigns value 30 to *age*; and the last prints the field *age*.

2.1.10 Typedef-name

C allows you to define your own data type name. By using the keyword *typedef*, you create a new name with existing data types. A typedef does not create a new data class, nor does it reserve any storage. It allows for the creation of a user-qualified data type. The new data type can be used to declare a variable. The general form of a typedef definition is:

```
typedef type-specifier identifier;
```

The *type-specifier* can be any data type, such as int, char, and float. The *identifier* is the new name you give to the new type. For example, to create a new data type name DOLLAR, having the same characteristics as type float, you would use

```
typedef float DOLLAR;
```

Now you can use this new type DOLLAR to declare a variable (e.g., rent):

```
DOLLAR rent;
```

The compiler recognizes rent as a float variable.

What is the advantage of creating a new data type based on an existing one? It allows the programmer to define types that reflect the intended use. Previously, we defined a type DOLLAR and used it to declare a variable rent. This approach adds to the self-documentation of your code and helps in the maintenance efforts later on.

The next program further illustrates the definitions and use of user-defined data types. At the top you will see three statements with the keyword typedef. The first defines the new type DOLLAR as float; the second defines the type NAME as an array of 30 characters; the third one, EMP_REC, uses a structure construct in its definition. This structure has three fields, where the first two variables surname and salary use previously defined data types NAME and DOLLAR. The third variable age is of the type int. The following statement

```
EMP_REC employee[ EMP_NUM ];
```

is a declaration of the array employee with EMP_NUM(100) elements of the type EMP_REC. Assuming that the array has been initialized, the body of the program shows how to access each element and field of the array employee. The variable i indexes through the array employee and the dot operator (.) is used to access each field.

```
/*******************************************************
This program illustrates typedef
*******************************************************/

#include <stdio.h>

#define EMP_NUM 100
typedef float DOLLAR;
typedef char NAME[30];
typedef struct      {
                    NAME surname;
                    int age;
                    DOLLAR salary;
                    } EMP_REC;

EMP_REC employee[ EMP_NUM ];

main()
{
    int i;
    for ( i = 0 ; i < EMP_NUM ; i++ )
      printf( "Name is %s, Age is %d, Salary is %f \n",
            employee[i].surname, employee[i].age,
            employee[i].salary);
}
```

2.2 STORAGE SPECIFIER

There are four ways of indicating to the compiler how a variable is to allocate memory for a variable. You do so with one of the class-specifiers:

auto

static

extern

register

The following discussion is about these class-specifiers. In using them, it is important to pay attention to whether a variable is 'local' or 'global' in relation to a function where it is used. A local variable when declared within the body of a function is local to the function. Variables declared outside a function are called global variables. The time of memory allocation and duration of the variable depends on whether it is local or global.

2.2.1 Class-Specifier auto

When storage class is not specified, the default is the auto class. This storage class is most commonly used. All local variables in a function are declared as *automatic* local variables. Their durations are transient, "created" at the time the function is called and lasting as long as the function is being executed. Such a variable *cannot* be accessed by other functions. When declaring a local variable within a function, it is more precise to declare it with the auto specifier; however, it is rarely used explicitly.

In this example, the variables n and limit in the count function are declared as *auto* storage class. Both of them are local to count function and last as long as this function is executed. The for-loop

```
for ( n=0; n < limit ; n++ );
```

simply increments n from 0 to the value of limit, which is 10:

```
count()
{
    auto int n;
    int limit = 10;
    for ( n=0; n < limit ; n++ );
}
```

2.2.2 Class-Specifier static

A variable declared with a static specifier is permanently established. There are two ways of using the static storage class: local and global.

The static local variables: When you use static specifier to declare variable within a function or block of code, the compiler creates a local but permanent data object. It is only known to the function where it is declared. Therefore, a static local variable cannot be referenced outside the function where it is declared. Such a variable retains its value from one execution of the function to the next.

The following example shows how a local `static` variable is used. In `prt_num` function, the local variable `number` is declared as a local `static` variable and is initialized to value zero. When `prt_num` function is first called in `main`, a value 10 is added to 0 and printed. The next time, value 10 is added to 10 and printed.

```
/*********************************************************
Program to illustrate a local static variable
*********************************************************/

# include <stdio.h>

void prt_num();

main()
{
    prt_num();
    prt_num();
}

void prt_num()
{
    static int number = 0;
    number = number + 10 ;
    printf( "Number is %d \n", number );
}
```

The output is:

```
Number is 10
Number is 20
```

The static global variables: When you use a `static` class-specifier to declare a variable outside a function, the compiler creates a global and permanent data object. Such a variable is known only to functions below the variable declaration within the file. It is different from global variables with `extern` storage class, which will be discussed later. Static global variables are not accessible to functions in another file.

The following example shows how a `static` global variable is used. In File 1, the variable `number` is declared as a global variable, initialized to zero. In the same file, `prt_num1` function prints the variable `number` after adding value 10 to it. In File 2, the variable `number` is defined again as a global variable, but initialized to the value 100. The `prt_num2` function also prints the variable `number` after adding value 10 to it. In `main` function, both `prt_num1` and `prt_num2` functions are called, but the results are different. In `prt_num1` 10 is added to 0, while in `prt_num2`, 10 is added to 100. The reason for this difference is that `number` is declared in two separate files.

File 1

```
/************************************************************
Program to illustrate a static global variable
************************************************************/
# include <stdio.h>
static int number = 0;
void prt_num1();
void prt_num2();

main()
{
    prt_num1();
    prt_num2();
}
void prt_num1()
{
    number = number + 10 ;
    printf( "Number is %d \n", number );
}
    File 2

    static int number = 100;
    void prt_num2()
{
    number = number + 10 ;
    printf( "Number is %d \n", number );
}
```

The output is:

```
Number is 10
Number is 110
```

2.2.3 Class-Specifier extern

Generally, a C program can be divided into several parts. Each part resides in a separate file (data set or PDS member). Each part, called a source module, is made up of many functions that are compiled separately. At link-edit time, all the modules are pull together into a executable program.

It is possible that variables are declared in one module, but accessed by functions in another module. To allow such a global access to a data object, you use the storage-specifier extern. A global variable is declared to be outside a function, using the keyword extern. If a declaration is found in a module without a class-specifier, but is outside a function, the default is *always* a global variable.

The compiler allocates memory for all extern storage class just before program execution begins. This memory is freed after the program terminates. If a variable with extern is declared in one file, this variable is available to all functions after it is within that file. However, if you want to access the same variable from a function in another file, you have to declare the variable with the `extern` specifier again in that file.

In this example, we have the `main` function in File 1 and the `counter` function in File 2. The global variable `first` is declared in file 1 without any storage-class specifier.

File 1

```
/**********************************************
This program illustrates extern variables
**********************************************/
# include <stdio.h>
int first; /* global declaration of first */

main()
{
  int count, last;

  first = 10 ;
  last  = 20 ;
  count = counter(last);
  printf( "First = %d, last = %d, and count = %d \n",
      first, last, count );
}
```

File 2

```
/**********************************************
This program counts from first to last
**********************************************/
counter ( int last )
{
  int i, count;
  extern int first; /* declaration of variable first */

  count = 1;
  for ( i = first; i < last; i++ )
    count++;
  return ( count );
}
```

The output is:

`First = 10, last = 20, and count = 11`

The `main` function and the global variable `first` are found in the same file; therefore, `main` can access `first` without a declaration. However, the `counter` function, found in another file, also references the variable first, but needs a declaration with `extern` specifier.

A declaration can appear at the beginning of a block (as in the `counter` function of the above example) or outside a function (only once in one file). In the `counter` function the for-loop is used to count from the value of `first` to the parameter `last`. The `count` is returned to the calling function.

2.2.4 Class-Specifier register

The register class only applies to variables of type int, char, and float. The register specifier requests that the compiler stores the declared variables in the register of the CPU, rather than memory, where variables are normally stored. This kind of storage expedites operation on a variable. It is useful to maximize the speed in a critical part of a program, where a variable is heavily used (e.g, to control a loop). It is used as a local variable and is therefore transient. It cannot be used as a global variable, but can be passed as a parameter to a function.

If the register storage class is properly used, it can significantly enhance the performance of a function. There are only few general purpose registers available to the compiler. Therefore, the number of register class variables at any given time is limited. This number depends on the compiler you are using.

```
/****************************************************************
This program illustrates register storage class
****************************************************************/
main()
}
    int limit = 10000;
    count1 ( limit );
    count2 ( limit );
}
    count1 ( register int l )
{
    register int n;
    for ( n=0; n < l ; n++ );
}
    count2 ( int l )
{
    int n;
    for ( n=0; n < l; n++ );
}
```

In this example, variables l and n in count1 function are declared with class-specifier register. The for-loop

```
for ( n=0; n < l ; n++ );
```

is to count from 0 to the value of l, which is 10000. Also, in the count2 function the variable *n* is declared as auto. Generally, you would take advantage of the register storage class where the same variable is referenced many times and where access to CPU registers take much less time than memory access. The count1 function will take less execution time than the count2 function.

2.3 DECLARATORS

A *declarator* specifies a data object. All declarations must have declarators, each having exactly one identifier. It is this identifier (variable-name) that is declared as having a certain type and a storage class. For example, the following data declaration uses message as the declarator:

```
static char message[] = "Hello universe";
```

The storage class of this data object is static, and its type is char. In a program, every time the identifier message appears, it will have these characteristics. In C, there are two ways of controlling access or changes to a data object. These attributes are: volatile and const.

Volatile   By using the attribute volatile in a declaration, you are telling the compiler that this variable's value may be changed by ways not explicitly specified in the program. For this reason, the compiler will not optimize the portion of the code where the variable is used, leaving the original intent inact.

The general form of volatile definition is:

```
volatile storage-specifier variable-list;
```

One illustration of its use is where a variable holding real-time data is updated by a subroutine of the operating system. In the following example, the variable clock is declared as a volatile data object. It is assumed that the variable clock is updated every tenth of a second by a routine outside this program. This program prints, in tenths of seconds, the elapsed time to increment variable i 10000 times.

```
/******************************************************
Program to illustrate volatile variable
******************************************************/
#include <stdio.h>

volatile int clock;

main()
{
    int time,i;

    time = clock;
    for( i = 0; i < 10000 ; i++ );
    printf( "Elapsed time is %d \n", clock - time );
}
```

Const   There are situations when you do not want the content of a variable to change. Although it may not be intented, it could happen inadvertently, causing a programming error. To avoid any alteration happening to a variable, you can declare a variable with const attribute.

The general form of const definition is:

```
const storage-specifier variable-list;
```

Such a definition will explicitly declare the variable as a constant. The compiler will flag any attempts to modify a variable declared as const. In the following statements, the variables version and name are declared as const:

```
const float version = 1.20 ;
const char name[] = "Softek International";
```

2.4 INITIALIZERS

An *initializer* is a way of setting the initial value of a data object. It is an option that is included during the declaration of a variable. An initializer is made up of the assignment symbol (=), followed by the initial expression. We have already looked at several initializers. In the following declaration statements, variables are declared and set to initial values, version is set to the value 1.20, name to string constant "Softek International," and number to the value 100:

```
const float version = 1.20;
char name[] = "Softek International";
static int number = 100;
```

Global variables are only initialized once, before the start of your program. In the following example, global variables first and last are set to values 10 and 20, respectively. However, local variables with auto storage class are initialized every time a function is called. If you do not use the initializer, all global variables are set to 0. However, the variable count in the counter function is set to 1 every time the function is called.

```
/*****************************************************************
This program illustrates local and global initializations
*****************************************************************/
#include <stdio.h>
static int first = 10, last = 20; /*global declaration
        of first and last */
main()
{
    int count;
    count = counter();
    printf( "First is %d,  last = %d and count = %d \n",
                first, last, count );
}
int counter()
{
    int i, count = 1;
    for ( i = first; i < last; i++ )
        count++;
    return (count);
}
```

The initializer helps to simplify your code; it can also reduce the size of your program.

3

Expressions and Operators

This chapter explains the use of expressions and operators in C. An expression is a sequence of operators, constants, function names, function calls, any objects, and pointers of any type. Any combination of these various pieces can be a valid part of an expression. The general classes of expressions are:

    Lvalue expressions

    Constant expressions

    Primary expressions

C language is rich in built-in operators. Each operator is a symbolic character that tells the compiler to execute certain mathematical or logical tasks. There are five general classes of operators. They are:

    Unary operators

    Binary operators

    Conditional operators

    Assignment operators

    Comma operators

During the course of the discussion of expressions and operators, references will be made to data types or groups of data types. The following lists the types that collectively belong to a group.

Groups	Types
Integral	character
	enumeration
	integer
Arithmetic	integral
	floating-point
Scalar	arithmetic
	pointers
Aggregate	arrays
	structures
	unions

Before delving into expressions and operators, we will first look at the importance of precedence and associativity of operators in evaluating an expression.

3.1 PRECEDENCE AND ASSOCIATIVITY

The compiler follows precise rules when performing an operation. To avoid the risk of misuse, a programmer must consider these rules as essential information. Table 3.1 lists all the operators that we will discuss in this chapter in order of precedence and associativity for each class of operators. The precedence determines the order in which operations are performed. Table 3.1 is arranged from the highest to the lowest precedence. At the top are primary operators, which have the highest priority. The comma operator, at the bottom of the list, has the lowest precedence. Within a given group, such as multiplicative operators (*, /, and %), all have the same priority. Now, let's have a look at how the compiler applies the built-in precedence rule.

In the expression

```
a - b * x / y
```

the multiplication and division operators have higher precedence than subtraction. Therefore, the expression b * x/y is calculated first, and the result is subtracted from x.

However, you can change the precedence by explicitly stating the grouping of the operands with parentheses. The previous expression is rearraged to

```
( a - b ) * ( x / y ).
```

Then the subtraction and division have the same precedence and are evaluated before the multiplication.

The associativity rule establishes how an operation is evaluated. If it is "left-to-right," the operators are evaluated from left to right. The "right-to-left" rule implies that the operators are performed from right to left.

TABLE 3.1 Precedence and Associativity

Precedence	Operators	Associativity
Primary	. -> ( ) [ ] –	left-to-right
Unary	- + ! - ++ –	right-to-left
	(typename) & *	
	sizeof	
Multiplicative	* / %	left-to-right
Additive	+ -	left-to-right
Bitwise Shift	< < > >	left-to-right
Relational	<= >= < >	left-to-right
Equality	!= ==	left-to-right
Bitwise AND	&	left-to-right
Bitwise XOR	¬	left-to-right
Bitwise OR	|	left-to-right
Logical AND	&&	left-to-right
Logical OR	||	left-to-right
Conditional	?:	right-to-left
Assignment	= += -= *= /=	right-to-left
	<<= >>= %= &=	
	¬= |=	
Comma	,	left-to-right

3.2 LVALUE EXPRESSION

A data object is a piece of memory that can be modified. The lvalue, refering to an object, is an expression. For example, in the expression

```
y = 50;
```

the identifier y is assigned the value 50; therefore, it is changed. The left operand of this assigment expression yields lvalue y. In addition to the assignment operator, other operators, such as the address operator, the increment operator, and the decrement operator, also require an lvalue as an operand. In the expression

```
*ptr++;
```

the pointer variable *ptr is an lvalue. A modifiable lvalue is an object that has array type or constant type.

3.3 CONSTANT EXPRESSION

The value of a constant expression is determined during the compilation of a program. This value cannot be changed during program execution. Integer constants, character constants, floating-point constants, enumeration constants, and other constant expressions are all considered constituents of a constant expression. For example, in the expression

```
y = 50;
```

the value 50 is an integer constant.

In C language, a constant expression is required in the following cases:

1. The `case` keyword must be followed by a constant expression in a `switch` statement.
2. To specify the size of an array.
3. An enumeration identifier must be assigned a constant expression.
4. To assign initial values to external or static variables.
5. In the #if preprocessor statement.

The first three situations require that the constant expression must be one of the following:

> Integer constants
>
> Character constants
>
> Enumeration constants
>
> Casts to integral types
>
> `sizeof` expression

In the same situations, you can only use the following operators:

> Arithmetic operators
>
> Bitwise operators
>
> Relational operators
>
> Conditional expression operator

In the fourth case, all the above rules of constants and operators are valid. However, the initializer of an external declaration must evaluate to either a constant or an address of a `static` or `extern` object (plus or minus an integral constant expression) that is already declared. In the following statements

```
static int x[20];
```
```
extern int *xp = &x + 5;
```

the expression

```
&x + 5
```

is valid because x is declared as an array and xp is declared as an external pointer variable.

For the fifth situation, the constant expression is placed after the #if, and the same constant and operator rules apply.

3.4 PRIMARY EXPRESSION

There are four primary expressions:

    Parenthesized expression

    Function call

    Array element specification

    Structure and union specification

All the primary operators are grouped from left to right, and all have the same precedence.

3.4.1 Parenthesized Expression ( )

As seen before, C's precedence mechanism forces execution of certain operations before others. In the example

```
x - y * z ;  /* multiply first */
```

the multiplication of y and z will be done before the subtraction. You can change the order of the operation with parentheses. If you want the subtraction done first, you can force the compiler to do so by enclosing subtraction in parentheses—for example,

```
( x - y ) * z ;  /* subtract first */
```

If you parenthesize the multiplication:

```
x - ( y * z );
```

it will not change the normal order of calculation—that is, multiplication first and subtraction next.

Parenthesized expressions are used to explicitly state how operands and operators are grouped together. This allows you to change the order in which the compiler will evaluate an expresion.

3.4.2 Function Call ( )

A function call is a primary expression followed by a list of arguments enclosed in parentheses. The list may be empty, or it may contain one or more expressions. Multiple expressions are separated by commas. The following shows various function calls:

```
sort ();
counts( x+y, y+10 );
read( buffer, length );
```

Each expression of the argument list is evaluated and becomes the argument of the function. For example, x+y and y+10 will be first calculated and passed as values to the counts function. The values of actual parameters, such as x and y, are never changed, however, assigning the value to the parameter changes the value within the function.

If you wish to change the value of the parameter within a function, you pass a pointer to the variable rather than the value. Arrays and functions are always converted to pointers before they are passed as parameters to a function.

If a *function call* is defined as function returning type `int`, then in an expression the value returned by such a function is of data type `int`. Similarly, a primary expression defined to return type `float` will result type `float`.

3.4.3 Array Element Specification [ ]

An identifier followed by an expression enclosed by a pair of square brackets ([]) that refers to an element of an array. Such a primary expression is a pointer, and the subscript type must be an integer value. The compiler converts the expression within the brackets into an address of the array element. In the example

```
horses[ y + 2 ]
```

expression `y + 2` is first evaluated, yielding an integer value. This value is then used to calculate the memory location of element `y + 2`.

3.4.4 Structure and Union Specifications (. or ->)

A primary expression followed by a dot (.) followed by an identifier is an expression. The primary expression must be a variable name defined as structure or union type. The identifier must be a member within the structure or union. The following is a dot expression:

```
employee.name
```

A primary expression followed by an arrow operator (—>) followed by an identifier is an expression. The primary expression must be defined as a pointer to structure or union type. The identifier must be a member within the structure or union. The following is an arrow operator expression:

```
employee->name
```

3.5 UNARY OPERATORS

All computer languages have operators called binary arithmetic operators, which require two operands. A unary operator acts on only one value. The following are unary operators:

    Increment ++

    Decrement --

    Unary Plus +

Unary Minus -

Logical Negation !

Bitwise Negation ~

Address &

Indirection *

Cast

sizeof

All these unary operators have the same precedence. In an expression with many unary operators, the compiler groups them in the right-to-left order.

3.5.1 Increment ++

The increment operator (++) simply adds 1 to the operand. After the statement

```
y++;
```

is executed the value of y is incremented by one.

But, if the operand is a pointer, the increment depends on the size of the data object it is pointing to. Let's say intp is an integer pointer variable. The statement

```
intp++;
```

will increase the value of intp by 4, since an integer occupies four bytes. Or, if pointer variable structp is declared as pointer to a structure of size 20 bytes, the example

```
structp++;
```

will add value 20 to structp.

The increment operator can be placed before or after an operand. In an expression with several operands, the position of ++ is significant. If you place ++ before the operand, the operand is first incremented and then used in the expression. In the example

```
y = ++x + z;
```

value 1 is first added to variable x, then the result is added to variable z, and the final sum is placed in variable y.

If you place ++ after the operand, the current value of the operand is first used in the expression, and then its value is incremented. In the example

```
y = x++ + z;
```

the current value of x is added to z, the result is placed in y, and then x is incremented by 1.

3.5.2 Decrement --

The decrement operator (--) simply subtracts 1 from the operand. After the statement

    y--;

is executed, the value of y is decremented by 1.

But if the operand is a pointer, the decrement depends on the size of the data object it is pointing to. Let's say intp is an integer pointer variable. The statement

    intp--;

will decrease the value of intp by 4, since an integer occupies four bytes. Or, if pointer variable structp is declared as pointer to a structure of size 20 bytes, the example

    structp--;

will decrease the value of structp by 20.

The decrement operator can be placed before or after an operand. In an expression with several operands, the position of -- is significant. If you place -- before the operand, the operand is first incremented and then used in the expression. In the example

    y = --x + z;

value 1 is first substracted from variable x, then the result is added to variable z, and the final result is placed in variable y.

If you place -- after the operand, the current value of the operand is first used in the expression, and then its value is decremented. In the example

    y = x-- + z;

the current value of x is added to z, the result is placed in y, and then x is decremented by 1.

3.5.3 Unary Plus +

The unary plus operator (+) does not change the value of the operand. In fact, this operator is rarely used. The operation of the statement

    +x;

will not change the value of x.

3.5.4 Unary Minus -

The unary minus operator (-) multiplies the value of the operand by -1. When the unary minus is applied to an operand, the sign of the value is switched. For example, if variable number has value 10, then

```
-number;
```

will change the value to -10. If `number` has value -10, then

```
-number;
```

will change the value to 10.

3.5.5 Logical Negation !

The logical negation operator (!) is used to test if the value of an expression is false. The expression is first evaluated and, if it is 0 the logical negation operator yields a 1. If the result of the negation is non-zero, the negation operator returns a 0. The result of the logical negation operator is always of type `int`. In the following statements, the variable `flag` is tested for a zero or non-zero value.

```
if ( !flag )
    printf( "flag is zero" );
else
    printf( "flag is non-zero" );
```

If the result of operation `!flag` is 1, then

```
printf( "flag is zero" );
```

is executed. Otherwise, this segment of program executes

```
printf( "flag is non-zero" );
```

Another use of the logical negation operator is to easily "flip" the value of a flag between 1 and 0—for example,

```
flag = !flag ;
```

will switch the value of `flag` to 1 or 0 depending on whether its value before the operation is 0 or non-zero.

3.5.6 Bitwise Negation ~

The bitwise negation operator (~) changes the content of every bit of the operand. All the bits that are 1's are changed to 0's, and all bits that are 0's are switched to 1's. The bitwise negation operator therefore produces the 1's complement of the operand. Let's say that `y` is declared as an `unsigned char` variable and has a value 10. The 8-bit binary representation of `y` is:

```
00001010.
```

Now the expression

```
~y;
```

will produce the binary value 11110101.

3.5.7 Address &

The address operator (&) produces the memory address of the operand. For example, the statement

```
py = &y;
```

assigns the memory location of variable y to py. It is assumed that py is declared as a pointer variable to the same type as y.

The operands of the & operator can be variables or array elements. But it is illegal to have *bitfield* or *register* variables as operands of address operator.

3.5.8 Indirection *

The indirection operator (*) uses as its operand the address to data object. The operand must be a pointer variable, and the result depends on the data type. The following statements first declare a and b as int variables and then pa as an integer pointer variable:

```
int a,b;
int *pa;
```

The statement

```
b = *pa;
```

assigns the value pointed to by pa to b. In this case, the result of the operator * is an integer value. The following sequence of statements:

```
pa = &a; /* assign address to a to pa */
b = *pa; /* assign content of pa to b */
```

demonstrates how to assign address and contents of variable a, which is the same as

```
b = a;
```

3.5.9 Cast

The cast operator converts the value of an expression to a specific data type. To do so, you place the parenthesized name of the data type before the operand. For example, you declare z as an integer and you want the result of expression z/5 to be a type float. To guarantee that the compiler yields a fractional component, you use cast operator. In the statement

```
price = (float) z/5 ;
```

the value z/5 is assigned to variable price, which is declared as a float.

3.5.10 sizeof

The sizeof operator gives the size of an operand in number of bytes. The operand can be a variable or type, but it cannot be bitfield or function. The following program prints the sizes of variables i, name, and record, declared as integer, array of 40 characters, and structures, respectively. Also, it prints the sizes in bytes of data types float and int long.

```
/*********************************************************
This program illustrates the sizeof operator
*********************************************************/
#include <stdio.h>

main()
{
    int i;
    char name[40];
    struct data    {
                    char name[40];
                    int number;
                    } record;

    printf( "size of i is %d\n", sizeof(i) );
    printf( "size of name is %d\n", sizeof(name) );
    printf( "size of record is %d\n", sizeof(record) );
    printf( "size of float is %d\n", sizeof(float) );
    printf( "size of double is %d\n", sizeof(double) );
}
```

The output is:

```
size of i is 4
size of name is 40
size of record is 44
size of float is 4
size of double is 8
```

3.6 BINARY OPERATORS

A binary operation requires two operands. A binary expression is made of two operands seperated by a binary operator. In C there are many binary operators. The precedence of all of them are not the same. The evaluation of binary expressions is done according to the precedence rule listed in Table 3.1. However, if an expression has many operators of the same precedence, the compiler will evaluate them in the left-to-right order.

The following sections describes each binary operator and its operation.

3.6.1 Multiplication *

The multiplication operator (*) calculates the product of two operands. In the statement

```
result = x * y ;
```

x is multiplied by y and the result is placed in the variable `result`.

The * operator is treated as associative. An expression with several multiplications may be rearranged by the compiler, although sub-expressions are enclosed by parentheses. The expression:

```
result = x * y * z ;
```

can be interpreted in three different ways:

```
result = ( x * y ) * z ;
result = x * ( y * z ) ;
result = ( x * z ) * y ;
```

3.6.2 Division /

The division operator (/) calculates the quotient of two operands. In the statement

```
result = x / y;
```

x is divided by y and the result is placed in the variable `result`.

If you use two positive integers as operands, the compiler will ignore any remainder produced by the division operation. For example, in the expression 9/4 the result is 2, discarding the remainder .25.

But, if one of the operands has a negative value, truncation will occur in the result. The usual arithmetic conversion, on operands discussed later in this chapter, are performed by the compiler.

3.6.3 Remainder %

The remainder operator (%) produces the remainder when two operators are divided. For example, the result of expression

```
9 % 4
```

is 1.

The type of both operands must be integer.

3.6.4 Addition +

The addition operator (+) produces the sum of the operands. For example, in the expression

```
a + b
```

the value of a is added to b. If there are many addition operators in an expression, the operators are grouped in left-to-right order.

The operands can be integers, floating-points, and pointers. If one operator is an integer and the other is a pointer, the compiler first converts the integer operand to an address offset and then does the addition. The result is an address of an data object. For detailed discussion on pointer arithmetic, refer to Chapter 7.

3.6.5 Subtraction -

The subtraction operator (-) produces the difference of the operands. In the expression

```
a - b
```

the value of b is substracted from a. If there are many subtraction operators in an expression, the operators are grouped in left-to-right order.

The operands can be integers, floating-points, and pointers. In case an integer is substracted from a pointer, the compiler computes the operation in the following steps:

1. The integer type operand is converted to an address offset.
2. After the subtraction is done, the result is an address of the same type as the pointer operand.

For more detailed discussion on pointer arithmetic, refer to Chapter 7.

3.6.6 Bitwise Left and Right Shift << >>

The shift operators (< < and > >) literally shift the bits of the left operand. The right operand is the number of places (bits) the left operand is to be shifted. The left shift operator < < moves bits towards the left, while the right shift operator > > moves bits towards the right. The shift operators are grouped in left-to-right order.

The operands must be integer values. The right operand is always converted to integer value, while the type of the result is the same as the left operand.

In the expression

```
x << 2;
```

the variable x, declared as type short, is shifted left by two positions.

The following shows the content of x in binary and decimal representations before and after the left shift operation:

```
0000  0000  0000  0011    3   (before)
0000  0000  0000  1100   12   (after)
```

Every shift to the left has the same effect as multiplying the value by two. The right end of x is filled with 0's.

In the expression

```
y >> 2;
```

y, declared as type short, is shifted by 2.

The following shows the content of y in binary and decimal representations before and after the right shift operation:

```
1100  0000  0000  0000   49152  (before)
0011  0000  0000  0000   12288  (after)
```

Every shift to the right has the same effect as dividing the value by 2. The left end of y is filled with 0's.

The results of a shift operator are undefined if the right operand is a negative value or is greater or equal to the number of bits of the left operands. If the right operand is a 0, the left operand is unchanged.

3.6.7 Relational < > <= >=

The relational operators (< > <= >=) compare two operands for a valid relationship. The result of the relational operators is either 1, if the relationship is true; otherwise, it is 0. The operands can be of arithmetic type or pointers of the same type. If the operands are arithmetic type, the usual arithmetic conversion (discussed later) on operands are performed by the compiler. The relational operators are grouped in the left-to-right order.

The following shows the result of each relational expression:

x < y	has the value 1 if x is less than y, otherwise 0.
x < = y	has the value 1 if x is less than or equal to y, otherwise 0.
x > y	has the value 1 if x is greater than y, otherwise 0.
x > = y	has the value 1 if x is greater than or equal to y, otherwise 0.

3.6.8 Equality == !=

The equality operators (= = !=) compare two operands for equality. The result of the equality operators is either 1, if the relationship is true; otherwise it is 0. The operands can be arithmetic type or pointers of the same type. It is also legal to have one operand as a pointer and the other as a null pointer or integer with value 0.

If the operands are of arithmetic type, the usual arithmetic conversion on operands are performed by the compiler. The equality operators are grouped in the left-to-right order.

The following shows the result of each equality expression:

x == y	has the value 1 if x is equal to y, otherwise 0.
x != y	has the value 1 if x is not equal to y, otherwise 0.

3.6.9 Bitwise AND &

The bitwise AND operator (&) compares the values of the operand bit by bit. If the bit of the fist value is 1 and the corresponding bit of the second value is also 1, the result is 1; otherwise, it is set to 0.

In the statement

z = x & y;

a bitwise comparison of y and x are done, and the result is placed in z. If x and y had values of 16645 and 51850, respectively, then 16-bit binary representations after the operation are:

x	0100	0001	0000	0110
y	1100	1010	1000	1010
z	0100	0000	0000	0010

If the corresponding bits of x and y are 1, the bit in the same position of y is 1; otherwise, it is 0. In an AND operation, both operands must be an integral type.

3.6.10 Bitwise Exclusive OR ¬

The bitwise exclusive OR operator (¬) compares the values of the operand bit by bit. If the bit of both values is 1 or 0, the corresponding bit of the result is 0; otherwise, it is set to 1.

In the statement

```
z = x ¬ y;
```

a bitwise comparison of y and x are done, and the result is placed in z. If the x and y had the values 16645 and 51880, respectively, the 16-bit binary representations of x, y, and z after the operation are:

x	0100	0001	0000	0110
y	1100	1010	1000	1010
z	1000	1011	1000	1100

If the corresponding bits of x and y are not the same, the bit in the same position of z is 1; otherwise, it is 0. In an exclusive OR operation, both operands must be of integral type.

3.6.11 Bitwise Inclusive OR |

The bitwise inclusive OR operator (|) works in the following ways: for corresponding bits of both operands, if either or both is a 1, the corresponding result bit is a 1; otherwise, it is set to 0.

In the following statement, a bitwise comparison of y and x is done, and the result is placed in z:

```
z = x | y;
```

If x and y had values 16645 and 51880, respectively, the 16-bit binary representations of x, y, and z are:

x	0100	0001	0000	0110
y	1100	1010	1000	1010
z	1100	1011	1000	1110

In an inclusive OR operation, both operands must be an integral type.

3.6.12 Logical AND &&

The logical AND operator (&&) checks two operators for non-zero values. If both have non-zero values, the result of the AND operation is 1; otherwise, it is 0. Both operands must be scalar types. In an expression, the AND operators are grouped in the left-to-right order.

For the logical expression

x && y

the following gives the result of three different pairs of x and y.

result	x		y
0	0	&&	0
0	0	&&	3
1	5	&&	2

In the first two cases, the result is 0 because x is 0 in both cases. In the third case, the result is 1 because both x and y have non-zero value.

3.6.13 Logical OR ||

The logical OR operator (||) checks two operators for non-zero value. If either has a non-zero value, the result of an OR operation is 1; otherwise, it is 0. Both operands must be scalar types. The logical OR operators are grouped in the left-to-right order. For the logical expression

x || y

the following shows the results of logical or operation for three of pairs x and y values.

result	x		y
0	0	&&	0
1	5	&&	2
1	0	&&	3

The first result is 0 because both x and y are 0's. The last two results are 1's because either 1 or both x and y are non-zeroes.

3.7 CONDITIONAL OPERATOR ?:

The conditional operator (?:) is among the most unique operators in the C language. It requires three operands and two symbols. The first operand is placed before the question mark (?), followed by the second operand and the colon (:) and the third operand after the colon.

The general form of a conditional expression is:

condition ? expression1 : expression2

The compiler first evaluates the *condition*, which is usually a relational expression. If the result from the evaluation of the *condition* is non-zero, *expression1* is evaluated, and the result is the value of the condition expression. If *condition* is 0, then *expression2* is evaluated and it is the value of the conditional expression.

The conditional operator is best understood by looking at an example to determine the maximum of two values: x and y. The usual way of programming this function is:

```
int max( int x, int y )
{
    int z;

    if ( x > y )
        z = x;
    else
        z = y ;
    return ( z );
}
```

The same logic can be programmed by using the conditional operator. For example, the following statement accomplishes the same task as the above *max* function:

```
z = ( x > y ) ? x : y ;  /* z = max(x,y) */
```

The conditional expression can be any expression, and it is enclosed in parantheses only for the sake of readability. First, the expression (x > y) is calculated. If it is true (that is, non-zero) the x is assigned to z; otherwise, y is assigned to z.

The conditional expression works according to the following rules:

1. The conditional operand must have scalar type.
2. The second and third operands can be any of these types:
   a. Arithmetic type.
   b. Same structure type.
   c. Same union type.
   d. Same pointer type.
3. The result of the conditional operator has the same type as the second and third operands.
4. If the second and third operands are arithmetic types, the usual arithmetic conversion (discussed later) on operands are performed by the compiler.

3.8 ASSIGNMENT OPERATOR =

The assignment operator (=) gives a value to the left operand after evaluating the right operand.

In an expression with many assignment operators, they are grouped in right-to-left order. The C language has two kinds of assignment operators:

1. Simple assignment
2. Compound assignment

3.8.1 Simple Assignment

The simple assignment simply takes the value of the right operand and gives it to the left operand.

The types of both operands must have:

1. Arithmetic type.
2. Same structure type.
3. Same union type.
4. Pointers to same type.

The left operand can be a pointer and the right operand a NULL pointer (0). If both operands are arithmetic types, the usual arithmetic conversion (discussed later) on operands are performed by the compiler,.

The following statements are some of the examples of assignment operators:

```
employee.age = 50 ;
employee.hours = regular + overtime ;
ptr = &prices[10] ;
chr = name[i] ;
x = y = z = 0 ;
value = 2.55 + 10 ;
*p = 's' ;
```

3.8.2 Compound Assignment

An expression with compound assignment contains two operators: An assignment operator and binary operator. The following is a list of all compound assignment operators.

Operator	Example	Equivalent Expression
+=	x += y	x = x + y
-=	x -= y	x = x - y
*=	x *= y	x = x * y
/=	x /= y	x = x / y
%=	x %= y	x = x % y
<<=	x <<= y	x = x << y
>>=	x >>= y	x = x >> y
&=	x &= y	x = x & y
¬=	x ¬= y	x = x ¬ y
|=	x |= y	x = x | y

3.9 COMMA OPERATOR ,

A simple comma expression has two operands, seperated by a comma—for example,

    x, y

is a comma expression. The compiler first evaluates x and then y. The value and type of the expression is y. However, a single expression can have a number of expressions separated by commas—for example:

    i ++, y = 5, max(y, b), 1--

You can use a comma expression as a parameter-list when calling a function. In the following function call, a, s+t, and new (x) are parameters separated with commas:

    find_max(a, s+t, new(x));

Another place where you can use a comma operator is in a for statement, as in the following program.

```
/************************************************
This program illustrates the comma operator
************************************************/
#include <stdio.h>
main ()
{
    char str = "dad" ;
    int c, i, j ;

    for ( i = o, j = strlen( str ) - 1 ;
          i <j;
          i ++, j-- )
    {
        c = str[i];
        str[i] = str[j];
        str[j] = c ;
    }
}
```

Before the loop starts, i is set to 0 and expression strlen(str) - 1 is calculated and placed in j. Each time the for-loop is executed, i is incremented by 1 and y is decremented by 1.

3.10 CONVERSIONS

The C compiler does *conversions* while evaluating many of the operators. Let's say a value of type short int is added to int value, the short int is first converted to type int before the addition takes place.

Conversions are done during the following operations:

- Arithmetic operations
- Type conversion (cast operator)
- Function calls
- Assignment operations

3.10.1 Arithmetic Conversions

In arithmetic expressions, a 'lower' type is promoted to a 'higher' type during conversion and before the expression is evaluated. If either operand is one type, the other operand is converted according to the list below.

One operand is	The other is converted to
long double	long double
double	double
float	float
long int	unsigned long int
unsigned long int	unsigned long int
unsigned int	unsigned long int
long int	long int
unsigned int	unsigned int

If both operands are type `int`, the result is also type `int`.

3.10.2 Type Conversions

When a `cast` operation conversion takes place, the `cast` operator explicitly changes the type of an expression and assigns it to a variable of another type.

3.10.3 Function Conversions

When passing arguments to functions, conversion take place. Expression of type `char` and `short int` become `int`, and `float` becomes `double`.

3.10.4 Assignment Conversions

In an assignment operation, when the operands are of different types, conversion takes place. It is possible that information is lost during such conversion. The assignment conversion rule is that an operand of lower type is promoted to a higher type. The result of the expression also has the higher type. The conversion is according to the hierarchy of types.

long double > double > float > unsigned long > unsigned > long > int.

You can convert a pointer that is pointing to one data type to a pointer that is pointing to a different type.

4

Control Flow

It is the program-control statements of any language that gives power and flexibility to a computer. In essence, the control statements are the strength of a language; they dictate the flow of a program execution. They are powerful building blocks of programs. C has a rich and diverse set of control statements. This chapter explains the basics of the control flow of these statements. It also shows how you can use them effectively to produce versatile and robust programs.

Before we go any further, let's say a few words about the three types of statements used in C. A statement may consist of one of the following:

1. A single statement.
2. A block statement.
3. An empty statement.

A *single* statement is simple valid C statement followed by a semi-colon. For example, the following are three single statements:

```
i = 1 + 2;
for( 1 = 0 ; i < 10 ; i++ );
printf( "Wonderful World of C" );
```

A *block* statement consists of definitions, declarations, and statements grouped together as one statement. A block statement is enclosed with a single set of braces—for example:

```
if ( x > 0 )
{
    int y = 10 ;
    printf( "value of y = % d \n", y );
}
```

An *empty*, or *NULL*, statement performs no operation. It is simply a semi-colon (;). For example, this for-loop has an empty statement (between the parantheses are required expressions, which are not considered statements).

```
for( i = 0; i < 100 ; i++ );
```

C has seven kinds of statements:

> if
>
> switch
>
> for
>
> while
>
> do/while
>
> break
>
> continue
>
> goto

4.1 LABEL

Before we discuss statements, let's look at the concept of label. A label is placed before a statement. A label is an identifier to which control is transferred; it is not a statement. There are three kinds of labels: plain label, case label, and default label. The plain label is used with a `goto` statement, and case label and default label are used in `switch` statement. We will discuss labels in more detail in association with statements in the rest of this chapter.

4.2 IF STATEMENT

The `if` statement allows a statement to be executed only after a condition is met. It consists of an expression, `else` clause, and statements.

The general form of the `if` statement is:

```
if ( expression )
        statement;
else
        statement;
```

The `else` is an optional clause. The conditional expression is first evaluated; when the result is TRUE (non-zero), the statement associated with `if` is acted upon. If the expression evaluates to FALSE (0), and else exists, the computer will execute the statement or the block of statement forming part of the else. In other words, only statements associated with if or statements associated with else are executed—never both. The expression can be any valid C expression, which can include relation and logical operators, functions, and pointers. In this section we will give examples of various expressions that can be used with an if statement.

In the next example, an if statement is used to check whether a variable has a 0 or non-zero value. The program first reads a number from the standard input stream using scanf function and places it in the variable num. Next, it prints the value of num if it is non-zero. Otherwise, it prints the message "Number is zero."

```
\*****************************************************
 This program illustrates the if statement
 *****************************************************/

#include <stdio.h>

main()
{
    int num = 0;

    scanf( "%d \n", &num );

    if ( num )
        printf( "Number is %d \n", num );
    else
        printf( "Number is zero \n" );

}
```

We can replace num with a relational expression num != 0 and the result would be the same—for example:

```
if ( num != 0 )

    printf( "Number is %d \n", num );

else

    printf( "Number is zero \n" );
```

In the next program, the conditional expression of the if statement consists of both relational and logical operators. A character is read by the *getchar* function and placed in variable chr. The expression of the if statement is to test if a character is numeric. According to the EBCDIC table, all numeric characters are between '0' and '9'. When the expression

```
( chr > '0' && chr <= '9' )
```

is evaluated to be FALSE (0), the message "Character is not numeric" is printed; otherwise, the numeric character is printed.

```
\*******************************************************
  This program illustrates if statement
  ******************************************************/

#include <stdio.h>

main()
{
    char chr;

    chr = getchar();

    if ( chr > '0' && chr <= '9' )
        printf( "Numeric character is %c \n", chr );
    else
        printf( "Character is not numeric \n" );
}
```

4.2.1 Nested If

In C, you can use if as an object of another if statement or an else clause. Such an arrangement is called nested ifs. Confusion arises when there are many nested ifs. You may have a problem associating the else with the right if, especially when at some level the else clause is dropped. The simple rule is to associate an else with the closest preceding if statement. Both if and else statements must be within the same block. Braces are used to override the normal association or simply to make your code more readable.

The general form of a two-level nested if is:

```
if ( expression )
        if ( expression )
            statement;
        else
            statement;
else
        if ( expression )
            statement;
        else
            statement;
```

A nested if can have many levels, and, as mentioned earlier, the else clause is optional.

The next program segment has a nested if statement as the object of the first if statement. Here the first pair of braces is not necessary, but is used to clarify the code. However, the second pair is necessary, as the `printf` function and `return` statement belong to the same block.

```
if ( scanf( "%c", &chr ) != EOF )
{
    if ( chr > '0' && chr <= '9' )
            printf( "Numeric character is %c \n", chr );
    else
            printf( "Character is not numeric \n" );
}
else
{
    print f("Input Error\n");
    return;
}
```

4.2.2 If-else-If Ladder

The general form of the *if-else-if* ladder is:

```
if( expression )
        statement;
else if ( expression )
        statement;
        •
        •
        •
else
        statement;
```

In a *if-else-if* ladder, the evaluation of expression starts from the top. As soon as an expression is found to be TRUE (non-zero), the associated statement is executed and the rest of the ladder is skipped. If none of the expression is found to be TRUE, the *statement* linked to the last `else` is executed.

In the following example, a message is printed when the input character is one of the following:

1. Numeric character.
2. Space character.
3. Plus sign.
4. None of the above, default.

```
\*****************************************************
 This program illustrates the if-else-if ladder
 *****************************************************/

#include <stdio.h>

main()
{
    char chr, * strp = " " ;
    int y;
    if ( scanf( "%c", & chr ) ! = EOF )
    {
       if ( chr >= '0' && chr <= '9' )
       {
          *strp = chr;
          y = atoi( strp );
          printf( "Number is %d \n", y );
       }
       else if ( chr == ' ' )
          print f( "Space character \n" );
       else if ( chr == '+' )
          printf( "Plus sign \n" );
       else
          printf("Not numeric character, space or + \n");
    }
    else
       printf( "Input Error " );
}
```

4.3 SWITCH STATEMENT

The switch statement is a multiple-branch decision statement. This statement not only replaces some forms of *if-else-if* ladder construction discussed earlier, but also infuses clarity and elegance to a program. A switch statement consists of an expression, labels, and statements.

The general form of the switch statement is:

```
switch( expression )
{
     case constant1:
          statement;
             break;
     case constant2:
          statement;
             break;
               •
               •
               •
default:
          statement;
```

switch body

The expression of the `switch` statement must evaluate to an integral type. The `switch` body, enclosed with braces, has `case` labels, statements, and `default` labels. The `case` label consists of a keyword `case`, followed by an integer or character constant and a colon. Following the `case` label, you can have an empty statement, single statement, or block of statements.

Starting from the top, the expression is checked against the constants successively. If a match is found, control is transferred to the statement associated with that constant. Execution will continue until a `break` statement is encountered or the end of the `switch` body is reached. If there is no match, the program executes the optional `default` statement. If a `default` label is not present, no action is taken if no match occurs. The `break` statement is not part of the `switch` statement, but it is used to stop execution of the statement sequence of the `case` clause.

There are a few things to keep in mind when using a `switch` statement:

1. The expression and constants must have integral type. And each constant must be different.
2. There must be only one `default` label.
3. A `switch` body can have definitions and declarations.
4. A `case` clause can have a `switch` statement. Therefore, nested `switch` is allowed.
5. A `case` clause can be empty.

One way of using a `switch` statement is to process a menu selection. In the next program, a menu of three items is printed. Then it reads a selection character.

```
\*********************************************************
This program illustrates the switch statement
**********************************************************/
#include <stdio.h>
main()
{
    char key;

    printf( "1. Add Customer Record \n");
    printf( "2. Change Customer Record \n");
    printf( "3. Delete Customer Record \n" );
       printf( " Enter a selection (1, 2 or 3) \n");
       printf( " Press any other key to skip \n" );

    key = getchar() ; /* read the selection from the
            standard input stream */

    switch( key )
    {
        case '1':
            CustAdd();
            break;
```

```
        case '2':
            CustChg();
            break;
        case '3':
            CustDel();
            break;
        default:
            printf( "No Selection Made \n" );
    }
    return;
}
```

The variable key is compared to each character constant: '1', '2', and '3'. If there is a match, the corresponding function is called. For example, if it is '1', CustAdd function is called. Upon return from CustAdd function, the switch statement is terminated because of break statement, and control is transferred to the next statement, which is return. Similarly, CustChg and CustDel functions are called if key is '2' or '3', respectively.

In case of no match—the input character is not '1', '2', or '3'—the message "No Selection Made" is printed to the standard output stream. This is as a result of executing the statement associated with the default label.

The following program illustrates an empty case clause and case clause having one or more statements. Note that the constants are both integer and character constants. For example, '1', '2', and '3' are character constants, and decimal 244 (EBCDIC code for '4') and SPACE defined as hex 40 are integer constants.

```
\***************************************************
This program illustrates the switch statement
****************************************************/
#include <stdio.h>
#define SPACE 0x40  /*EBCDIC code for space character*/
main()
{
    int y;
    char key, *strp = " " ;
    key = getchar();
    switch( key )
    {
        case '1':
        case '2':
        case '3':
            printf("Key is %c", key );
            break;
        case 244: /*EBCDIC code for '4' */
            *strp = key;
            y = atoi( strp );
            printf( "Number is %d ", y );
```

```
                break;
         case SPACE:
                printf( " Key is space bar " );
                break;
      }
}
```

The `case` clauses with constant '1' and '2' have no statements; therefore, they use the same code as the `case` clause with constant '3'. This shows that different conditions can use the same portion of a program. In the fourth `case` clause, the constant is an integer constant 244. This `case` clause has three statements. The first is

```
*strp = key;
```

to move the input character into a string. The second is a call to `atio` function to convert the key stroke from a character to integer value, which is placed in y. Next, the converted integer y is printed. The fifth `case` label has an integer constant representing a space character. Note that this `switch` statement does not have a `default` label. This means that the `switch` statement does not execute anything if none of the five conditions are met.

4.4. FOR STATEMENT

The general form of the `for` statement is

```
for ( expression1; expression2; expression3 )
        statement ;
```

This statement has up to three expressions, enclosed in brackets, and statements whenever needed. The `for` statement can have an empty statement, a single statement, or a block of statements. More than one statement must be enclosed in a pair of braces. It forms the body of the for-loop.

Expression1 is evaluated only once before the loop starts. It can be used to initialize a variable to control the loop. *Expression2* is evaluated every time the body is executed. The result of *expression2* determines when to exit the loop. If it yields a zero value (0), the statement of the for-loop is *not executed* and control goes to the next statement of the program. Otherwise, the statement is executed. The computer evaluates *expression3* every time, but only after the statement of the loop is executed. It can be used to increment, decrement, or initialize variables that determine whether to exit or continue the loop.

Any or all of these expressions can be ommitted, but in each case it affects how the loop is executed. Later, we will discuss some of the variations of the for-loop. First, we want to show you a simple example of the for-loop.

In the following program, the for-loop is used to print numbers 1 through 5 to the standard output stream. First, the variable i is set to value 1. Next, the expression i <= 5 is evaluated. If it is TRUE (1), the value is printed; otherwise, the loop terminates. Everytime after i is printed with `printf` function, it is incremented by 1. The loop stops when i reaches the value 5.

CONTROL FLOW

```
\*********************************************
  This program illustrates for-loop
**********************************************/

#include <stdio.h>
main()
{
    int i;

    for( i = 1; i <= 5; i++ )
        printf( "%d ", i );

}
```

The output is:

1 2 3 4 5

In a for-loop, C does not restrict you in the composition of expressions, as long as they are valid. In the following example, *expression1* set i to 5, *expression2* tests if i greater than 0, and *expression3* decrements i by 1. In this case, the *statement* (call to printf function) prints numbers in descending order from 5 through 1.

```
for ( i = 5; i > 0 ; x-- )
    printf( "%d ", i );
```

C allows many variables of the for-loop that can add power and flexibility to your programs. You can omit the first expression, but you have to ensure that the variable controlling the loop is properly initialized before the execution of the for-loop. If not set properly, undesired result may occur. In the following situation, i is set to 5 before the loop starts.

```
i = 5;
for ( ; i > 0 ; x-- )
    printf ( "%d ", i );
```

In the next example, the second expression is missing. When this expression is ommitted, the compiler replaces the expression with a non-zero constant. Therefore, the loop will be executed infinitely. To break out of the loop, you use the break, as shown here:

```
for ( i = 0 ; ; i++ )
{
    if ( i > 5 )
        break;
    printf( "%d ", i );
}
return;
```

This will end the loop when i is greater than 5 and give control to the next statement in the function, namely

```
return;
```

Note that there is more than one statement associated with this for-loop; therefore, the loop is enclosed in braces.

Other ways to end a for-loop are by using return and goto statements. Return will terminate the function, while goto will transfer control to a portion of the function identified by a label. Break and goto are discussed later in this chapter. The return statement is discussed in greater detail in Chapter 5.

You can include a for statement within another one, thus forming many levels of nested for-loops. The next example uses two levels of for-loops to initialize a two-dimensional array called table. The outer for-loop increments i by 1 from 0 to 10. Before every increment of i, the inner loop increments j from 0 to 20. The body of the inner loop first calculates the sum if i and j, and places it in the ith and jth element of the array table.

```
\*********************************************
This program illustrates two levels of for-loop
**********************************************/

#include <stdio.h>

main()
{
    int table[10][20] ;
    int sum, i, j;

    for ( i = 0 ; i >= 10; i++ ) /* outer loop */
        for ( j = 0 ; j >= 20 ; j++ ) /* inner loop */
      }
            sum = i + j ;
            table[i][j] = sum ;
      }
}
```

So far we have seen *expression1* and *expression3*, having only one part. But they can have many parts. In the following example, the initialization expression sets x to 0 and y to 1. Also, the *expression3* first increments y by 1, and x becomes the sum of the y and 5.

```
for ( x = 0, y = 1; y <= 5 ; y++, x = y + 5 )

    printf( "y = %d, x = %d \n", y, x );\
```

An empty for-loop does not have any statement. For example,

```
if ( i = 0 ; i > 1000 ; i ++ );
```

4.5 WHILE STATEMENT

A while statement consists of an conditional expression and statement.
The general form of the while statement is

while(expression)

    statement;

The statement consists either of an empty statement, a single statement, or a block of statements, forming the body of the while-loop.

The expression determines the duration of the loop. Before every iteration, the expression is evaluated. If it yields a FALSE value (0), the loop is terminated. Otherwise, the statements of the body are executed. This allows you to repeatedly do a task within a program until a specific condition is met. You can break out of the while-loop by using the break, return, or goto statement.

The following example is a simple program to determine the length of a string and the number of spaces. Using the while-loop, the program scans the character array string until a NULL character is found. The expression of the while-loop checks if the ith element is '\0'. If it is TRUE, the body is executed. In the body, counter spaces is incremented by 1 when a space character is encountered. Next, the index i is incremented by 1 when the ith element of array string is '\0', and then the loop is terminated. The variable i has the length of the string, and spaces has the number of spaces in the string. Both counts are printed before the program ends.

```
\***********************************************************
This program illustrates the while-loop
************************************************************/

#include <stdio.h>

#define SPACE ' '

main()
{
    char string[] = "This is a complex world";
    int i, spaces ;

    i = 0;
    spaces = 0;

    while( string[i] != '\0')
    {
       if ( string [i] == SPACE )
            spaces++;
       i++;
    }
    printf( "length of string is %d \n", i );
    printf( "number of spaces are %d \n", spaces);
}
```

The output is:

```
length of string is 23
number of spaces is 4
```

4.6 DO/WHILE STATEMENT

The do/while statement consists of statement and an conditional expression.
The general form of the do/while statement is:

```
do
{
        statement;
} while( expression );
```

The do/while statement executes the body of the loop, statements between braces, and then evaluates the expression. The *body* is made of either an empty statement, a single statement, or a block of statements. If the expression of the while clause evaluates to non-zero, the loop is executed again; otherwise, the loop ends.

Unlike for- and while-loops, the do/while-loop executes the body at least once, regardless of the form of the expression. The loop can also be ended with a break, return, or goto statement within the body of the do/while-loop.

One possible use of the do/while-loop is to process a menu selection. The following program first prints all the items of a menu and then enters the body of the do/while-loop. Within the body, the program accepts a key, which is executed at least once. The switch statement is used to process the selection. For example, if the key is '1', CustAdd function is called, and CustChg and CustDel functions are called if key is '2' and '3', respectively. The expression of the while clause checks if the key is '4'; if it is, the loop is terminated. Otherwise, it reads another key from the standard input stream and does another iteration.

```
\***********************************************************
  This program illustrates the do/while-loop
 ***********************************************************/

#include <stdio.h>

main()
{
        char key ;

        printf("1. Add Customer Record \n");
        printf("2. Change Customer Record \n");
        printf("3. Delete Customer Record \n");
        printf("4. Exit \n");
        printf(" Enter Selection (1,2,3 or 4) \n");
```

```
        do
        {
            key = getchar();  /* read the selection */
            switch( key )
            {
                case '1':
                    CustAdd();
                    break;
                case '2':
                    CustChg();
                    break;
                case '3':
                    CustDel();
                    break;
            }
        } while (key! = '4');
}
```

4.7 BREAK STATEMENT

The break statement has been used earlier in this chapter to terminate loops and switch statements. The break statement can be placed within the body of do, for, while, and switch statements. Any loop or switch statement is immediately terminated, without testing the conditional expression when a break statement is encountered.

The general form of a break statement is

break;

When a loop or switch statement is ended with a break, the control moves to the next statement outside the loop or switch body. Within nested statements, break terminates only the lower level of the loop or switch statement. A break statement cannot be used outside a loop or switch body.

The following program illustrates how to use a break within a while-loop by stopping a search when the first space character within a string is found. The while-loop scans a character array called string. It starts from the first element and continues as long as the ith element is not a NULL character ('\0'). Within the loop body, when the first space character is encountered, the loop is ended after printing the position of the space in the string. The loop exits, regardless of the conditional expression of the while statement. If the ith element is not a NULL or space character, the variable i is incremented by one.

```
\***********************************************************
 This program illustrates a break statement
 ***********************************************************/

#include <stdio.h>

#define SPACE ' '
```

```
main()
{
      int i, rc;
      char string[] = "It is a wonderful world";
      i = 0 ;
      while ( string[i] != '\0' )
      {
         if ( string[i] == SPACE )
         {
            printf( "Space character is at index %d \n", i );
            break;
         }
         i++;
      }
}
```

The output is:

```
Space character is at index 2
```

The above program with a break statement can be coded using a do/while-loop. For example,

```
do
{
      if ( string[i] == SPACE )
      {
            printf( "Space character is at index %d \n", i );
            break;
      }
      i++;
} while ( string[i] != '\0' );
```

4.8. CONTINUE

A continue statement forces the next iteration of a loop to happen. The general form of the continue statement is:

continue;

Within the body of the do, for, or while statement, the current iteration stops when continue is executed and control is passed to the expression of the loop. If it is a for statement, the third expression is executed, followed by the second expression.

The following program illustrates how to use the continue statement to count non-blank characters in a string array. This for-loop scans the character array string starting from the first element until the NULL character is found. Every time the body of the loop is executed, the ith element is tested. If it is a blank character, the rest of the loop is skipped by using the continue statement. The next iteration starts after incrementing the index i and testing if the ith element is not NULL. If it is a non-blank character, a counter count is incremented by 1.

Within nested statements, the continue statement ends the current iteration of the loop where it is found. The continue statement can only be used within a loop body.

```
\***********************************************************
 This program illustrates the continue statement
 ***********************************************************/

#include <stdio.h>

main( )
{
    int count, i ;
    char string [] = "This is a very vast universe" ;

    count = 0;

    for ( i = 0 ; string [i] != '\0' ; i ++ )
    {
       if ( string[i] == ' ' )
            continue;
       count++;
    }
    printf( "Number of non-blank characters is %d \n", count );
}
```

The output is:

```
Number of non-blank characters is 23
```

4.9 GOTO STATEMENT

Because of the emphasis on structured programming techniques, goto has fallen out of favor among programmers. Although it is possible to avoid goto entirely in any programming situations, there are times when use of the goto statement simplifies and clarifies a program. However, with the rich control verbs of C, there may never be a need to use the goto statement.

The general form of the goto statement is

```
goto label;
```

The goto transfers control unconditionally to a statement associated with a label.

This program scans the character array string for the first space character. Upon finding it, the control is transferred to the label found, where the position of the space character is printed.

```
\***************************************************
This program illustrates the goto statement
****************************************************/
#include <stdio.h>
# define SPACE ' '
main()
{
    int i;
    char string[] = "Humanity will live in harmony" ;

    i = 0;

    while ( string[i] != '\0' )
       {
            if ( string[i] == SPACE )
                go to found ;
            i++;
       }
    not_found: printf( "Space character not found \n" );

    return;
    found: printf( "Space character is at index %d \n", i );
}
```

The output is:

```
Space character is at index 8
```

5

Why Function?

Function is the building block of a program. It allows a major program task to be divided into smaller tasks. In C, this concept of partitioning is materialized by writing subprograms or functions, which are more manageable. Each function is designed to do a very specific job.

The function construct lends itself to the top-down method of programming. Breaking down big tasks into smaller portions also has other benefits. They are easier to write, maintain, and debug. Besides, short programs are easy to read and understand, and are self-documenting.

There are many aspects to writing functions. In this chapter we will discuss the definition and declaration of functions, passing parameters, returning values or pointers, and calling functions. Before we delve into these and many other technical sides of functions, it is important to remember few practical points.

One is that a function should be as general as possible, such that it can be called from many parts of a program. For example, functions to format date and time can be used in many parts of the program. As you progress in your development as a C programmer, you will have many of these general purpose functions. They can be placed in a library to be used by any C programming situation. A general rule to writing programs that are general and reusable is to make each function do one task. This may mean that some of them are short, with just few statements. The general rule of thumb is to keep programs large enough to fit on one page.

5.1 main( )

A C program must have a `main` function. We have seen this function in many examples throughout this book. Program execution always begins with `main`, which in turn can call other functions. The `main` follows all the function rules, described later in this chapter, but have a few unique points. The name of main should be in lower case letters. Also, a program must only have one main function. The main function has two parameters. The usual names of these parameters are argc and argv, although they can have many other names. These parameters are for the users to pass arguments to a C program.

The first parameter, argc, has the type int and is the number of arguments passed to a program. The second parameter, argv, is an array of pointers to strings. The value of argc represents the number of pointers in the array argv. The first element of the array (argv[0]) always points to the program name. If no argument is passed to the program, the value of argc is 1. The strings passed to main function are null-terminated.

The following program, called *product*, receives two values from the user and prints the product. It has only one main function.

```
\***********************************************************
This program illustrates the function main()
************************************************************/

#include <stdio.h>

main(int argc, char *argv[]))
{
    int x, y, product;

    if (argc < 3 )
    {
       printf( "Input Error \n" );
       return;
    }
    /* convert from string to numeric */
    x = atoi( argv[1] );
    y = atoi( argv[2] );

    product = x * y ;
    printf("%d multiplied by %d is %d \n", x, y, product );
}
```

The program first checks the number of arguments. If it is less than three, the program exits after printing an error message to the standard output stream.

Next, it converts the two numeric input strings to integers by calling the atio function. After the conversion, the first argument is placed in variable x and the second one in y. After multiplying them, it prints the input values and their product. After this program is compiled and link-edited without error, it can be used.

The following is a CLIST command to call the product program:

```
CALL PRODUCT '123 456'
```

The parameters argc and argv would have the following values.

Object	Value
argc	3
argv[0]	pointer to "PRODUCT"
argv[1]	pointer to "123"
argv[2]	pointer to "456"
argv[3]	pointer to NULL

5.2 FUNCTION DEFINITION

A function definition describes all aspects of a function. It specifies the storage class, name, any parameter, and its body. It also denotes the type of data, if any, that is returned from the function. There should be only one definition for each function in a program. This should not be confused with function declaration, which can be several in a program for the same function. Function declaration is discussed later in this chapter.

The general form of function definition is:

storage-class type function-name (parameter-list)
parameter declaration list
{
    body ⟶ *declaration*
            ⟶ *statement*
}

Storage-class: In a function definition, only two storage classes can be used. They are `extern` and `static`. The storage class describes the scope of the function. It is optional; when not included in a definition, the default storage class is `extern`. A function with storage class `extern` can be called from anywhere in the program. But a storage class `static` limits reference to a function only to the source file where it is found.

In the next program, `main` and `product` functions are defined in source FILE 1. And `PrtResul` function is defined in FILE 2. The storage class of `main` function is `extern` and technically accessible from FILE 2. However, the storage class of `product` is `static` and can only be called from FILE 1. The storage class of `PrtResul` function is `extern`; therefore, it can be called from any source file, namely FILE 1.

```
FILE 1
    \***********************************************************
    This program illustrates function definition
    ************************************************************/
    long result;
    void PrtResul();
    long product( int x, int y );
```

```
main()
{
    long product( int x, int y);

    result = product( 456711, 2233441 );
    PrtResul() ;
}

static long product( int x, int y )
{
    return (y * x);
}
```
FILE 2
```
#include <stdio.h>
void PrtResul()
{
    extern long result;
    printf( "Result is %1", result);
}
```

Type: The type of a function defines the type of value that a function returns. Any type is valid for a function—for example, `void`, `int`, `char`, `pointer`, `float`, or any user-defined type. The type specifier is optional; if none is included in a function definition, the default is type `int`. In the last program, *product*, the types of return value of each function are as follows.

Type	Function
int	main( )
long	product( )
void	PrtResul( )

The `main` function returns an integer value, while `product` function returns long integer value. A type `void` means that the function does not return any value.

Function-name: The function-name is an identifier that names a function. The ANSI C standard has no limit on the number of characters in an identifier. However, various compilers have imposed limits by allowing a minimum number of significant characters. The IBM C/370 compiler, for example, limits the significance to 31 characters for internal function names. Such functions are defined with storage class `static`. For functions with storage class `extern`, only eight characters are allowed. Function names longer than eight characters are truncated during linkage, and this may result in unresolved external name errors.

An identifier can have upper or lower characters. Although underscore (_) is allowed as part of a name, it is translated to another character, depending on the compiler, which is acceptable in the MVS environment. You should avoid using any reserved words. They are language keywords, such as `if`, `while`, `return`, and so on. Also, you should not name your functions the same as the function names declared in the include files of C library functions.

Parameter-list: A function is an isolated and self-contained unit of code. One way that a a function receives data from outside is through parameters (the other way is through global variables). The parameters are holders of values that are passed to the function being called. A parameter-list is also called formal parameters. In the previous definition of product function, there are two parameters x and y.

A parameter-list should consist of at least the name of the parameters, each separated by a comma. It can also describe the type and storage class. Only the storage classes register and auto are allowed. If the storage class is missing, the compiler gives the parameter the default class auto. In the next example, timer function has one parameter, with type int and storage class register.

```
void timer( register int tick )
{
    •
    •
    •
}
```

A parameter-list is optional. If a function is to receive no value, use the keyword void—for example:

```
message ( void )
{
    printf( "E.T. phone home" );
}
```

Any data type can be specified, but if omitted, the default is int. For example, in the following definition

```
void timer ( tick )
{
    •
    •
    •
}
```

parameter tick has type int and storage class static.

The following program further illustrates various ways of using parameter-list. It has five functions with varying number of parameters to list name and quantity of inventory. The PrtHead function has no parameter, and StuffRec function has two parameters—recp and str. The first parameter recp is a pointer to a data object declared as a user-defined type `Inventory_rec`, while `str` is declared as an character array.

In this program, structure `Inventory_rec` is first defined and used to declare variable `inventory`. In `main` function, data set TEST.INVENTOR.FILE is first opened. Then, each record is read and placed in the structure variable `inventory` (fields `ITEM` and `QUANTITY`) by `StuffRec` function. The `PrtDet` function prints each field. Finally, `PrtTotal` function prints the total number of records from the data set.

```
\************************************************************
 This program illustrates function definition
 ************************************************************/

#include <stdio.h>

/* inventory record */
typedef   struct
              {
                   char ITEM [20]; /* name of item */
                   int  QUANTITY; /* quantity of item */
              } Inventory_rec;

#define     SIZE         80
#define     NULLPTR      ((char *) 0)

main()
{
    Inventory_rec inventory;
    char line[ SIZE ], *lineprt ;
    int count ;
    FILE *fh;
    void PrtHead(void);
    void PrtTotal(int count);
    void StuffRec(Inventory_rec * recp, char str[]);
    void PrtDet(Inventory_rec *recp);

    if ( ( fh = fopen( " 'TEST.INVENTOR.FILE' ",
       "r, blksize = 9040, lrecl = 80, recfm = FB" )
                                         == NULL )
    {
       printf( "Error opening file TEST.INVENTOR,FILE \n" );
       return;
    }

    /* print heading */
    PrtHead() ;
    count = 0;

    do
    {
       /* read a line from file */
```

```
                lineprt = fgets( line, SIZE, fh );
                if ( lineptr != NULLPTR )
                {
                        StuffRec( &inventory, line );
                        PrtDet( &inventory );
                        count ++ ;
                }
        } while ( lineptr != NULLPTR )

        PrtTotal( count );
}
/* print the header */
void PrtHead( void )
{
    printf( "Inventory List \n" );
    printf( "%-20s %s\n\n", "Item", "Quantity" );
}

/* move data from line buffer to inventory record */
void StuffRec( Inventory_rec *recp, char str[] )
{
    sscanf( str, "%s %d", recp->ITEM, &recp->QUANTITY );
}

/* print inventory information */
void PrtDet( Inventory_rec *recp )
{
    printf( "%-20s %d \n", recp-> ITEM, recp->QUANTITY );
}

/* print total number of items */
void PrtTotal( count )
{
    printf( "Total number of items are %d \n", count );
}
```

Parameter Declaration List: If the parameter-list consists of only names of the parameter, a declaration of each parameter is required. Let's look again at a function we have seen before:

```
void StuffRec(Inventory_rec *recp, char str[])
{
        •
        •
        •
}
```

This parameter-list can be rewritten thus:

```
void StuffRec (recp, str)
Inventory_rec * recp;
```

```
    char str[];
    {
        •
        •
        •
    }
```

Now `StuffRec` function has both a parameter-list and a parameter declaration list. The parameter declaration must have a type and parameter name.

Header: A header consists of storage class, data type, function name, and parameter-list—for example, this header

```
static void StuffRec(Inventory_rec *recp, char str[])
```

has storage class `void`, data type `static`, function name `StuffRec`, and a parameter-list with `recp` and `str`. The storage class and data type are optional.

Function body: A function body may consist of a single statement, a block statement, or an empty statement. Also, it may contain declaration. The body is always enclosed in braces. Earlier in this chapter, we saw several examples of function bodies. The `main` function has several declarations and statements, while `StuffRec` function has a body made of a single statement and no declaration. The following illustrates an empty body:

```
void dummy(void)
{
}
```

5.3 FUNCTION PROTOTYPE

Functions should be declared before using them. The declaration syntax, according to ANSI C standards, is called function prototype. A function prototype establishes the type of the return value and the name of the function and its parameters. It is a good practice to use function prototype, thus allowing the compiler to check for any discrepancies between the use and definition of functions. By not using them, the compiler assumes default values, which may result in programming errors. The default type of a function return value is `int`.

The general form of function prototype is:

type function-name (parameter type list);

Both types can be any valid data object type corresponding to the types of the function definition. The function name is the actual function identifier.

The minimum requirement for a parameter type is to list, in proper order, the data types of parameters, separated by commas. However, you can also add the identifier of each parameter type; it does not serve any purpose except add documentation to a function declaration.

For example, we have seen several function prototypes in an earlier program. They are:

```
void PrtHead(void);

void StuffRec( Inventory_rec *recp, char str[] );
```

The function prototype is new from ANSI C; traditionally, a parameter type list is not allowed in function declaration. The above examples would look like this:

```
void PrtHead();

void StuffRec();
```

Although ANSI compilers tolerate the old way of declaring functions, the use of function prototype is highly preferred.

Function declarations can be placed in an include file. In fact, the include files of the C standard library have function prototypes. Similarly, you can have your own include file for each function library you build, which should have function prototypes.

Here are few examples of function prototypes from include file stdio.h.

```
int ungetc( int c, FILE *stream );

FILE *tmpfile( void );

int sscanf( const char *buffer, const char *format,
argument-list);
```

5.4 CALLING FUNCTIONS AND PASSING VALUES

The execution of a function starts by invoking or calling it. As mentioned earlier, the very first function to be called is main. The main function in turn calls other functions. The control is passed to the called function. Upon completion of the task, the control is returned to the calling function. In the next example, when main function calls sum function, control goes to sum to calculate the sum of numbers. When returning from sum, control is passed to the next statement of main, which is the printf function, to print the sum b.

```
\***********************************************
This program illustrates a function call
***********************************************/

#include <stdio.h>
main()
{
    int a = 10, b, sum( int number );

    b = sum( a );
    printf( "sum = % ", b )
    printf( "a = %d", a );
}
```

```
int sum( int number )
{
    int sum;

    for ( sum = 0; number > 0;-number )
        sum += number ;
    return sum;
}
```

A function is invoked by its name and a correct list of arguments, enclosed in parentheses. This list of arguments must match in type to the parameter-list of the function. Arguments and parameters are two sides of the same coin. A calling function passes arguments, while parameters are defined during the definition of a function. As mentioned earlier, if function prototypes are used, the compiler will check the compatibility of arguments and parameters.

In C, arguments are passed by a technique known as "call-by-value." This means that each argument is first evaluated and a copy of the value is passed to its corresponding parameter. In other words, the original argument value of the calling function is not changed. Let's refer to the previous program, which illustrates the concept of "call-by-value." In main, the value of a is passed to sum. This value is received by the parameter number of sum, which is decremented until it is 0. But the value of a remains the same (10) after the execution of sum.

When an array is an argument, the pointer to the first element of the array is passed, but not the element of the array. In this case, the receiving function is capable to read or change any element of the array. The argument is passed by *reference*. When StuffRec (with arguments &inventory and str []) was called earlier, the compiler converts the expression str[] into a pointer automatically. But, in case of the first argument, an address operator (&) is placed in front of the structure inventory. Therefore, by using the operator &, the compiler passes the address of structure inventory. Passing the address allows the called function to change or read its content. As in StuffRec, each record field of inventory is initialized.

An argument list can be empty—for example:

```
PrtHead();
```

A function call can be an argument. In statement, for example,

```
printf( "Sum is %d", sum( a ) );
```

sum(a) is an argument of printf function.

Few words must be said about calling the printf function, the most commonly used C function. This function has two arguments. The first is a format string, and the second is a varying number of arguments. The printf function matches the list of arguments and their types from the format string. If these two arguments are not compatible, the function will fail badly. The caller must provide the right number of arguments to match the data types and the number indicated in the format string.

5.5 RETURN STATEMENT

A return statement unconditionally terminates the execution of a function, and control goes back to the calling function. The general form of return statement is:

```
return( expression );
```

The expression is optional, and, after it is evaluated, its value is passed to the caller. The data type of the expression is specified in the *header*. If the type of the expression is different than the type in the header, a conversion of the return value takes place. A calling function does not have to use the return value.

The expression is enclosed in parentheses, although it is not required. If a return statement does not have an expression, the function simply stops without returning any value. If the definition of a function has a return type void, the return statement cannot have an expression.

The following illustrates a few return statements:

```
return;              /* returns no value              */
return -x;           /* returns negated value of x    */
return -1;           /* returns value -1              */
return ( y*z );      /* returns the result of (y*z)   */
```

A function is not required to have a return statement. The execution of a function ends when the end of the body (the last brace) is reached. In the example,

```
void print_message( void )
{
    printf( "Honey, they shrunk my pay \n" );
}
```

the control goes back to calling function after executing the printf function.

But a function can have many return statements. The IsAlpha function, in the next example, has two return statements.

```
/* function to check if a character is alphabetic */
int IsAlpha( char c )
{
    if ( ( c >= 'a' && c <= 'z' ) ||
         ( c >= 'A' && c <= 'Z' ) )
        return 1;
    else
        return 0;
}
```

The return statement is a normal way of terminating a function. There are several functions in C library that are suitable for abnormal situations. They are atexit, exit, and abort.

5.6 RECURSION

A recusion happens when a function calls itself directly or indirectly. To illustrate recursive programming, let's look at the task of printing a number as a character string. First, we'll write this program in the traditional way. The printd function of the next program takes an integer as its input and prints one digit at a time.

```
\*************************************************
This program prints numbers as a character string
**************************************************/
#include <stdio.h>
main()
{
    void printd( int number );

    printd( 123 ); /* call the function */
}
/* print number */

void printd( int number )
{
    char s[20];
    int i;

    /* if number is negative, make it positive */
    if ( number < 0 )
    {
      putchar( '-' );
      number = -number ;
    }

    i = 0 ;
    /* convert from number to character string */
    while ( number > 0 )
    {
      s[i] = number % 10 + '0' ;
      number /= 10 ; /* discard the right digit */
      i++;
    }

    /* print the digits, starting from the last converted digit
       to the last */
    for ( i--; i >= 0 ; i-- )
      putchar( s[i] );
}
```

The function first converts a negative number to a positive. Then it converts the right-most digit to a character constant and stores it in a character array. After all the digits are done, it prints each character starting from the last converted one to the first.

An alternative way is to use the recursive approach. The printd function calls itself to convert the number into a character string, then it prints them one at a time.

```
/* print number using recursion */
void printd( int number )
{
    int i;
    /* if number is negative, make it positive */
    if ( number < 0 )
    {
       putchar( '-' );
       number = - number;
    }

    i = number / 10 ;  /* drop the last digit */

    if ( i != 0 )
       printd( i ) ; /* call itself              */
    putchar( number % 10 + '0' );
}
```

In the printd function, the input number is checked. If it is negative, a dash (-) is printed and the number is made positive. The number is divided by 10 and then passed to the printd function in a recursive manner. The following shows how the function calls itself and the number is passed as argument.

```
printd( 123 )
call printd( 12 )  ⟶  printd( 12 )
                       call printd( 1 )  ⟶  printd(1)
                                             putchar('1')
                       putchar('2')  ⟵  return
putchar('3')  ⟵  return
return
```

In the main function, the printd function is called with value 123 as argument. The second time, when printd i is called, the value is 12 as argument. But, in the third time, printd is not called again, because i = 1. Therefore, in this call it prints character '1' and returns. Next, '2' is printed, then '3', and then control goes back to main.

Recursion does not save any storage, as each function call gets a new allocation of its variables. Nor is the code faster. The reason for using recursion is to produce compact function that is usually easy to write and understand.

6

Input and Output

The core of C language does not support input and output to external devices. Unlike COBOL or PL/I, it does not have verbs to read from and write to files or to display and accept data from consoles. It is hard to imagine writing a program without any input and output tasks.

The architects of C designed this language with portability in mind, allowing programs developed in one system to be moved easily to other computer environments. For this reason, the I/O capabilities have been moved from the core to the standard library accompanying the language. This library has functions that perform the same tasks regardless of the hardware and software environment.

The library is a repository of a very rich and diverse assortment of I/O and other functions. This chapter gives only an overview of some of the most often used input and output facilities. For more details of functions, refer to Chapter 20.

There are three main reasons for writing this chapter. They are:

1. The C I/O concept is different from other languages. Here we discuss some of the important issues that would make programming in C easier. We will explain the C concept of *streams* and how they are associated with *files*.
2. To give an overview of the most commonly used I/O operations, such as:
    a. File access.
    b. Operation on files.
    c. Formatted and unformatted input and output.
3. The file structures in MVS are different from PC-DOS and UNIX environments. For example, when handling an MVS file (data set), one has to be mindful of many physical descriptions, such as file format, record length, blocksize, and duration. Also, the naming conventions of MVS files differ from other systems.

Since C does not have I/O commands, this chapter is to acquaint the reader with read and write tasks of sequential files. Functions for random access such as `fseek`, `fgetpos`, `fsetpos`, `ftell`, and `frewind` are discussed in Chapter 20. For VSAM files, refer to Chapter 13. Also, many other functions are mentioned in this chapter, for more detail information refer to Chapter 20.

6.1 STREAMS AND FILES

C has a unique approach to I/O systems. Portability, being one of the strengths of C, provides a consistent interface to devices across many computer environments. It makes I/O programming independent of the characteristics of the actual device. To provide a uniform interface, C has an abstract concept called *stream*. With each stream is associated an actual device called a *file*. The following section explains streams and files and their relation to each other.

6.1.1 Streams

ANSI C requires that I/O operations use buffered file systems to make different devices look like streams. This way, streams behave the same way, and programming I/O operations is much easier. The same function can be used to write to a disk file, terminal, printer, or plotter.

There are three types of buffering that are associated with stream processing. A stream may be unbuffered—that is, each character is transmitted immediately. When a stream is fully buffered, characters are transmitted only when a block is full. A line buffered stream is transmitted when a new line character is encountered. However, you can call a flush function, called `fflush`, to write data from the buffer to the file any time you want to.

Each stream has its own default buffer. You can control the mode and the size of the buffer by using library functions: `setvbuf` and `setbuf`. The buffering-system applies to a variety of devices, such as terminals, tape drives, and disk drives.

There are two kinds of streams: text and binary.

6.1.1.1 Text Stream

A *text* stream is a series of characters that form a line. Each line can have zero or more characters terminated with a newline character. During input or output to a text stream, the C library functions may add, alter, or even delete some special characters. Therefore, there may not be a one-to-one correspondence between the characters your program reads or writes and the actual data in the device.

There are many cases when such translation can happen. Every time a line is added or updated to a file, a newline character is removed. Conversely, when a record is read and passed on to your program, the newline character is inserted at the end of the record.

When you open a file as a fixed-length record format, there are several things to remember. When appending a record, it is always padded with blank characters to the end of the record. When reading a record, any trailing blanks are discarded at the end of the record. But, if it is an update operation and the replacement record is longer than the file, the record is updated up to its record size. If the replacement record is shorter than the record, the remaining record is padded with blanks. If the record format is variable or the length is undefined, padding occurs on output. Conversely, blanks are removed on input.

6.1.1.2 ASA files

An *ASA* file is a printable file that contains a control character (' ', '0', '-', '1', or '+') in the first column of each line. The C I/O library functions have a way of translating a sequence of characters into these control characters. The following lists the escape sequences and their corresponding control characters of an ASA file.

Escape Sequences	Control Characters
'\n'	becomes a ' ' (skip one line)
'\n\n'	becomes a '0' (skip two lines)
'\n\n\n'	becomes a '-' (skip three lines)
'\f'	becomes a '1' (new page)
'\r'	becomes a '+' (over print character)

When reading from an ASA file, the control characters are converted to escape sequences. This translation will happen *only if* you specify the recfm as fba during an open file operation. Also, the mode of the text file must be one of the following: r, w, r+, or a+—for example:

```
FILE *fh;
fh = fopen( "'MY.FILE.ASA'", "w, recfm=fba" );
```

6.1.1.3 Binary Stream

A *binary* stream is a series of bytes representing the full range of binary values. Unlike a text stream, during input or output, the data is not altered. There is a one-to-one correspondence between the characters your program reads or writes and the actual data in the external device. In binary mode, the I/O functions do not recognize a record boundary; it is left up to you to determine.

If the record format is fixed-length, the last record, on closing a file, is padded with NULL bytes to fill it to the record size. On read, any padded NULL characters of the last record is passed on to the program. On append, previously padded characters are not overwritten. Rather, the record is added after the last character, which may be a padded NULL character.

6.1.2 Files

A stream is associated with an external file by *opening* the file. This process will either create a new file, treat an existing file as new, open a file to read, or open a file to update or append. It is only after the file is opened that it is ready for an exchange of data between your program and the external device. All streams behave the same way, but all files do not have the same capacities. For example, you can randomly access a disk file, but not a terminal.

For every file that can handle random access, there is a *file-position indicator* associated with it. The indicator is initialized on opening and is moved up once upon reading or writing a character.

Each file has a file-control structure of the type FILE. The definition of this structure is found in the include file stdio.h. As we will see later, you must declare a pointer variable for the structure FILE, which is initialized during an open operation of a file, and contains all the neccessary information about the file. Therefore, it is neccessary to include this file in the program where I/O operations are performed. Before the start of the main function, three text streams are automatically opened—standard input stream stdin, standard output stream stdout, and error stream stderr.

A file is disassociated from a stream by closing the file. During this process the stream is flushed. It means that the content of the buffer is written to the file, assuming the stream is opened as output. It is a good habit to close all files before terminating a program. However, any opened file is closed after your program terminates, successfully or not.

6.2 FILE ACCESS FUNCTIONS

This section describes the following file access functions:

- Open a file.
- Close a file.
- Read and write.
- Memory file.

6.2.1 Open File

The C library function to open a file is called fopen. Its two main functions are to open a stream and to connect the stream with a file. The declaration of the fopen function is:

`FILE *fopen(char * filename, char *mode);`

Unlike PC-DOS and UNIX, opening a stream in MVS is a complicated process. There are many details to keep in mind while using fopen function. There are different points to remember when opening files for access under TSO or batch environments.

If the open is successful, fopen will return a file handle. A file handle is a pointer to a structure FILE and is used to associate a stream with a file. The structure FILE is defined in the header file stdio.h. This structure must never be changed. This file handle is subsequently used to read or write data or do other tasks related to a file that require a file handle. If not successful, `fopen` returns the NULL pointer.

The `filename` must always point to a string of characters that contains a valid data set name (DSNAME) or a data definition name (DDNAME). Unlike PC-DOS or UNIX, the *filename* can have three different forms: partially qualified DSNAME, fully qualified DSNAME, and DDNAME. All these forms are discussed next.

1. Partially qualified DSNAME
   A `filename` can be a DSNAME with quotes, like any string in C language. In the next two statements, to open a file,

   ```
   FILE * fh;

   fh = fopen( "ACCOUNT.DATA", "r");
   ```

   the DSNAME is "ACCOUNT.DATA", which is a partial name of the data set. In this case the DSNAME is prefixed with your account number (or user ID). If your user ID is Z0110SH, the actual filename would be:

   ```
   Z0110SH.ACCOUNT.DATA
   ```

   The lower case characters of filename are translated to upper case.

2. Fully qualified DSNAME
   There are situations when you have to use data sets that are not prefixed by your used ID. To specify the full DSNAME, enclose the *filename* string with single and double quotes. In this example,

   ```
   FILE *fh;

   fh = fopen( "'TEST.ACCOUNT.DATA(MONDAY)'" , "r");
   ```

   the full name of the data set is specified, which is TEST.ACCOUNT.DATA. You can open a member of a PDS, such as MONDAY.

3. DDNAME
   The `filename` of `fopen` function can be a string of characters specifying the DDNAME. Of course, the DDNAME must reference to a valid file outside your program. This can be done using TSO ALLOCATE or JCL DD statement. In this case, the `filename` consists of a prefix "dd:" and the DDNAME, both enclosed with double quotes. In this example,

   ```
   FILE *fp;

   fp = fopen( "dd: ACCOUNT(MONDAY)", "r");
   ```

   ACCOUNT is a DDNAME, and MONDAY is a member of the PDS that the DDNAME is referencing. To link the DDNAME ACCOUNT with a PDS, you write the following statement under TSO:

   ```
   ALLOCATE FILE(ACCOUNT) DATASET('TEST.ACCOUNT.DATA')
   ```

Under batch mode, to declare the DDNAME ACCOUNT used in the above C statement, you write a JCL DD statement, which can be similar to:

`// GO.ACCOUNT DD DSN=TEST.ACCOUNT.DATA,.`

The `mode` of the `fopen` function is a pointer to a string, containing the mandatory open status and, optionally, characteristics of the data set. Table 6.1 is a list of the code for each open status and a description for each one.

Table 6.2 lists all the options you can include as part of the `mode` of the `fopen` function. With `mode`, you can optionally include attributes of the data set you are using. If you omit any one of them, the compiler uses the default value.

In the following statements,

```
FILE *fh;
fh = fopen( " 'TEST.ACCOUNT.DATA' ", "r,blksize=9040,
                                      lrecl=80, recfm=FB" );
```

the `fopen` function will attempt to open the file TEST.ACCOUNT.DATA. The argument `mode` indicate a read status with `blksize` as 9040, `lrecl` as 80, and

TABLE 6.1 A List of Legal Values of Open Status

Type	Description
"r"	Open an existing text file for reading.
"w"	Create or open a text file for writing. If the file exists, its content is deleted.
"a"	Open a text file to append at the end of the file. Create if it does not exist.
"r+"	Open an existing text file for reading and writing.
"w+"	Create or open a text file reading and writing. If the file exists, its content is deleted.
"a+"	Open a text file to read or append at the end of the file. If the file does not exist, create it.
"rb"	Open an existing binary file for reading.
"wb"	Create or open a binary file for writing. If the file exists, its content is deleted.
"ab"	Open a binary file to append at the end of the file. Create if it does not exist.
"rb+" or "r+b"	Open an existing binary file for reading and writing.
"wb+" or "w+b"	Create or open a binary file for reading and writing. If the file exists, its content is deleted.
"ab+" or "a+b"	Open a binary file to read or append at the end of the file. If the file does not exist, create it.

TABLE 6.2. Options as Part of Mode Argument of Function FOPEN

Option	Description
blksize	The maximum length in bytes of the physical block of records.
lrecl	The length in bytes of fixed-length records or variable-length records.
recfm	File formats. The valid values are: F: Fixed-length, unblocked records. FB: Fixed-length, blocked records. V: Variable-length, unblocked records. VB: Variable-length, blocked records.
type	The type of the file to be opened. The valid types are: memory: The file is temporary and memory resident. record: The file is opened only for sequential record I/O.

recfm as FB. If a file is opened successfully, the return is a non-zero value, which is a pointer to the structure FILE; otherwise, it is a NULL pointer.

When using fopen, if you do not specify the lrecl, blksize, and recfm values, default values are set. The following gives all the defaults for the optional parameters. The defaults for recfm to open an output file are as follows.

File type	Format	Files
Text	VBA	Spool (printer)
	U	Terminal
	VB	Others
Binary	FB	All

The defaults for lrecl and blksize to open the file as output, if both are not specified, are as follows.

recfm	lrecl	blksize
F	80	80
FB	80	*
V	**	max
U	0	max

The defaults for blksize to an open file as output, if lrecl is specified but blksize is ommitted, are as follows.

recfm	blksize
F	lrecl
FB	***
V	max
U	lrecl

max values are 6144 for disks, 32760 for tape, and 80 for card punches.
* Maximum multiples of 80, but no more than the *max* value of device.
** Greater than 1028 or maximum blksize.
*** Multiple of lrecl, but no more than the *max* value of the device.

The defaults for lrecl to open a file as output, if blksize is specified but lrecl is ommitted, are as follows.

recfm	lrecl
F--	blksize
V--	maximum of 1028 or blksize - 4
U	0

If you are opening a file to read or append, it is best not to specify the recfm, lrecl, and blksize. This will force the function to use the existing file attributes. The risk of including these options is that, if the parameters are wrong, the open function will fail.

In MVS environment, there are several restrictions that you must be aware of while using fopen function. They are:

1. Tape files cannot be opened for update.
2. An open to partitioned data set (PDS) member will fail when using modes a, ab, a+, a+b, ab+, w+, w+b, or wb+.
3. A PDS can be opened to read its directory. In this case, lrecl, blksize, and recfm should not be specified.

6.2.2 Close File

After opening a file using the fopen function, you must close the file with the fclose function. The general form to declare fclose is

    int fclose(FILE *fh);

where variable fh is a pointer to structure FILE, which must contain a file handle returned by the fopen function.

The fclose function returns zero value upon a successful close operation. In case of failure, the return is a non-zero value. Any problem relating to closing a file can be determined by using the ferror function. It is important to explicitly close all files in your program before returning control to the operating system. Although all files are automatically closed when a program terminates normally or abends, there is always a risk of losing data or corrupting the file.

6.2.3 Read and Write File

Any read or write operation on a file must be preceded by opening the file, using the fopen function. The fread and fwrite functions, found in the standard C library, allow you to read and write blocks of data, respectively.

The general form to declare these functions are:

```
int fread( char *ptr, size_t size,
                 size_t nmemb, FILE *stream );
int fwrite( char *ptr, size_t size,
                 size_t nmemb, FILE *stream );
```

In the fread function, ptr is a pointer to a buffer where the function places the data after fetching it from the file. In the fwrite function, ptr points to the memory from where the function writes data to the file. In both cases size is the length in bytes of a single member (or record); nmemb is the count of members to read or write. The stream is a pointer to the structure FILE previously returned from the fopen function.

The following program is a simple example of how to use the open, close, read, and write functions.

```
/**********************************************************
This program illustrates record I/O
**********************************************************/
#include <stdio.h>
#include <stdlib.h>

main()
{
FILE *fh_in, *fh_out ;
char buffer[80];

/* open the input file */

if (( fh_in = fopen( " 'TEST.EMPLOYEE.DATA' ",
        "rb, type=record, lrecl=80, recfm=fb") ) == NULL )
{
      printf( "Error opening file TEST.EMPLOYEE.DATA \n" );
      return;
}

/* open the output file */
if (( fh_out = fopen( " 'TEST.EMPLOYEE.BAK' ",
        "wb, type=record, lrecl =80, recfm=fb") ) == NULL )
{
      print f( "Error opening file TEST.EMPLOYEE.BAK \n" );
      fclose( fh_in );
      return;
}
```

```
while( !feof( fh_in ) )
{
        fread( buffer, sizeof(buffer), 1, fh_in );
        fwrite( buffer, sizeof(buffer), 1, fh_out );
}

fclose( fh_in );
fclose( fh_out );
}
```

This program first declares two variables, `fh_in` and `fh_out`, as pointers to structure FILE. These variables will hold the file handles of the input and output files when they are opened later. Also, a buffer to hold 80 characters, called `buffer`, is also declared, which is used to store data from the input file. Next, the program opens a data set TEST.EMPLOYEE.DATA as an input binary file. If the open operation is successful, the variable `fh_in` is initialized; otherwise, it exits after printing a message. The data set TEST.EMPLOYEE.BAK is opened as an output binary file. If successful, the variable `fh_out` is initialized; otherwise, it exists after printing a message and closing the input file. Before running this program, both these files must be allocated with 80 bytes record size and fixed-block record format.

Then it reads a record of data into the variable `buffer` and writes the content of this buffer to the output file. This continues until the end of the input file is reached. The expression `!feof( fh_in )` in the while-loop checks for the end-of-file indicator of the input file. The `feof` function returns a non-zero value if the EOF flag is set, which is when the loop terminates. Before exiting `main`, both files are closed.

There are a few points to be mentioned that may be of interest to a programmer when using these two read and write functions. If the record length specified, when the `fread` function is called, is less than the actual length of the record being read, only a partial record will be read. Subsequent read will point to the next record.

If in the `fwrite` function, the record length is less than the minimum size allowed for an output file, the write operation fails. If the total number of output bytes is greater than the actual file record size, the data is truncated and only one record is written. Upon update, the output byte count must be the same as the current record length of the file.

Both write and read functions return an integer value. If either operation fails, a zero value is returned; otherwise, this value represents the number of bytes read or written.

6.2.4 Memory File

The IBM C/370 compiler has an interesting feature: memory file. A memory file, as the name implies, is created in memory with the `fopen` function. You designate the `type` of the `mode` as memory—for example:

```
FILE *mfp;
mfp = fopen( "TEMP.DATA", "w+, type=memory" );
```

This memory file is a stream just like any other. Therefore, you can do operations like read and write exactly the way you would do with other kind of files.

Since such a file resides in memory, there are a few characteristics to keep in mind while using it.

1. It is a temporary file that exist until the program terminates normally or abends, or is deleted by `remove` function.
2. A memory file can be accessed within and outside of the function that creates it.
3. You can close the file using the `fclose` function, but this function does not erase it.
4. If a memory file exists, there is no need to include option "type=memory" in the arguement `mode` of the `fopen` function.
5. The memory file yields high performance of speed.

6.3 OPERATIONS ON FILE

This section describes the following file operations:

- Delete a file.
- Rename a file.
- Create a temporary file.

6.3.1 Delete a File

To delete a data set, you use the standard library function `remove`. The general declaration form is:

```
int remove( char *filename );
```

As mentioned earlier in this chapter, `filename` is a string of character in three different forms. They are:

1. Partially qualified DSNAME.
2. Fully qualified DSNAME.
3. DDNAME.

In the first two cases, the `remove` function deletes the file. In the third case, it removes the file and deactivates the DDNAME. The `remove` function returns a zero value if the operation is successful; otherwise, it returns a non-zero value.

There are many reasons why a delete operation will fail. Some of them are:

1. The filename is incorrect.
2. The file is opened by your program.
3. The file is being used by another program.

The `remove` function cannot be used to delete a PDS member.

6.3.2 Rename a File

To rename a data set, you use the standard library rename function. Its general declaration form is:

```
int rename( char *oldname, char *newname );
```

The current name is passed to the function as oldname. Of course, it must exist. The newname points to the new filename. The rename function returns a zero value if the operation is successful; otherwise, it returns a non-zero value. The rename function cannot be used to rename a PDS member.

6.3.3 Temporary File

There are two functions to create temporary files: tmpfile and tmpnam. The tmpfile function will automatically create a binary stream. The stream is associated with a temporary file, which is removed when the program terminates. The tmpnam function will yield a data set name that is valid and unique.

6.4 FORMATTED INPUT AND OUTPUT

The standard C library has functions that allow formatted input or output to external devices, such as terminals and disks. The format capabilities will give you control over how the information is sent or received from files or the standard I/O stream. The following lists the functions to do formatted I/O.

Function	Description
printf( )	Output formatted data to the standard output stream.
scanf( )	Input formatted data from the standard input stream.
fprintf( )	Output formatted data to a file.
fscanf( )	Input formatted data from a file.

6.4.1 Standard I/O Streams

The function that prints to the standard output stream is printf, which we have seen in many examples since the start of this book. The complementary one—to receive data from the standard input stream—is scanf. Since the data comes from or goes to the standard I/O streams, these functions do not require a stream to be declared and opened. As mentioned earlier, streams for standard I/O (stdin, stdout, and stderr) are automatically opened before your program begins execution. The printf function uses stream stdout, and scanf uses stdin.

The general declaration forms are:

```
int printf( char *format, arg1, arg2, ... argn );
int scanf ( char * format, arg1, arg2, ... argn );
```

In both cases you need two arguments: format string and argument list. For a more detailed explanation of these arguments, refer to Chapter 20.

The following programs demonstrate the use of `printf` and `scanf` functions. First, in this program, three variables—quantity, product, and price—are declared. Next, within the body of the while-loop the `scanf` function reads three values from the standard input stream. The inputs are the quantity, the description of the product, and the price, which are stored in the respective variables. Then these values are printed to the standard output stream with the `printf` function. The while-loop terminates when the input value for quantity is 0.

```
/************************************************************
This program illustrates formatted standard I/O
************************************************************/

#include <stdio.h>
#include <stdlib.h>

main()
{
    int quantity = 10 ;
    char product [20] ;
    float price ;

    while ( quantity > 0 )
    {
        scanf("%d %20s %f",
              &quantity, product, &price );
        printf( Output: %d, %20s, %10.2f \n",
              quantity, product, price );
        printf( "To stop enter zero (0) value for
              quantity \n");
    }
}
```

A zero or negative value for quantity will terminate this program. Note that the argument list of `scanf` must be addresses.

6.4.2 File I/O

The function to write to a file is `fprintf`. To receive formatted data from a file, you use `fscanf`. In both cases, in addition to a format string and argument list, you have to pass a file handle. For more details about these arguments, refer to Chapter 20. This file handle is returned by calling `fopen`.

Their general declaration forms are:

```
int fprintf( char * format, arg1, arg2, ... argn, *fh );

int fscanf ( char * format, arg1, arg2, ... argn, *fh );
```

In the program we first declare working variables quantity, product, and price, and two pointer variables, fh_in and fh_out, to hold files handles.

Next we open a data set TEST.INPUT.DATA as input binary file. This data set must be allocated with an 80-byte record size and fixed-block record format. If the open operation fails (`fopen` returning NULL), the program prints an error message and exits. If it is successful, the variable `fh_in` is initialized with the file handle. Similarly, a data set TEST.OUTPUT.DATA is opened as a binary output file. If the operation is successful, the variable `fh_out` is initialized. Otherwise, it exits after closing the input file and printing an error message.

```
/***********************************************
This program illustrates formatted File I/O
***********************************************/

#include <stdio.h>
#include <stdlib.h>

main()
{
    int quantity = 0 ;
    char product[20] ;

    float price ;
    FILE *fh_in, *fh_out ;

    /* open the input file */
    if (( fh_in =fopen( " 'TEST.INPUT.DATA' ",
       "rb, lrecl=80, recfm=fb")) == NULL )
    {
       printf( "Error opening file TEST.INPUT.DATA \n" );
       return;
    }
    /* open the output file */
    if (( fh_out = fopen ( " 'TEST.OUTPUT.DATA' ",
            "wb, lrecl=80, recfm=fb")) == NULL )
    {
       printf( "Error opening file TEST.OUTPUT.DATA \n" );
       fclose( fh_in );
       return;
    }

    while( !feof( fh_in) )
    {
       fscanf(fh_in, "%d %20s %f \n",
              &quantity, product, &price );
       fprintf(fh_out, Output: %d, %20s, %10.2f\n",
              quantity, product, price );
    }
    fclose( fh_in );
    fclose( fh_out );
}
```

In the body of the while-loop, we use the fscanf function to read from the input file and write to the output file with fprintf. This loop terminates when the end-of-file condition of the input file is reached. This condition is checked by the expression !feof(fh_in) as part of the while statement. The feof function returns a non-zero value if the EOF flag is set. It is assumed that each record read has these three fields: quantity of product, description of product, and price. Before exiting, this program closes both files.

6.5 UNFORMATTED INPUT AND OUTPUT

In the standard C library, there are functions to read and write unformatted strings of characters or a character to and from the standard I/O streams and files. As mentioned earlier, the functions for I/O use the streams stdin, stdout, and stderr. The following is a list of functions to perform unformatted I/O.

Function	Description
getchar( )	Reads a character from the terminal; waits for carriage return.
gets( )	Reads a string of characters from the terminal.
putchar( )	Writes a character to the terminal.
puts( )	Writes a string of characters to the terminal.
fgetc( )	Reads a character from a file.
fgets( )	Reads a string of characters from a file.
fputc( )	Writes a character to a file.
fputs( )	Writes a string of characters to a file.

The following program reads a string from the standard input stream and writes it to an output file, 'TEST.OUTPUT.DATA'. The input is first opened and, if successful, the while-loop is executed. The input data is placed in the variable buffer by the gets function and then the fputs function writes the content of buffer to the stream pointed to by fh_out. The read and write loop continues until a character '.' is typed in the first column of the input. Before the exit of the program, the output file is closed.

```
/***********************************************
This program illustrates unformatted File I/O
***********************************************/
#include <stdio.h>
#include <stdlib.h>

main()
{
    char buffer[80] ;
    FILE *fh_out ;
```

```
    /* open the output file */
    if (( fh_out = fopen( " 'TEST.OUTPUT.DATA' ", "w"))
                        == NULL )
    {
       printf("Error opening file TEST.OUTPUT.DATA \n" );
       return
    }
    while( buffer[0] != '.' )
    {
            gets( buffer );
            fputs( buffer, fh_out );
    }

    fclose( fh_out );
}
```

7

Pointers

We have discussed pointers in earlier chapters in relation to function and data definition. Because of their common use in C programming, we want to look at this topic again to gain a deeper understanding, which hopefully will lead to a better appreciation of pointers. The concept of pointers requires a clear and sound comprehension; lack of it can frustrate your programming efforts and result in bug-ridden programs. It is easy to misuse a pointer: you expect it to do certain things, but the compiler interprets it differently, and the consequences can be disastrous.

Although the discussion in this chapter will show you the correct use of pointers, you should also read Chapter 9 on Pitfalls. This chapter focuses on common mistakes in pointer usage and will make you more aware of some of the situations to avoid. A pointer is a variable that has an address that points to another variable. They should be distinguished from integers.

In C, pointers can be very useful, but using them carelessly can lead to hard-to-understand programs or to a pointer pointing to wrong data objects. But, with a sound understanding of how pointers can be used, they are a powerful tool. It will add flexibility to programming because C provides you with an elegant pointer mechanism.

This chapter explores various ways of using pointers. You will see many illustrations of how simplicity and clarity can be achieved by using pointers. The topics to be covered are:

- Dynamic memory allocation.
- Pointer arithmetic.
- Pointers and functions.
- Pointer and string.
- Array of pointers.

7.1 DYNAMIC MEMORY ALLOCATION

The standard C library provides functions to request memory from the system. This must not be confused with data object declaration in a program, which sets the storage class, type, and a variable-name. Variables and constants are declared during compilation, allocated just before executing main function of your program and used during run-time. Such memory is fixed in size, from the start until the end of the execution of the program.

Unlike variables, memory allocation (and deallocation) happens while your program is running. Although requested memory can be viewed as an array of one dimension, subscript cannot be used to access elements of the array. The only way to reference such memory is by a pointer. Each allocation is a contiguous storage space.

In this section we will first introduce the standard library functions for dynamic memory allocation, and then show where allocated memory is found during the run-time of a program. Following this, we will describe functions to maintain a memory file, where pointers are extensively used.

7.1.1 Functions

The following describes the C library functions to acquire and free storage space from your program. There are four such functions: calloc, malloc, realloc, and free. Although these functions will be fully described in Chapter 20, we will touch upon them briefly, as they are used later in this chapter to demonstrate use of pointer.

void *calloc (size_t n, size_t size);

The calloc function reserves memory space for an array. The parameter n is the number of elements, each having a length of size bytes. The calloc function initializes each element to value zero.

Upon a successful allocation of memory calloc function, returns a pointer to the base address of the space; otherwise, it returns NULL pointer.

void *malloc(size_t size);

The malloc function reserves size bytes in length. This function does not initialize the memory storage. The malloc function returns a pointer to the base address, if enough memory is found; otherwise, it returns NULL pointer.

void *realloc(void *ptr, size_t size);

The realloc function changes the size of a previously reserved storage space by malloc or calloc. The original space is kept unchanged, and the new space is not initialized. The parameter size is the length in bytes of more memory requested. The ptr is the pointer to the base address of an allocated memory. A successful reallocation returns a pointer to the memory, or NULL, if it could not find more memory.

void free(void* ptr);

The free function returns an allocated storage to the system. The parameter ptr must point to a base address previously returned by calloc, malloc, or realloc.

7.1.2 Heap Storage

When an allocation function is called, the memory you requested is found in an area called heap. The heap storage comes to exist only if malloc or calloc is encountered in a program, either directly or indirectly.

Now, let's look at where the heap memory fits in the storage during the run-time. This describes only the heap area for the IBM C/370 (version 1.2) compiler. The region of your C program, when it is running, can be divided into three areas: load module, initial storage area (ISA), and residual storage. Among other things, the residual storage contains the heap area only if memory allocation is requested by your program or library function.

The size of the heap area increments to satisfy the allocation requests, and this space decreases as memory is freed. By using the HEAP option during run-time, you can control the initial size of heap storage; the default is 4K. With the HEAP option, you can also specify the size of subsequent increments. If this option is not used, the default is 4K.

If you run into any difficulty when using the memory allocation facility of C library routines, you can get a report of the memory status during run-time by using the REPORT option during run-time. It gives useful information regarding ISA, stack storage, and heap storage.

7.1.3 Memory File

This section describes some of the ways pointers can be used to manipulate memory. To demonstrate this, we have written a simple yet complete program to manage a memory file. As you will see, several functions are written to accomplish this. A memory file is used to copy disk file to memory, where it can be accessed using pointers. Such a file has many advantages, and the most important one is that you can access any byte of this file directly. You can also sort it and search for a pattern of character or any record. Of course, it speeds up the process if a file is in memory. The following describes the functions defined here to complete this program. They are main, mf_ist, mf_read, and mf_getrp. Before proceeding, we'll briefly describe the definitions found at the top of the program listing. After the include preprocessor directives, there are six definitions of constants. Following this, there is a definition of a new data type called UCHAR, and then a structure called mfile_struct, which holds information of an instance of a memory file is defined. The structure is defined as follows:

```
struct mfile_struct
{
    struct mfile_struct *id;        /*memory file instance id */
    int         fmaxrow;            /* maximum number of
                                       rows requested */
    int         fmaxcol;            /* maximum number of columns
                                       requested */
    int         rows_full;          /* number of rows filled */
    UCHAR*mf_data_ptr;              /*pointer to data storage */;
};
```

Using this structure, a new data type is defined, called MFILE, in the following way:

```
typedef struct mfile_struct MFILE;
```

main( )

This example is to demonstrate how to use a memory file. The following steps are accomplished:

1. Create a memory file instance with 40 records, each 80 bytes long.
2. Read a disk file called 'MY.NAME.FILE' into this memory file.
3. Print each record of the file to the standard output stream.
4. Release a memory file instance.

MFILE *mf_ist(int row, int col)

This function creates an instance of a memory file. Many such instances can be spawned. It requests two storages: instance memory and data buffer. The input parameters are the maximum number of rows and columns that the file should have. If successful, the function returns a pointer to a structure data type MFILE. Otherwise, NULLPTR (NULL pointer) is returned to the caller. The mf_ist function accomplishes the following steps:

1. Requests storage for the memory file instance, using malloc function.
2. Initializes fields id, fmaxrow, fmaxcol, and rows_full.
3. Requests storage for data buffer, using calloc function. Initializes mf_data_ptr field.
4. If step 3 is successful, it returns the pointer to the memory file instance. Otherwise, it frees the storage for memory file instance and returns NULLPTR.

int mf_rls(MFILE *mfptr)

This function releases all storage for a memory file instance. The instance memory and data buffer are freed using the free function. The parameter for mf_rls is mfprt, a pointer returned by mf_ist function. It returns RC_FAIL if instance id is not correct; otherwise, it returns RC_SUCCESS. The following steps are taken:

1. Check the instance id.
2. Free the data buffer.
3. Free the memory file instance.

int mf_read(MFILE *mfptr, char *fptr)

This function reads a disk file into a memory file previously created by mf_ist. Each record of the input file is read into the row of the data buffer. It returns RC_FAIL if instance id is not correct or could not open the input file. The parameters are mfptr (a pointer to a memory file instance) and fptr (a pointer to an input data set name). In this function, pointers are used extensively. In addition to the input parameters being pointers, local variables, such as rc, fh, and lineptr, are declared as pointer type. The following steps are taken:

1. Check instance id.
2. Open the input file.
3. Read records from the input file until end-of-file is reached. Place each record into data buffer row.

UCHAR *mf_getrp(MFILE *mfptr, row)

This function returns the pointer to a row. The parameters are mfptr and row. If row is greater than rows_full or if the instance id is not correct, it returns NULLPTR. Otherwise, it returns the address pointing to the start of the row.

```
/****************************************************
This program illustrates memory allocation and dellocation
****************************************************/

#include <stdio.h>
#include <stdlib.h>
#include <string.h>

#define RC_FAIL       -1       /* return code for failure */
#define RC_SUCCESS    0        /* return code for success */
#define NULLPTR       ( (MFILE *) 0) /* null pointer to
structure MFILE            */
#define EOS           '\0'    /* end-of-file escape sequence */
#define ROWS          40      /* number of rows in memory file*/
#define COLS          80      /* number of columns in memory file */

typedef      unsigned      char UCHAR ;

struct mfile_struct
{
    struct mfile_struct *id;    /* memory file instance id */
    int             fmaxrow;    /* maximum number of rows
                                   requested */
    int             fmaxcol;    /* maximum number of columns
```

```c
                                    requested */
    int     rows_full;   /* number of rows filled */
    UCHAR   *mf_data_ptr;/* pointer to data storage */
};

typedef struct mfile_struct MFILE;
MFILE *mf_ist( int row, int col );
int mf_read( MFILE *mfptr, char *fptr );
int mf_rls( MFILE * mfptr );
UCHAR *mf_getrp( MFILE *mfptr, int row );

main()
{
    MFILE *mfptr;
    int row = 0, rc;

    /* 1. create a memory file instance with 40 rows
       and 80 columns */
    if ( ( mfptr = mf_ist( ROWS, COLS ) ) == NULLPTR )
    {
        printf("Could not create memory file\n");
        return;
    }

    /* 2. read a disk file into memory file */
    rc = mf_read( mfptr, "'MY.NAME.FILE'" );
    if ( rc == RC_FAIL )
    {
        printf("mf_read failed \n");
        mf_rls( mfptr );
        return;
    }

    /* 3. print each line of the file to standard output
       stream */
    while ( row <= mfptr->rows_full )
    {
        printf( "%s", (char * ) mfgetrp( mfptr, row ) );
        row++;
    }
    /* 4. release the memory file instance */
    mf_rls( mfptr );
}

/* create a memory file instance */

MFILE *mf_ist( int row, int col )
{
    MFILE *mfile_ptr ;
```

```c
    /* 1. request memory for the memory file instance */
    mfile_ptr = malloc( sizeof ( MFILE ) );
    if ( !mfile_ptr ) /* if allocation fails, return */
        return NULLPTR ;

    /* 2. initialize the id, row, and column fields */
    mfile_ptr->id = (MFILE *) mfile_ptr;
    mfile_ptr->fmaxrow = row ;
    mfile_ptr->fmaxcol = col ;
    mfile_ptr->rows_full = 0 ;

    /* 3. request memory for data buffer */
    mfile_ptr->mf_data_ptr = calloc( row, col );

    /* 4. if successful return the pointer to memory file
                         instance to caller */
    if ( mfile_ptr->mf_data_ptr )
        return mfile_ptr;

    /* 5. if request fails, free instance memory and
       return NULLPTR */
    else
    {
        free( mfile_ptr ); /* free memory */
        return NULLPTR ;
    }
}

/* release storage for memory file instance */
int mf_rls( MFILE *mfptr )
{
    /* 1. check the instance id */
    if ( mfptr != mfptr->id )
        return RC_FAIL;

    /* 2. free data buffer */
    free( mfptr->mf_data_ptr );

    /* 3. free the memory file instance */
    free( mfptr );

    return RC_SUCCESS;
}

/* read a file into a memory file */

int mf_read( MFILE *mfptr, char *fptr )
{
    char *rc ;
    FILE *fh ;
    UCHAR *lineptr ;
```

```c
        int col = mf->fmaxcol, count = 0;

    /* 1. check instance id */
    if ( mfptr != mfptr->id )
    {
        printf( "memory instance incorrect\n");
        return RC_FAIL;
    }

    /* 2. open the input file */
    if ( ( fh = fopen( fptr, "r, type=record" ) )
            == NULL )
    {
       printf( "error opening file %s\n", fptr );
       return RC_FAIL;
    }

    lineptr = mfptr->mf_data_ptr;

    /*3. read records from input file until end-of-file
       is reached. Place each record into data buffer
       row */
    do
    {
       /* read a line from file */
       rc = fgets( lineptr, col, fh );
       if ( rc != NULL )
       {
            lineptr = lineptr + col ;
            count++;
       }
    }while ( (rc != NULL) && (count <= mfptr->fmaxrow ));

    mfptr->rows_full = count ;
    fclose( fh );
}

/* return the pointer to row */
UCHAR *mf_getrp( MFILE *mfptr, int row )
{
    if ( mfptr-> id !=mfptr || row > mfptr->rows_full )
       return NULLPTR;
    else
       return mfptr->mf_data_ptr
            + ( row *mfptr->fmaxcol );
}
```

7.2 POINTER ARITHMETIC

The are few arithmetic operations that can be performed on pointers. These operations are:

- Increment and addition.
- Decrement and subtraction.
- Comparison and assignment.

7.2.1 Increment and Addition

The increment and addition operators for pointers were briefly discussed in an earlier chapter. Here we'll discuss it further, keeping in mind how these two operators affect the pointer, as well as the data it points to. One of the most common mistakes in using pointer arithmetic is not knowing when you are working with an address or data.

Let's first start with declaring and initializing an array of intergers and a pointer of type `int`. The variable x is an array of five integers, and xp is a pointer to an integer data object.

```
static int x[5] = { 1, 2, 3, 4, 5 };
static int *xp;
```

Now, let's assign to the pointer the address of x[0],

```
xp = &x[0] ;
```

Let's say that the memory storage of x starts at location 100 decimal and xp at 500. Therefore, the address and content of each array element and pointer xp will look like this:

variable	location	content
x[0]	100	1
x[1]	104	2
x[2]	108	3
x[3]	112	4
x[4]	116	5
xp	500	100

Note: Each integer occupies 4 bytes.

To increment xp to point to the next element, the statement is:

```
xp++;
```

After its execution, xp will have 104 or point to x[1]. Also, you can use a pointer indirectly to do operations on any element of the array x—for example,

```
*xp += 2;
```

will add value 2 to x[1] (assuming xp is pointing to x[1]), and this element will have 4 after the execution.

variable	location	content
x[1]	104	4

But, if the expression

```
xp + 1
```

is executed, the operation is done on the pointer and not on the data. The reason for this is that the indirection operator(*) is not used. In this context, the value 1 represents one element of the array, and xp will now have the value 108 or the address of x[2].

Now, if we had

```
xp = xp + i ;
```

where i is a variable of type int and has the value 2, the pointer will be increased by two elements. It will have the value 116 or address of x[4].

variable	location	content
xp	500	116

The expression (*xp)++ will increment the content of the array by 1, the same as

```
*xp += 1 ;
```

The parentheses are necessary; without them, the pointer is incremented instead of the array element it points to. This is because unary operators (such as * and ++) are evaluated right to left.

Now, let's say that xp is pointing to x[0] and statement

```
*(xp + 2)++;
```

is executed. Because of the indirection operator (*), the emphasis is on the content (an element of the array). In this situation, the expression (xp + 2) is first calculated to point to the element x[2]. Also, this element is incremented by one.

We have only used an array of integers to demonstrate increment and addition, but the same principle applies to any data type, such as character or structure arrays. To illustrate pointer arithmetic, let's look at a programming situation to calculate the checksum of a record. The CheckSum function receives a pointer to a record of data and the length of the record. The value of each byte of the record is added to an accumulated sum. The record is scanned by a pointer incremented until the length of the record is reached. This function returns the complement of the sum.

```
/***********************************************************
This program illustrates use of pointers
***********************************************************/

unsigned char CheckSum( char * rp, int length );

typedef struct
{
    char name[20];
    int age;
    char address[30];
    unsigned char check_sum;
} EMP_REC;

EMP_REC employee;

main()
{
    employee.check_sum = check_sum( ( char * ) & employee,
            sizeof( employee ) ) ;
}

/* calculate the check sum of a record */

unsigned char CheckSum( char *rp, int length )
{
    char*s;
    unsigned char sum;
    int i;

    for ( s = rp, sum = 0, i = 0;
          i < length ; s++, i ++ )
        sum += *s;
    return( ~sum );
}
```

7.2.2 Decrement and Subtraction

The decrement and subtraction of pointers work the same way as the increment and addition, described previously, except that the pointer and the data are affected negatively. To illustrate this point, let's declare an array y with five elements and a pointer yp, both of type double.

```
double y[5] = { 1.1, 1.2, 1.3, 1.4, 1.5 };

double *yp;
```

Let's initialize the pointer to the address of y[3],

```
yp = &y[3];
```

Let's say that variable y is located at memory address 100 and yp at 500. The memory map will look like this:

Variable	Location	Content
y[0]	100	1.1
y[1]	108	1.2
y[2]	116	1.3
y[3]	124	1.4
y[5]	132	1.5
yp	500	124

Note: Each data type double occupies 8 bytes.

The statement

    yp—;

will decrement the pointer by one element to 116, which is element y[2].
However, the statement

    *yp =- 2 ;

will subtract two from the content of the memory it is pointing to, while yp remains unchanged. This is because of the indirection operator (*). After execution, if yp is pointing to y[2], the value of the element will be -.7 (1.3 - 2) and py will still have 116.

Variable	Location	Content
y[2]	116	-.7
yp	500	116

Now, let's see what happens when an integer is substracted from a pointer—for example:

    py - j ;

In this context, an integer variable j represents the number of elements of the array. If j is 2, the expression will subtract two times the number of bytes of each element from py.

    yp - (2 * 8)

If yp is 116 (pointing to y[2]), the yield will be 100 pointing to y[0].

The expression (*yp)—has the same effect as *yp -= 1—it decrements the content pointed to by py. The parentheses are necessary; without them the pointer will be decremented and not the element of the array. This is because unary operators (such as * and—) are evaluated from right to left.

In an expression, it is possible to affect both the pointer and data object—for example,

    *(yp - 2) ;

will first subtract the number of bytes occupied by two elements from yp and then decrement the content of that address by one. If yp is 116 (pointing y[2]), the previous statement will decrement the content of the address 100 or y[0] by 1. The pointer subtraction is valid only if both are pointing to the elements of the same array. The result is the number of elements.

The following function, which determines the length of a string, demonstrates pointer subtraction. The strlen function scans the string until a NULL character is found, while incrementing a pointer. When the end of the string (indicated by '\0') is reached, the difference between the old and the new gives the number of characters. This strlen function is called as a parameter of printf function.

```
/***********************************************************
This program illustrates pointer subtraction
***********************************************************/
#include <stdio.h>

char string[] = "The world is but one country";

main()
{
    printf( "length is %d" , strlen( string ) );
}

/* return length of a string */

int strlen( char *str )
{
    char *p = str;

    while ( *p != '\0' )
        p++;
    return ( p - str );
}
```

The output is:

length is 28

7.2.3 Comparison and Assignment

In the previous example we used the while-loop:

```
while ( *p != '\0' )
        p++;
```

The expression *p != '\0' uses a pointer variable p to compare each element of a character array with '\0'. Similarly, other operators can be used to compare data object by pointer variable. They are:

<, >, <=, >=, ==, and !=.

These operators can be applied not only to data, but also to pointer comparison and assignment.

Similarly, pointers can be compared. For example, let's say that p and q are pointers pointing to different elements of the same array. Then the expression (p < q) compares pointers. Also, the expression (*p < *q) compares data pointed by p and q.

You can assign an address of a data object to a pointer—for example, we saw earlier

```
yp = &y[3];
```

which assigns the address of the fourth element of y to yp. Pointers can be used to assign data. If

```
yp = &y[1];
```

and

```
xp = &y[2];
```

(where yp and xp are pointer variable), then

```
*py = *px
```

is the same as

```
y[1] = y[2];
```

7.3 POINTERS AND FUNCTIONS

Another area where pointers are frequently used is with functions. There are three such areas:

- Pointer as a function argument.
- Function returning a pointer.
- Pointer to a function.

The first two have been touched upon briefly in earlier chapters, and are commonly used in C programs. Although the third is rarely used, it gives you as a programmer more capability and flexibility.

7.3.1 Pointers as Function Arguments

In C, arguments to functions are passes by "call-by-value." This prevents the called function from changing the value of the variable of the calling function. But there are numerous programming situations where you may want a called function to change the value of a variable. Consider the mf_read function we saw earlier. This program changes two memory areas. One is the field rows-full of the memory file record, which loads the data buffer with records from the input file. To accomplish this, this function receives a pointer to the memory file instance. Therefore, the calling function must pass an argument `mfptr` to `mf_read` (known as "call-by-reference").

In fact, this function has two pointer parameters, as seen in the following function prototype:

```
int mf_read( MFILE * mfptr, char *fptr);
```

Similarly, functions can receive pointers of any data type, such as `float`, `int`, `structure`, and so on. In the next `flip` function, variables `x` and `y` are defined as type `float`. When calling this function, the address of these two variables are passed. This is done by using the address operator `&x` and `&y`.

In the `flip` function, the parameters that receive these values are defined as pointers to type `float`.

```
/***********************************************************
This program illustrates pointers as function arguments
***********************************************************/
main( )
{
    float x, y ;
    x = 1.1 ;
    y = 2.2 ;
    flip( &x, &y );
}
void flip ( float *xp, float *yp )
{
    float temp;

    temp = *xp ;
    *xp = *yp;
    *yp = temp ;
}
```

7.3.2 Function Returning Pointers

Returning a pointer allows you to overcome the limitation of returning only one item—value or reference. It gives a function the facility to return any number of data objects.

The `mfist` function, which we looked at earlier, in this chapter returns a pointer to type `MFILE`. This pointer is a memory address pointing to a structure called `struct_mfile`. The `mf_ist` function initializes all the elements. The calling program can use any of these values and pointers, namely:

```
int *id
int fmaxline
int fmaxrow
int row_full
UCHAR *mf_data_ptr
```

This illustrates that, with a pointer, the mf_ist function returns three values and two pointers.

Returning pointers, especially to arrays and structures, are very common to C programming. In fact, the C function library has many such examples. A few of them are:

```
/* return a pointer to a file structure */
FILE *fopen( const char *filename, const char *type );
/* returns a pointer to a buffer */
char *fgets( char *string, int n, FILE *stream );
/* returns a pointer to a structure result */
struct tm *gmtime( const time_t *time );
/* returns a pointer to a reserved space */
void *malloc( size_t size );
```

7.3.3 Pointer to a Function

In C, it is possible to have a pointer to a function that is different from a function returning a pointer. As we will soon see, the declaration of such a pointer is special, but the pointer works the same way as any other pointer. It contains the address of a function, which can be used in many different ways.

The general form to declare a pointer to a function is:

```
storage-specifier type-specifier (*variable-name) ();
```

The storage-specifier denotes whether a pointer is a local or global variable. The type-specifier establishes the data type that the function is returning. The variable-name is the identifier of the pointer. The parentheses around the variable-name is essential to make the identifier a pointer to function. Without them, the declaration is for a function rather than a pointer. This is important and should be clarified with an illustration. The following declares a variable-name func_ptr:

```
int (*func_ptr) ();
```

as a pointer. However, the following declares func as a function returning a pointer to an integer:

```
int * func();
```

You must keep in mind these two distinctions—pointer to a function and a function returning to a pointer—when declaring functions.

The following program illustrates the declaration of an array of pointers to functions and how each function pointed by each element of the pointer array is called.

We start by defining a new data type called FPI (Function Pointer Integer). The asterisk (*) denotes that it is a pointer, and the parentheses around *FPI makes it a pointer to a function. Also, the type int assumes that the function will return an integer value.

The next statement declares an array, called `funcptr[]`, of type FPI and storage class `static`. There are three elements in this array, each initialized with an address of a function. Notice that the parentheses following the function names are omitted. It is the next statement

```
int CustAdd(), CustDel(), CustChg();
```

that declares these functions, which tell the compiler that these identifiers are function names.

```
/************************************************************
This program illustrates function pointers
************************************************************/

#include <stdio.h>

typedef int (*FPI) ();

static FPI funcptr[] =
{
    CustAdd;
    CustDel;
    CustChg;
};

int CustAdd(), CustDel(), CustChg();
int i;
char c, *string = " " ;

main()
{

    printf( " Customer File Maintenance \n" );
    printf( "0 - Add Customer \n" );
    printf( "1 - Delete Customer \n" );
    printf( "2 - Change Customer \n" );
    printf( " Make a selection ( 0, 1 or 2 ) :" );

    c = getchar();
    if ( c < '0' && c > '2' )
    {
       printf( "Selection %c is not correct\n", c );
       return; /* return if selection is wrong */
    }

    *string = c;
    i = atio( c ); /* convert character to integer */

    (funcptr[i]) () ; /* call a function */
}
```

The `main` function first prints a menu. Then a selection is made by entering a key (0, 1 or 2). The key is received in variable c by calling `getchar` function. If the key is none of the selection characters, the program exits. Otherwise, the key is placed in a string and converted to int using atio function and then placed in i. Finally, i is used as an index to the array funcptr, to call a function pointed by an element, using the statement

```
(funcptr[i]) ();
```

7.4 POINTER AND STRING

We discussed the basics of character array in Chapter 2 (Data Declaration). It covered declaration, initialization of arrays. Here we want to look at character array again, to emphasis the use of pointer with string. A string is a series of characters in an array.

In data processing, text (also called string) is frequently handled; therefore, it makes sense to view a series of characters as string. C does not regard string as a data type. The compiler treats a series of characters as a string only if it is terminated with a NULL character, '\0'. Overlooking this fact can lead to fatal errors. Many of the string functions of C standard library use the end-of-string terminator for processing. Some are strcpy, strcmp, and printf. During initialization of a character array, it is important to remember when the compiler adds a NULL character.

In the following declaration:

```
static char str1[5] = {'n', 'e', 'v', 'e', 'r'};
```

the compiler does not add a NULL character after 'r'. This variable should not be used in the above functions. But, in the following declaration of the variable str2, the initialization characters are enclosed in double quotes.

```
static char str2[] = { "Universal Participation"} ;
```

After the last character 'n', a NULL character is added by the compiler. This variable str2 can be used with the string functions. The distinction is that the first character variable str1 was initialized with character constants; therefore, it does not have end-of-string terminator, while the variable str2 is initialized with a string constant and has an end-of-string terminator.

In string functions (strcpy, strcmp and printf) or any other function that receives string as parameters, the pointers are passed as arguments for processing. Such functions use pointers to scan arrays, instead of using array subscript. In the example that follows, strcpy function copies string s2 to s1.

In the main function, both string variables s1 and s2 are declared. After the strcpy function is called, both strings are printed on the standard output streams.

```
/*********************************************
This program illustrates pointers and array
*********************************************/

#include <stdio.h>
```

```
main()
{
    char s2[] = "Global Village" ;
    char s1[20] ;

    strcpy( s1, s2 );
    printf( "%s %s\n", s1, s2 );
}
void strcpy( char *strp1, char *strp2 )
{
    while ( ( *strp1++ = *strp2++ ) != '\0' );
}
```

In strcpy, the character being copied is also tested for a NULL character. The while-loop stops when a NULL character is encountered.

7.5 ARRAYS OF POINTERS

An array can be declared as having a pointer data type. One situation is having an array of strings. If this array is seen as rows and columns, all the number of columns of each row must be the same. For example, a declaration might look like this:

```
#define ROWS 3
#define COLS 5
static char furniture [ROWS][COLS] =
{
    "Table",
    "Chair",
    "Sofa"
} ;
```

The variable furniture has 3 rows and 5 columns. The rows are initialized with string constants: "Table," "Chair," and "Sofa."

In the next example, fields[] is a one-dimensional array, and each element is initialized with a pointer to a string. In the declaration, the asterisk (*) preceding the fields[], makes it an array of pointers. The lengths of the strings are not the same. For example, fields[2] points to string "Prov" and fields[3] points to "Postal Code:". Such an array is called a ragged array.

The show_fld_names function illustrates how to use a pointer array. It prints each string to the standard output stream. The array fields is indexed from first element using a subscript i until NULL pointer (NULLPTR) is found.

```
/************************************************
This program illustrates pointer array
************************************************/

#include <stdio.h>
#define NULLPTR ((char *)0)
```

```
static char *fields[]=
{
    "Name:          First:          Middle:",
    "City:",
    "Prov:",
    "Postal Code:",
    "Phone (H):     (B):",
    NULLPTR
};

main()
{
    show_fld_names( fields );
}

static void show_fld_names( char *fld[] )
{
    int i = 0 ;

    while ( fld [i] != NULLPTR )
    {
       printf( "%s\n", fld[i] );
       i++;
    }
}
```

The following shows each element of the array `fields[]` having a pointer to a string.

Array	String
fields[0] ——>	"Name: First: Middle:"
fields[1] ——>	"City:"
fields[2] ——>	"Prov:"
fields[3] ——>	"Postal Code:"
fields[4] ——>	"Phone (H): (B):"
fields[5] ——>	NULLPTR

8

Preprocessor Directives

In C, a preprocessor step takes place before compilation, which looks for directives to be followed during compilation. Theses directives, coded with keywords, are instructions to the preprocessor. As we will discuss in details the different preprocessor directives, you will notice that they add power to the development of software. The preprocessor provides you with these benefits:

- Include files.
- Define macros.
- Conditional compilation.
- Pass information to the compiler.
- Line numbering of source program.
- Generate compile error messages.

In using the preprocessor directives, there are few general rules that must be followed. A directive starts with the number sign #, and it must be the first character on the line. The # can be preceded by white spaces; it need not be on column 1.

If a directive has to be extended over more than a line, a continuation maker \ must be used. The marker must be the last character on a line.

8.1 #include

The #include directive causes the preprocessor to replace the line in a program with the content of a specified file. The #include directive has the form:

```
#include "filename"
```

or

```
#include <filename>
```

We have used the #include directive numerous times in this book, and the most common ones are:

#include <stdio.h>

#include <stdlib.h>

Later, we will discuss when to enclose the filename with double quotation marks or angle brackets (<>), but first let's look at what an include (also called header) file contains. Generally, a header file contains other preprocessor directives, data declarations, function prototypes, macros, or other #include directives. There are two kinds of header files. One kind comes with the C compiler, such as *stdio.h* and *stdlib.h*. These files should not be changed. The others are for your own programs, which multiply and grow, depending on the needs of the software design.

The file *mydef.h* is an example of an include file, and it contains the following lines:

```
/*mydef.h*/
#include <stdio.h>
#include <stdlib.h>
#include <string.h>

#define RC_FAIL      -1        /* return for failure           */
#define RC_SUCCESS   0         /* return code for success      */
#define NULLPTR      ( (MFILE *) 0) /* null pointer             */
#define EOS     '\0'  /* end-of-string                          */

typedef     unsigned char UCHAR;

struct mfile_struct
{
    struct mfile_struct *id; /* memory file instance id     */

    int      fmaxrows;    /* maximum number of rows          */
    int      fmaxcols;    /* maximum number of columns       */

    int      rows_full;   /* number of rows filled           */
    UCHAR    *mf_data_ptr;/* pointer to data storage         */
};

typedef     struct mfile_struct MFILE;

/* function prototypes */

MFILE *mf_ist( int row, int col );
int mf_rls( MFILE *mfptr );
int mf_read( MFILE *mfptr, char *fptr );
int *mf_getrp( MFILE *mfptr, int row );
```

It has #include directives, other preprocessor directives (#define), structure definition, data type definitions, and function prototypes. Next is an example of how to use this include file *mydef.h*.

```
/***************************************************************
This program illustrates use of preprocessor #include directive
***************************************************************/
#include "mydef.h"
main()
{

}
```

During compilation of the program, the preprocessor will replace the line #include "mydef.h" with the content of the file *mydef.h*. Notice that we used double quotation marks instead of angle brackets. The next discussion is about how the compiler reacts to these two ways of enclosing the filename.

The convention is to enclose the system include files that come with the C compiler with brackets, such as

```
#include <stdio.h>
```

The double quotation marks are used for a user-defined include file—for example:

```
#include "mydef.h"
```

The preprocessor searches the specified path in two ways: via compiler option, and DD statements in your JCL stream.

For system include files, the libraries specified in the SEARCH compilation option is scanned first. If a file is not found, the libraries of the SYSLIB DD statements are searched next.

The preprocessor looks for user include files in the libraries mentioned in the LSEARCH option of the compiler. If the file is not found, the libraries of the SYSLIB DD statements are searched next. Failing to locate a file in user libraries, the preprocessor attempts to find it in the system libraries.

The filename can be a fully qualified DSNAME and must be enclosed in single as well as double quotation marks. Such a file name can also have a PDS member. If the filename appears with single quotation marks, the preprocessor will not search any library. In the following example,

```
#include "'USER1.INCLUDE.MYDEF'"
```

will attempt to open and read the data set 'USER1.INCLUDE.MYDEF'.

If the single quotation marks are not used, the normal search rule is followed. You should also be aware of the following translation of the filename that takes place to conform with MVS naming convention.

1. All lower case characters are translated to upper case.
2. Filename is truncated to eight characters.
3. Every underscore (_) is replaced with @ character.
4. The filename is stripped of all characters from the first period (.) until the end. Therefore, <stdio.h> becomes STDIO., for example.

If you use a DDNAME, the preprocessor will only use the file associated with the DDNAME. In the next example, MYLIB is a DDNAME.

```
#include "DD:MYLIB"
```

8.2 #define AND #undef

The #define directive has two forms: simple and complex. The complex form is called a macro, which will be discussed later. The simple form is:

```
#define identifier token_string
```

The preprocessor replaces all the occurrences of the *identifier* with the *token string*. This only happens in the source file where the definition of the identifier occurs. In the following example, COUNT is associated with a number 5. A #define directive does not use any storage area.

```
#define COUNT 5
main()
{
    int i;
    for( i = 0; i <= COUNT ; i++ )
        printf( "New World Order\n" );
}
```

The output is:

```
New World Order
New World Order
New World Order
New World Order
New World Order
```

The preprocessor substitutes every occurrence of COUNT with the value 5—only once in this case.

There are many advantages in using #define directive. It adds clarity and portability to programs. The symbolic representation of constant is self-documenting. Consequently, it makes maintenance of software much easier than without it. Consider the following:

```
#define PI              3.14159
#define HRS_PER_WK      7*24
#define EOS             '\0' /* end of string terminator */
#define TRUE            1
#define FALSE           ~TRUE
#define MESSAGE         "Dawning Star"
#define COUNT 5
#define NEW_COUNT       (COUNT+30) /5
#define NULLPTR         ((char *) 0) /*null pointer */
#define TAB             '\t'   /* tab */
#define CR              '\r'   /* carriage return */
```

```
#define LF        '\n'   /* line feed */
#define SPACE     ' '
#define ZERO      0
```

These are only a few examples of how constants can be represented by meaningful identifiers.

The scope of a #define identifier lasts until the end of a source file unless it is nullified with an #undef directive. For example, the following directive

```
#define COUNT 100
```

defines COUNT as 100. And the next directive removes the identifier COUNT:

```
#undef COUNT
```

Following the #undef, the *identifier* cannot be substituted for previously defined code. However, the same *identifier* can be used again to represent the same or another constant.

The complex form of the #define directive is called a macro, the subject of our next discussion.

8.3 MACROS

A macro is a complex form of a #define directive. A complex macro receives from one to many parameters when it is invoked. A macro has a general form:

```
#define identifier(parameter1,...,parametern) token_string
```

There should be no space between the *identifier* and the left paranthesis. The parameters are separated by commas. The token_string is the replacement code. In the next macro definition of ADD, there are two parameters, a and b. The replacement code is (a+b). In the main function, this macro ADD is used to add variables x and y.

```
/************************************************
This program illustrates macro definition and call
************************************************/
#include <stdio.h>
#define ADD(a,b) (a+b)  /* macro to add */
main()
{
    int x = 1, y = 5;

    printf( "Sum of x and y is %d \n", ADD (x,y));
}
```

The output is:

```
Sum of x and y is 6
```

The scope of a macro lasts until the end of a source file unless it is nullified with directive #undef. Once removed, the same identifier can be reused to define another macro.

Macros are very useful in replacing function calls by in-line code, which lends to efficient programs. The following are a few such examples:

```
/* find the minimum of two values */
#define min(a,b) ( ( (a) < (b) ) ? (a) : (b) )
/* find the maximum of two values */
#define max (a,b) ( ( (a) > (b) ) ? (a) : (b) )
/* check if a character is alpha */
#define ISALPHA(c) ( ( ('a') <= (c) ) && ( (c) <= 'z') ) \
            ||' ( ('A') < = (c) ) && ( (c) <= 'Z') ) )
/* copy string s to d */
#define Copy(d,s) strncpy( d, s, sizeof(d) )
/* fill an array with zeroes */
#define Zero_array(a) memset( a, 0, sizeof(a) )
```

8.3.1 Predifined Macros

The C compiler provides five predefined macros. The name of each of these macros has two leading and trailing underscore (_) characters. Although they are available to you, these macros cannot be undefined by your program.

Predefined Macros	Return Values
__DATE__	A character string containing the date when the source file was last compiled. The date format is "Mnn dd yyyy" , where Mnn is the month (Jan, Feb, etc.) dd is the day, and yyyy is the year.
__TIME__	A character string containing the time when source file was last compiled. The time format is "hh:mm:ss."
__FILE__	A character string containing the source file name.
__LINE__	An integer representing the current line number.
__STDC__	A non-zero integer value indicating that implementation follows ANSI Standard C; otherwise, it is zero.

The following program prints the values of the predefined macros __LINE__, __FILE__, __DATE__, and __TIME__. It also prints the value of CONF, which is defined as "YES" or "NO," depending whether __STDC__ is defined or not.

```
/***********************************************
This program illustrates predefined macros
***********************************************/

#include <stdio.h>

#if __STDC__
# define CONF "YES"
```

```
#else
# define CONF "NO"
#endif

main( )
{
    printf( "Line   File   Date   Time   ANSI\n");
    printf( "%d     %s     %s     %s     %s\n",
             __LINE__, __FILE__, __DATE__, __TIME__,
                                           CONF );
}
```

8.3.2 Macros in ctype.h

One of the include files of C compiler is called *ctype.h*. It has many useful macro definitions for character testing and conversions. To use these macros in your program, add to the source file the preprocessor directive:

```
#include <ctype.h>
```

The macros are as follows.

Macro	Conditions returning non-zero (TRUE) value
isalpha(c)	c is an alphabet
isupper(c)	c is an uppercase character
islower(c)	c is a lowercase character
isdigit(c)	c is a digit
isalnum(c)	c is an alphanumeric character
isxdigit(c)	c is a hexadecimal digit
isspace(c)	c is a space character
ispunct(c)	c is a punctuation character
isprint(c)	c is a printable character
isgraph(c)	c is a printable character, except a space
iscntrl(c)	c is a control character

Macro	Conversion functions
toupper(c)	change c from lower to upper case
tolower(c)	change c from upper to lower case

8.4 CONDITIONAL COMPILATION

A conditional compilation directive causes the preprocessor to select or discard portions of a source program during a compilation. What should be passed on to the compiler depends on the conditions that the preprocessor evaluates.

There are many conditional compilation directives, and there are many ways of using them. One way is to write portions of program code that are applicable for different stages of the software life cycle: development, testing, and production. With conditional directives, you can "turn on" only part of your source code and discard the rest during a compilation. The preprocessor does the work of selecting the appropriate parts to suit each situation.

The C preprocessor allows the following conditional directives:

#if, #else, and #endif

#elif

#ifdef

#ifndef

8.4.1 #If, #else, and #endif

The #if directive is the start of a conditional compilation and ends when #endif is encountered. The general form of these two directives are:

```
#if constant-expression
    statements
#endif
```

The preprocessor evaluates the constant-expression and, if it is non-zero (TRUE), the following C statements, until the #endif directive, are passed to the compiler. If it is zero (FALSE), the following statements are not included for compilation.

The next program is a simple example of how #if and #endif are used in conditional compilation. This program illustrates how strategic portions of your program can be linked to debugging and testing by using preprocessor directives. In this example, the #if directive is used twice:

```
#if DEBUG >= 1
```

and

```
#if TEST >= 1
```

The expression DEBUG >= 1 will yield 1 because DEBUG is defined as 1. Therefore, the debug portion of the code will be included in the compilation.

The result of the expression TEST >= 1 will be 0, since TEST is associated with 0, and the test portion of the function will be ignored.

```
/************************************************
This program illustrates conditional compilation
************************************************/

#include <stdio.h>

#define DEBUG 1
#define TEST 0

main()
{
```

```
    FILE *fh;
/* debug code */
#if DEBUG >= 1
    if ( ( fh = fopen( "'MY.ACCOUNT.DATA'", "r" ))
                                        != NULL )
        return;
    else
        printf( "Debug file: MY.ACCOUNT.DATA \n");
#endif

/* test code */
#if TEST >= 1
    if ( ( fh = fopen( "'TEST.ACCOUNT.DATA'", "r"))
                                        != NULL )
        return;
    else
        printf( "Test file: TEST.ACCOUNT.DATA \n");
#endif

    fclose( fh );

}
```

The preprocessor allows an *if-else-endif* construct. Our previous example can be rewritten to initialize the variable in_file with a test or production file name.

```
/***********************************************
This program illustrates #if #else #endif
***********************************************/

#include <stdio.h>

#define TEST 1

#if TEST >= 1
    static char in_file[] = "'TEST.ACCOUNT.DATA'";
#else
    static char in_file[] = "'PROD.ACCOUNT.DATA'";
#endif

main()
{
    FILE *fh;

    if ( ( fh = fopen ( in_file, "r" ) ) != NULL )
        return;
    else
        printf ( "Input file is %s \n", in_file );
    fclose ( fh );
}
```

The output is:

```
Input file is 'TEST.ACCOUNT.DATA'
```

The *constant-expression* cannot contain a sizeof operator or a cast. It can contain a keyword defined, which can only be used with #if directive. The expression

```
defined(identifier)
```

yields a value 1 if the *identifier* has been previously defined by the preprocessor. Here is an example to illustrate the use of keyword defined.

```
#define TEST
#if defined(DEBUG)
        statements
#endif
#if defined(TEST)
        statements
#endif
```

8.4.2 #elif

The #elif directive is an *else-if* control construct. It is always preceded by #if directive and followed by none or many #elif directives, and finally followed by directive #endif.

The general form is:

```
#if constant-expression_1
        statements
#elif constant-expression_2
        statements
#elif constant-expression_3
        statements
#else
        statements
#endif
```

The #else directive is optional, and it must be placed just before the #endif directive. If the evaluation of constant-expression yields 1 (TRUE), the next #elif or #else will be included for compilation.

In the following example, identifiers DEBUG and TEST are defined and conditional directives are used to select only one of the three definitions and initialization of variable in_file[]. In this case, the preprocessor will send

```
          static char in_file[] = "'TEST.ACCOUNT.DATA'";
```
to the compiler because expression TEST >= 1 yields value 1.
```
#define DEBUG 0
#define TEST 1
#if DEBUG >= 1
    static char in_file[] = "'MY.ACCOUNT.DATA'";
#elif TEST >= 1
    static char in_file[] = "'TEST.ACCOUNT.DATA'";
#else
    static char in_file[] = "'PROD.ACCOUNT.DATA'";
#endif
```

8.4.3 #Ifdef

The #ifdef directive is to check whether an identifier has been defined as a macro by the preprocessor. If it is defined, the C statements immediately following the #ifdef directive are passed to the compiler. The general form is:
```
#ifdef identifier
    statements
#endif
```

In the following example, in_file is initialized to 'TEST.FILE' if DEBUG is defined as a macro by the preprocessor. Otherwise, it will be initialized to 'PROD.FILE'.
```
#ifdef DEBUG
    static char in_file[] = "'TEST.FILE'";
#else
    static char in_file[] = "'PROD.FILE'";
#endif
```

8.4.4 #Ifndef

The #ifndef directive is to check whether an identifier has not been defined as a macro by the preprocessor. If it is *not* defined, the C statements immediately following the directive #ifndef are passed to the compiler. The general form is:
```
#ifndef identifier
    statements
#endif
```

In the following example, `in_file` is initialized to 'TEST.FILE' if DEBUG is *not* defined as a macro by the preprocessor. Otherwise, it will be initialized to 'PROD.FILE'.

```
#ifndef DEBUG
    static char in_file[] = "'TEST.FILE'";
#else
    static char in_file[] = "'PROD.FILE'";
#endif
```

8.5 #PRAGMA

The preprocessor directive allows you to pass instructions to the compiler. The general form is:

```
#pragma tokens
```

The `tokens` are specific to the implementation of the C compiler that you are using. You can pass such information as title, comments, pagesize, and so on.

8.6 NULL DIRECTIVE

A `NULL` directive invokes no action by the preprocessor. The `NULL` statements consist of a single # on a line of its own.

8.7 #OPERATOR

The preprocessor operator # causes a formal parameter of complex macro definition to become a string. The following example illustrates the use of operator #. In the macro definition of `message`, the token x is preceded with #:

```
#define message(x)   #x
main()
{
    printf("Message is: %s\n", message(Peace has come));
}
```

The output is:

```
Message is: Peace has come
```

When the macro `message` is invoked, the operator # will enclose the argument with double quotes. After the execution of the preprocessor, the macro expansion will become:

```
    printf("Message is: %s","Peace has come\n");
```

8.8 ##OPERATOR

The preprocessor operator ## concatenates two parameters of a macro definition. In the next definition, operator ## is used to combine parameters a and b of macro CONCAT.

```
#define CONCAT(a,b) a##b
```

When the macro CONCAT is invoked, the arguments passed are joined together—for example:

```
CONCAT(100,220) is expanded to 100220
```

and

```
CONCAT(Hand,book) to Handbook
```

8.9 LINE CONTROL

The preprocessor #line directive renumbers the source lines. The #line directive has the form:

```
#line decimal-constant "filename"
```

The preprocessor assigns the source line, following the #line, the decimal-constant, as the line number. The filename is optional; if it is omitted, the current source file is assumed. The line number and file name are available to your program through macros __LINE__ and __FILE__. In the Function_1 and Function_2 functions, the current value of macro __LINE__ is printed. Note that the line number is set to 2000 and 3000 with #line directive just before each function.

```
/***********************************************************
This program illustrates a line directive
***********************************************************/
#include <stdio.h>
#line 1000
main()
{
    Function_1();
    Function_2();
}

#line 2000
static void Function_1()
{
    printf("Function_1: line number is %d\n", __LINE__);
```

```
        }
        #line 3000
        static void Function_2()
        {
                printf("Function_2: line number is %d\n", __LINE__);
        }
```

The output is:

```
Function_1: line number is 2002
Function_2: line number is 3002
```

8.10 #ERROR

The #error directive is to generate an error message and stop the compilation. The #error directive has the form:

    #error character

The #error directive is useful in detecting errors in conditional compilation. If the preprocessor passes a portion of your program, when it should not have, the #error directive gives you an appropriate message and terminates the compilation. In the following example, when the compiler reaches #error directive, it will show the message associated with it and stop:

    #error Program: LGLP701, this is test code, should \
                    not be compiled

9

Pitfalls in C Programming

As in learning anything, one is bound to make mistakes in the process of mastering a language. C is not an easy language to learn because of its potentially cryptic nature, and it incorporates many novel programming concepts. Therefore, one may fall into traps and pitfalls. Novice and experienced programmers alike are sometimes bewildered and confused, consequently stuck in a hole of despair. But with knowledge, experience, and insight, one could escape the agony of pitfalls.

Of course, it is impossible to list all of the possible traps and pitfalls in C programming. In this chapter we have dealt with some of the more common errors that programmers make.

9.1 HAZARDS OF USING POINTERS

Pointer is a hard concept to understand and use, even for assembly language programmers who use direct memory addressing. As such, pointers have caused a lot of confusion among novice C programmers. A common mistake in using pointers is to overlook details. The perception is blurred; you expect it to do something, and it does something completely different. Consequently, you are thrown into a turmoil. It is impossible to cover all the possible situations of mishandling pointers, but we'll cover a few examples that will give you an idea of some of the conceptual errors you may run into.

9.1.1 Uninitialized Pointer

Let's consider the next program where the `swap` function is invoked. At first glance, every statement looks correct and legal; it will even work without failure. But disaster is lurking in this code.

Although both contents pointed by pointer variables yp and xp are initialized to 10 and 20 before calling swap, there is an important step missing. Where are these pointers pointing to?

```
/*************************************************************
This program illustrates a danger of uninitialized pointers
*************************************************************/
#include <stdio.h>
main()
{
    int *yp, *xp;

    *yp = 10;
    *xp = 20;

    swap( yp, xp );
    printf( "%d %d \n", *yp, *xp );
}
void swap( int *i, int *j )
{
    int t;

    t  = *i;
    *i = *j;
    *j = t;
}
```

In other words, the pointers are *not* initialized, and when

```
*yp = 10;

*xp = 20;
```

are executed, the values 10 and 20 are stored in unknown addresses. A safer code would be:

```
main()
{
    int *yp, *xp;
    int  y, x;

    yp  = &y;
    xp  = &x;
    *yp = 10;
    *xp = 20;

    swap( yp, xp );
    printf( "%d %d \n", *yp, *xp );
}
```

In this case, pointers yp and xp are initialized with the address of variables y and x respectively.

9.1.2 Pointer and Array

In C there is a strong relationship between arrays and pointers. Understanding operations on arrays will also demystify the concept of a pointer. In fact, any subscript operation on an array can be directly substituted with a pointer operation. This can also be a source of confusion and programming errors. Any element of an array can be pointed to by doing a pointer arithmetic. Pointer arithmetic has been thoroughly discussed in Chapter 7. If you have any doubts in using pointers and arrays, we strongly suggest that you refer to it.

9.1.3 Pointer and String

When you define a character pointer variable, it does not allocate any memory for the string; it reserves space for the pointer only. The following code of main function can be catastrophic. The statement

```
char * name;
```

reserves memory for the pointer name, but it does not allocate any space for characters that we intend to copy. Notice that this variable is not set to any particular address. The strcpy function will copy the string str into an unknown memory location of pointer name.

```
main()
{
    char *name;
    char str[] = "New World Order";

    strcpy( name, str );
}
```

The danger is that this program may overwrite memory occupied by good data or code. Often, you would not see the disastrous effect immediately; one day, suddenly, the program does not work.

In such a situation, you must always reserve storage before copying. In the next program, enough memory space is allocated by calling malloc function and assigning its address to name. Then the content of string variable str is copied to this location.

```
main()
{
    char *name, *malloc();
    char str[] = "New World Order";

    name = malloc( sizeof(str) + 1 );
    strcpy( name, str );
}
```

9.2 ARRAY INDEXING

In C, the first element of an array has index 0 and not 1. A common mistake is to do the following.

```
/***********************************************************
This program illustrates a mistake in array indexing
***********************************************************/
main()
{
    int sqr[100], i;

    for (i = 1; i <= 100; i++ )
        sqr[i] = i*i;
}
```

In this program the for-loop increments i from 1 to 100 and indexes the array sqr. Consequently, the element sqr[0] is not initialized and the nonexistent element sqr[100] has been overwritten with a value. Such an incorrect initialization may destroy useful data used by your program. The correct way to write the code is like this:

```
for (i = 0; i < 100 ; i++ )
    sqr[i] = i*i;
```

9.3 STRING AND CHARACTERS

The printf function will fail badly in the following program fragment:

```
char alpha[] = 'a';
printf( "Alphabet is %s", alpha);
```

The reason is that printf looks for a NULL terminator '\0'. In the declaration and initialization of alpha, there is no end-of-string character after 'a'. However, the following code will work:

```
char alpha[] = "a";
printf( "Alphabet is %s", alpha);
```

The reason is that the compiler puts a NULL character after 'a'. In the former case, the single quotes mean that the initial value is a character constant. While in the second case, the double quotes indicate that the initial value is a string constant.

You can initialize a character array with character constants and add a NULL character at the end. This has the same effect as initializing the array with a string. For example, the following code

```
char alpha[] = 'h', 'e', 'l', 'l', 'o', '\0';
printf( "Alphabets are %s", alpha);
```

will work correctly. On the other hand, if you want to print just one character, use the character format-specifier %c—for example:

```
printf( "Alphabet is %c", alpha);
```

9.4 PASSING ADDRESS

One of the common errors in C is to pass a value when an address is expected. Earlier, we used the swap function, which receives pointers to intergers. In the next program, we use the swap function to demonstrate the incorrect way of passing pointers.

```
/********************************************
This program illustrates passing address
********************************************/
#include <stdio.h>
main()
{
    int a = 10, b = 20;

    swap( a, b );

    printf( "%d %d ", a, b );

}
void swap( int *i, int *j )
{
    int t;

    t = *i;
    *i = *j;
    *j =  t;
}
```

When

```
swap( a, b );
```

is executed, the value and not the address of arguments a and b are being passed. The correct call to swap is:

```
swap( &a, &b );
```

9.5 CASE SENSITIVE

In a switch statement, there is a risk of case labels flowing into each other unintentionally. This happens when you forget to break out of the switch loop at the appropriate place. Let's consider the next statement:

```
switch( control )
{
    case 0: printf("zero");
    case 1: printf("one");
    case 2: printf("two");
    default: printf("other");
}
```

It will compile and run without errors, and it will execute statement following a match between the value of control and the constant associated with case label. If control is 1, it will print

onetwoother

But, if this is not what you desired, you want to print "zero" only if control is 0, "one" if control is 1, "two" if it is 2, and "other" for anything else. Let's rewrite this statement:

```
switch( control )
{
    case 0: printf("zero");
        break;
    case 1: printf("one");
        break;
    case 2: printf("two");
        break;
    default: printf("other");
}
```

You can see that both statements are correct and legal, but the results are quite different.

9.6 = Is not = =

A common mistake in C programming is to use = instead of == or vice versa. This happens to novice as well as experienced programmers. The operator = is for assignment, while == is for comparison.

The statement

```
if (x = y )
    return;
```

may at times be desirable, but it can also be a typing error or misunderstanding.

Now, let's examine this statement. It will copy the value of y into x, and test that value. If it is non-zero (TRUE), it will return; otherwise, it will continue.

But the next statement has a different effect.

```
if ( x == y )
    return;
```

It will compare the value of x to y and return only if it is non-zero (TRUE).

9.7 & and | not && or | |

The operators & and | are bitwise operators. The operators && and | | are logical operators. Obviously, each category is different from the other. You may get away with substituting one for the other. Soon, we will see the results of using bitwise and logical operators.

The operators & and | work with bits, and they yield values that must be considered in binary notation. On the other hand, the logical operators test operands and the result is either 1 (TRUE) or 0 (FALSE).

Let's illustrate the difference by looking at a few examples. The expression (0 & 10) in

```
if (0 & 10 )
    return;
```

will give 0000, the result of the bitwise AND operation on binary 0000 and 1010. In the same statement, let's use the operator && instead:

```
if (0 && 10 )
    return;
```

The expression (0 && 10) will always be false, yielding value 0, because one of the operators is not non-zero. In this case, the evaluation of the expression will stop after checking only the first operand, which is 0.

Now let's look at bitwise (|) and logical (| |) OR operators. The expression (10 | 0) in the statement

```
if ( 10 | 0 )
    return;
```

will yeild binary 1010. The result is non-zero (TRUE); therefore, return statement will be executed.

But substituting the binary operator (|) for logical operator (| |) gives you the same result while executing the if statement. In the statement

```
if (10 || 0 )
    return;
```

the expression (10 || 0) gives a value of 1; therefore, the return statement will be executed. As you can see, although both bitwise and logical operators sometimes appear to work the same, both yield different results. These operators must be used with care and logical thinking.

9.8 WHAT HAPPENED TO ELSE?

It is easy to lose the intended purpose of else, and it happens for many reasons. Many levels of if-else ladder and cryptic C language syntax can easily give a "mirage" effect. You think that an else is there, but it is only your imagination. The compiler associates else to an if differently than you think; obviously, this creates confusion. To illustrate the misunderstanding of the compiler rules, let's look at the following example.

```
/********************************************************
This program illustrates dangling else
********************************************************/

#include <stdio.h>

main()
{
    int a = 10, b = 20, c;

if( a == 0 )
    if ( b == 0 ) return;
else
{
    c = a + b;
    printf( "%d %d %d", a, b, c );
}
```

Where does the else belong? At first glance, it seems it should go with the first if. Not according to C rules. An else clause is associated with the closest if statement. Let's rewrite the portion of the program with if statements:

```
if( a == 0 )
    if ( b == 0 ) return;
    else
    {
       c = a + b ;
       printf( "%d %d %d", a, b, c );
    }
```

If you are not sure about where an else does belong, use braces—without any cost—to clarify your code—for example:

```
if( a == 0 )
{
    if ( b == 0 )
    {
       return;
    }
    else
    {
       c = a + b ;
       printf( "%d %d %d", a, b, c );
    }
}
```

9.9 ADDRESSING MODE

When programming for the MVS environment, you must be aware of different addressing modes among various versions of the operating system. With the advent of MVS/XA, and later with MVS/ESA, the addressing range was extended from 24 bits (16 M bytes) to 31 bits (2 G bytes). This new addressing mode can cause unpredictable problems when old and new programs—some using below the 16 M bytes line—are linked together.

To avoid addressing mishaps, a program can be forced to reside and address below or above the line with an addressing mode (AMODE) specification (or default) for each CSECT and load module. Depending on the AMODE (24, 30, or ANYWHERE), a program has an addressing length of 24-bit addresses, 31-bit addresses, or both. The compiler can be installed below or above the address line. Similarly, an application program can have either or both ranges of addressing.

Problems arise when a C program has AMODE=31 and is calling existing programs below the line. This will result in unpredictable behavior. One solution is to have all programs operate in the same range. But this is not always possible if you want to take advantage of the extended addressing, as well as use exiting software. Many IBM products still run below the 16 M bytes boundary.

To get around this problem, an intermidiary program can be written to switch addressing mode between 24-bit and 32-bit addressing. In the next diagram, program pgm1 with AMODE=31 calls the intermediary program pgm2 with AMODE=31, which in turn calls program pgm3 with AMODE=24.

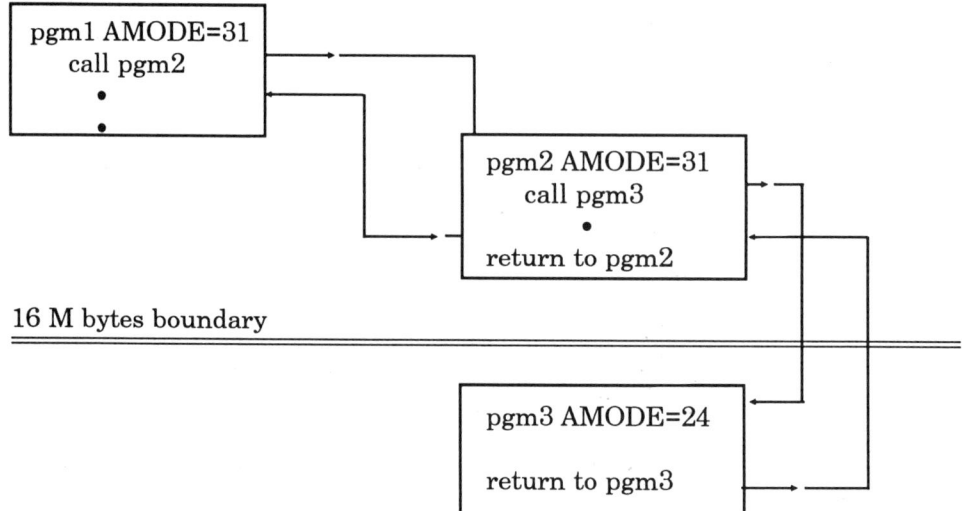

When considering the addressing mode, you should be aware of how the C compiler is installed—below or above the line. Not knowing this fact can cause you a lot of grief. During run-time, you can force the heap of a C program to reside below the line, with HEAP option.

10

Compilers and Compiling

The first section of this chapter surveys four mainframe C compilers, using the following criteria:

1. Availability of debugging tools.
2. Availability of development utilities.
3. Availability of full-screen application development support.
4. 370 support and special features.

A complete description of the compilers is beyond the scope of this book, so our discussion will be limited to the features of interest to mainframe programmers.

All of the compilers discussed adhere to the ANSI X3J11 standard. Some of them provide additional functions as part of the run-time libraries. Of course, if you use any of these additional functions, your programs may not be portable across computing platforms or compilers. There are programming techniques that allow you to minimize the impact of using compiler-specific functions when you want to port your programs to another environment. Some of these are discussed in the section on program portability in Chapter 0.

The second section of this chapter describes how you would compile a C program.

10.1 THE COMPILERS

The C compilers we will discuss are Waterloo C by WATCOM Products Inc., C/370 by IBM Corp., C for System/370 by Whitesmiths, Ltd., and SAS/C by SAS Institute Inc. The compilers produced by WATCOM, Whitesmiths, and SAS are established in the marketplace. SAS has used their C compiler to develop their own software. C/370 is IBM's implementation and is an important component of IBM's System Application Architecture (SAA).

10.1.1 Run-time Libraries

Each compiler provides a run-time library that may include extensions to the ANSI standard library definition. A run-time library is a collection of function declarations, macros, and type definitions that provide an execution-time environment for C programs. Input/output, storage allocation, and string manipulation are a few of the functions performed by library routines.

The extensions to the ANSI standard are useful and often necessary, if you intend to use existing MVS facilities. Functions such as issuing a TSO command, allocating data sets dynamically, accessing VSAM files, and issuing supervisor calls (SVCs) are available. This relieves you from having to develop similar functions and also improves your productivity.

10.1.2 Waterloo C by WATCOM Products Inc.

The debugger provides line mode and full-screen interfaces. You can walk through programs at the source level or at the machine code level. The functions of this debugger include setting breakpoints, changing variable values, redirecting a program, detecting a change in a variable value, and tracing a program. If your program fails while executing under the debugger, control is returned to the debugger. You can determine the cause of the abend, take corrective action, and continue testing.

Waterloo C provides three utilities to improve programmer productivity. They are:

1. A data set comparison utility that lists the differences between two data sets. You can use this to track down changes between two versions of a program, a document, or a data file.
2. A search utility that lists the occurrences of a character or a string of characters. Multiple members of a PDS or multiple files may be searched with one command.
3. A cross reference utility that lists all symbols found in OBJECT data sets. The listing also contains the name of the data set where the symbol is defined and any data sets that reference the symbol.

The ability to develop full-screen applications is provided via a panel library. The functions enable you to develop simple data entry applications or complex multi-window application interfaces.

The following is a partial list of the features available in the Waterloo C compiler that are designed to support and enhance program development in an MVS environment:

1. Extended addressing (XA) support—31-bit addressing.
2. Data is passed 'by reference' between C and non-C programs.
3. Reentrant (LPA eligible) programs.
4. Functions are available to issue TSO commands and MVS system macros.
5. Compiler diagnostic messages written to a terminal or to a file.

COMPILERS AND COMPILING   155

6. 370 Assembler source produced at compile time.
7. Will accept alternate characters for characters that may not be found on 3270-type terminals.
8. Access to the directory of a partitioned data set (PDS).
9. Some system-dependent portions of the run-time library are shipped in source format so that installations can modify these to suit their particular environments.
10. Run-time library may reside in the LPA.
11. Catalog access functions and control block mappings provided.
12. User signals provided.

10.1.3 C/370 by IBM Corp.

The debugger for C/370 is a separate program product that may be used to analyze both C and PL/I programs. It provides you with both a line mode and full screen interface. Programs can be walked through at the source level. You use program compile-time options to control the debugger's processing. Functions of the debugger include setting breakpoints, redirecting a program, detecting a change in a variable's value, and logging a debugging session for later replay.

The following is a partial list of the features available in the C/370 compiler that are designed to support and enhance program development in an MVS environment:

1. Extended addressing (XA) support—31-bit addressing
2. Data is passed 'by reference' or 'by value' to non-C programs.
3. Reentrant (LPA eligible) programs.
4. Function available to issue MVS system macros and program CALLs.
5. Compiler diagnostic messages written to a terminal or to a file.
6. 370 assembler source produced at compile time.
7. C/370 source programs may have line numbers.
8. VSAM file access support for all file types.
9. Access to the directory of a partitioned data set (PDS).
10. Use of a temporary file residing in memory, memory file, that can be used to provide high-speed data access.
11. IBM products with C/370 interfaces:
    a. GDDM—Graphical Data Display Manager, to display and print data.
    b. IMS—Information Management System provides database/data communication facilities.
    c. ISPF—Interactive System Productivity Facility provides services for developing full-screen applications in a TSO (Time Sharing Option) environment.
    d. DB2—relational database facility.
    e. Data Window Services—data object manipulation for MVS/ESA.
    f. CICS—Customer Information Control System provides data communication (MVS/ESA only).

12. Multitasking Facility allows you to implement applications to run as independent tasks, but does not require you to have an in-depth knowledge of MVS multi-tasking.
13. Large number of compile time options to tailor object module creation and program execution.
14. User signals available.

C/370 does not have built-in full-screen development support or development tools because of its ability to interface with existing IBM products. Products such as ISPF, CICS, and IMS allow you to produce full-screen applications in three different operating environments. The GDDM interface puts graphics capabilities in your hands. The MVS environment has a wealth of utilities that can be used by any programmer, regardless of what language is used to implement an application.

10.1.4. C for System/370 by Whitesmiths, Ltd.

This compiler provides a source level debugger with a line mode interface. The functions include setting breakpoints, displaying, modifying and printing variables, detecting when a variable's value changes, viewing the stack, and logging debugging session commands and output.

The following is a partial list of the features available in the C for System/370 compiler that are designed to support and enhance program development in an MVS environment:

1. Extended addressing (XA) support—31-bit addressing.
2. Data is passed 'by reference' between C and non-C programs.
3. Reentrant (LPA eligible) programs.
4. Program LINK function.
5. Compiler diagnostic messages written to a terminal or to a file.
6. 370 assembler source produced at compile time.
7. Registers used for frequently referenced data objects, which reduces access time.
8. C for System/370 source programs may be line numbered.
9. IMS (Information Management System) interface provides access to database and data communication facilities.
10. Large number of compile time options to tailor object module creation and program execution.
11. User signals available.
12. Names of external data objects have seven significant characters.

10.1.5 SAS/C by SAS Institute Inc.

The SAS/C compiler provides a source level debugger with a line mode interface. Functions include setting breakpoints, executing a single instruction, tracing a program, assigning and displaying values of data objects, trapping and correcting bugs that may cause your program to abend, and listing program source.

The SAS/C compiler provides a utility to convert a 370 assembler language dummy section, a DSECT, to its equivalent C structure definition. Like a C structure, a DSECT does not occupy storage; it is a map or description of storage. This utility can be useful when C and 370 assembler programs share storage.

With the SAS/C Full Screen Support Library you can develop simple or complex applications. You do not have to have in-depth knowledge of the 3270 programming environment to develop full-screen applications.

The SAS/C compiler has a number of features that support and enhance application development in an MVS environment. A list of some of these features follow:

1. Extended addressing (XA) support—31-bit addressing.
2. Data is passed 'by reference' or 'by value' between C and non-C programs.
3. Reentrant (LPA eligible) programs.
4. Compiler diagnostic messages written to a terminal or to a file.
5. 370 assembler source produced at compile time.
6. SAS/C source programs may be line numbered.
7. VSAM file access support.
8. Site customized representation of the following special characters: braces, square brackets, circumflex, tilde, backslash, vertical bar, and pound sign.
9. Digraph sequences for the special characters—two characters alternate forms.
10. Call-by-reference operator that produces an address of a variable or, when used with an array, an address pointing to the address of an array. Can be used to pass data between C and non-C programs.
11. Non-C language functions—can be used to interface with products such as ISPF and GDDM.
12. Compiler generated program patch area so that program maintenance can be applied via the AMASPZAP utility. Can be used to modify a load module or an object module.
13. Large number of compile time options to tailor object module creation and program execution.
14. Load modules can contain a copy of all required support routines.
15. In-line machine code interface allows the generation of SVCs and 370 assembler language instructions within a SAC/C program.
16. Systems Programming Environment—SAS/C used as a systems programming language, in much the same way as 370 assembler.
17. Generalized Operating System—SAS/C programs cannot execute in all MVS environments; with GOS you would write necessary support routines to be used by run-time libraries to request environment-specific services.

10.2 COMPILING

All of the vendors provide procedures to compile C programs, either in the foreground, under TSO, or in the background, via batch processing. To provide meaningful examples of the compile process, the CLISTs and JCL supplied by IBM are used. This is not intended to be an endorsement of the IBM compiler or procedures; those supplied by the other vendors provide similar functionality.

10.2.1 Compiling under TSO

The CC CLIST will compile a C program to produce object code. You may customize this CLIST, or you may write your own. The format of the supplied CLIST is:

> CC source OBJ(object) COPT(options) USERLIB(library) LISTING(list) where source is your C program. This can be a sequential file or a member of a PDS.
>
> OBJ(object) is the data set where the object code will be stored. If this is not specified, a data set name will be generated, using the source data set name and appending '.OBJ' to it. If the source data set was a PDS, the resulting object data set will be a PDS and the member name will be the same as the source member name.
>
> COPT(options) are the compile time options.
>
> USERLIB(library) is the library or libraries containing user header files.
>
> LISTING(list) is the data set where the program listing will be stored. If an asterisk(*) is specified, the output will be displayed on the terminal executing the CLIST. If this is not specified, a data set name is generated in the same manner as the object library data set name except that '.LIST' is appended.

When you execute CLISTs or commands under TSO, certain rules must be followed when specifying data set names or using special characters in text strings.

1. If the data set name is not enclosed in single quotes, the prefix value specified in your TSO profile is appended to the start of the specified data set name. The default prefix value is your TSO userid. A filename enclosed within single quotes is referred to as a 'fully qualified data set name'.
2. If spaces, commas, single quote marks, or parentheses are specified within an option, the entire text string must be enclosed within single quotes.
3. If single quotes are used inside a text string, two single quotes must be used for each single quote within the string.

The following examples show the use of the CC CLIST. The upper case characters are used to differentiate the data you enter from the command syntax. The userid is C5964JF.

In the first example, the program source is in a sequential data set named 'C5964JF.SAMPLE1.C'. It has line numbers in columns 73 to 80, inclusive.

```
CC sample1.c COPT('sequence(73,80)') LISTING(*)
```

The output from the compile, an object module, will be placed in a sequential data set called 'C5964JF.SAMPLE1.C.OBJ'. If there are any diagnostic messages, they will appear at your terminal.

In the next example, fully qualified data set names are used to specify the program source and where the object module will be placed. The source and the object files are partitioned data sets. The default compile options and listing data set name will be used.

```
CC 'z5987wf.test.c(first1)' OBJ('z5987wf.obj(first1)')
```

When the above command is executed, the listing will be placed in a data set named 'Z5987WF.TEST.C.LIST' with a member name of FIRST1.

The last example will show how to include user libraries in the compilation process.

```
CC sample2.c COPT('list,source') USERLIB(sample.lib)
```

When you execute this command, the object module will be placed in a sequential data set named 'C5964JF.SAMPLE2.C.OBJ'. The output will include an assembler-like listing of the module, as well as the C source. The library that will be searched for the user header (include) files is 'C5964JF.SAMPLE.LIB'.

10.2.2 Compiling with JCL

Job Control Language (JCL) is one method used to execute programs in MVS. The program to be executed is identified, as is the library where the program can be found. All input and output files are defined by using JCL. Refer to the *MVS JCL Reference Manual* for a complete description of the language and its uses.

There is an IBM-supplied catalogued procedure to compile a C program via JCL. You may customize the procedure, or you may write your own. You can use the following JCL to compile a C program, using the supplied procedure. It is assumed that the unmodified procedure is installed in a library accessible to all jobs.

```
//COMPILE JOB (accounting info)
  //STEP1 EXEC EDCC,INFILE='Z5987WF.SAMPLE1.C(FIRST1)'
```

With the above JCL, the program FIRST1 in a PDS named 'Z5987WF.SAMPLE1.C' will be compiled. The default compile options will be used.

11

Preparing Your Programs for Execution

In this chapter we will describe how you would create an executable version of your program for the TSO or batch environments. If your program is to run in another executable environment, such as CICS, or make use of database or data communication facilities, other processing may be necessary. Please refer to the appropriate product manual for your situation.

We will provide a description of the functions of the linkage editor and show you, by example, how to invoke it from a TSO session or by using JCL. We will also describe program attributes that can be assigned during linkage editor processing and discuss how to edit an existing load module.

For a complete discussion on the linkage editor, please refer to the *MVS Linkage Editor and Loader User's Guide*.

11.1 LINKAGE EDITOR

After successfully compiling your program, you must create an executable version of it. In an MVS environment, this step is performed by the linkage editor. The input to the linkage editor is an object module. An object module is created when you compile or assemble your program. The output of the linkage editor is a load module—your program in an executable format.

A load module can be made up of one or more object modules. Combining object modules to form a composite load module is one function of the linkage editor. The source languages of the object modules may differ, but they can still be combined to form a single load module.

The linkage editor can also modify an existing load module. You may want to update one program in a composite load module. You make the necessary updates to the source program and compile it. The newly created object module can replace the existing object module in the composite load module. All it takes is proper use of linkage editor control statements.

The linkage editor can also assign program attributes. These attributes affect where the load module can execute, above or below the 16M line, or whether the program can be reprocessed by the linkage editor. We will describe some of these attributes.

11.2 LINKING

All of the compiler vendors provide procedures to link-edit C programs, either under TSO or via batch processing. The commands, CLISTs, and JCL provided by IBM are used in our examples.

11.2.1 Linking under TSO

The procedure you use to link-edit your C program depends on whether or not the program is reentrant. A reentrant program is not self-modifying. This means that a single copy of this type of program can be executed by a number of different users concurrently. A full description of reentrancy is given in Chapter 15, "Advanced Programming Techniques." The CPLINK CLIST should be used to link-edit reentrant programs. If a program is not reentrant, the TSO LINK command should be used.

The format of the CPLINK CLIST is:

CPLINK OBJ(object) POPT(options) PLIB(libraries) LOPT(options)
  LIB(libraries) LOAD(library) where—OBJ(object) is a data set name
  or names that contain object modules compiled with the reentrant
  option or are not self-modifying.

POPT(options) pre-link utility options.

PLIB(libraries) pre-link utility input libraries LOPT(options) linkage editor options.

LIB(libraries) libraries searched to resolve external references.

LOAD(library) partitioned data set (PDS) to contain load module.

The pre-link utility options are:

NCAL/NONCAL—This option determines if the pre-link utility should use the automatic library call to resolve external references. NCAL means no automatic library call—the pre-link utility will not use the automatic library call to resolve external references. The default is NONCAL. The libraries specified with the PLIB keyword are used if the automatic library call mechanism is used to resolve external references.

MAP/NOMAP—This option determines if the pre-link utility will create a map of modifiable storage or 'writable static'. The default is MAP.

The format of the TSO LINK command is:

Link object LOAD(library) LIB(libraries) LOPT(options) where—object is the data set name or names that contain the input object modules.

LOAD(library) is where the load module will be placed. It must be a partitioned data set (PDS).

LIB(libraries) external references will be resolved, using these libraries.

LOPT(options) linkage editor options.

Please refer to the *TSO/E Command Language Reference* manual for a complete description of the LINK command.

The following examples will show you how to link-edit a program by using the CPLINK CLIST and the TSO LINK command.

In this first example, the signed on userid is Z5964WF. The object module has been compiled with the reentrancy option, and the default linkage editor options will be used. The upper and lower case characters are used to differentiate the data you enter from the command syntax.

```
CPLINK OBJ(c.obj(first1)) POPT(nomap)
```

The object module, FIRST1, must be in the data set named 'Z5964WF.C.OBJ'. The load module will be placed in a data set named Z5964WF.C.OBJ.LOAD with a member name of TEMPNAME. A map of the modifiable storage will not be produced.

In the second example, fully qualified data set names will be used for the object and load libraries.

```
LINK 'quik.c(test1)' LOAD('quik.c.load(test1)') LIB('ibm.sedchase',
'ibm.sibmbase')
```

The data sets specified in the LIB keyword are the IBM C/370 library and the PL/I-C common library and must always be specified in this manner when using the LINK command.

11.2.2 Linking with JCL

There are a number of supplied catalogued procedures to compile and link-edit a program via JCL. You can customize these procedures or write your own. There are different procedures used to link-edit reentrant and non-reentrant programs. The following examples will use the different procedures. It is assumed that the procedures are installed in a library accessible to all jobs.

```
//CMPLLINK JOB (accounting info)
  //STEP1 EXEC EDCPL,INPUT='QUIK.C(TEST1)',
```

```
//         OUTPUT='QUIK.C.LOAD(TEST1)'
```

The preceding job will invoke the pre-link utility to produce a reentrant load module.

```
//CMPLLINK JOB (accounting info)
//STEP1    EXEC EDCCL,INPUT='QUIK.C(SAMPLE1)',
//         OUTPUT='QUIK.C.LOAD(SAMPLE1)'
```

No pre-link step is included in the preceding example. The load module produced here will not be reentrant.

The following JCL stream could be used to link-edit programs.

```
//LKEDEDIT   JOB (accounting info)
//STEP 1     EXEC  PGM=IEWL,PARM='linkage editor parms'
//SYSPRINT   DD    SYSOUT=A
//SYSLMOD    DD    DSN=LOAD.LIB(FIRST1),DISP=SHR
//SYSUT1     DD    UNIT=SYSDA,SPACE=(1024,(200,20))
//SYSLIN     DD    *
input to the linkage editor
//
```

The JCL statements are explained below.

EXEC statement

The linkage editor program name is specified on this statement. The program attributes can be supplied via the PARM keyword.

SYSPRINT DD statement

Linkage editor diagnostic messages are written to the data set described by this statement.

SYSLMOD DD statement

The load module created by the linkage editor will be placed in this library. You may also reprocess an existing load module from this library.

SYSUT1 DD statement

This statement describes a work data set used by the linkage editor.

SYSLIN DD statement

This is the primary input to the linkage editor and may contain object modules and/or linkage editor control statements.

If you want to include modules from other libraries, you must add DD statements to define those libraries. Refer to the MVS *Linkage Editor and Loader User's Guide* for a complete description of the linkage editor.

11.3 PROGRAM ATTRIBUTES

Program attributes describe certain characteristics of the load module. This information is used mainly at program execution. We will provide a description of those attributes that are of importance in a C/370 environment. For a complete description of all program attributes, please refer to the *MVS Linkage Editor and Loader User's Guide*.

11.3.1 Addressing and Residency Modes

In an MVS environment, extended addressing (XA), and Enterprise System Architecture (ESA), data addresses can be composed of 24 bits or 31 bits. The addressing mode (AMODE) describes how a processor treats addresses as 24 bits or 31 bits. The residency mode (RMODE) specifies where a program can reside—in the 24-bit addressable area or anywhere in the 31-bit addressable area. When 24-bit addresses are used, the largest addressable area is 16 megabytes. This limit is known as the *16M line*. We will use this term throughout the book to describe programs or facilities that operate using 24-bit addresses. When 31-bit addresses are used, 2 gigabytes is the largest addressable area.

For C/370 programs, AMODE and RMODE are program attributes specified during linkage editor processing. The AMODE specifies the addressing mode in which a program expects to receive control. The RMODE specifies where a program is expected to reside.

The values for AMODE are:

24—This program expects to receive control in 24-bit addressing mode.

31—This program expects to receive control in 31-bit addressing mode.

ANY—This program can receive control in either 24-bit or 31-bit mode.

The values for RMODE are:

24—This program must reside below the 16M line.

ANY—this program can reside either above or below the 16M line.

When developing programs using C/370, you must be aware of how the C/370 library was installed. If the library was installed above the 16M line, your C/370 programs must have AMODE 31 specified. If the library was installed below the 16M line, there are no addressing mode restrictions. If you are developing mixed language applications, you must ensure that the addressing modes of all modules are compatible. If the C/370 program has AMODE 31 specified, all programs that make up the composite load module must have AMODE 31 specified as well.

There are AMODE/RMODE restrictions when using C/370 with other software products. You should refer to the *C/370 User's Guide* and the discussions on using

C/370 with other products, for the details. For a complete discussion on AMODE/RMODE, please refer to the *MVS System Programming Library: 31-Bit Addressing Manual*.

11.3.2 Not Editable Attribute

A load module that has this attribute cannot be reprocessed by the linkage editor. You cannot replace any portion of a composite load module that has this attribute. If a module with this attribute must be processed by the linkage editor, it must be recreated. If you are using the MultiTasking Facility (MTF) of C/370, the load module that contains all the subtask functions must NOT have this attribute.

11.3.3 Reusability Attribute

A load module is reusable when the same copy can be executed by more than one user, either concurrently or one at a time. A load module with the first of these attributes is reenterable and is serially reusable if it possesses the second attribute.

11.3.3.1 Reenterable Attribute

A reenterable load module is one that is not self-modifying or is not modified by any other module during its execution. A reentrant program may be executed by more than one user at the same time. If a composite load module is to be reenterable, all of the components that make up the load module must be reentrant. A reentrant load module is also serially reusable.

11.3.3.2 Serially Reusable Attribute

A serially reusable load module can be executed by only one user at a time. This type of load module may modify itself, but reinitializes all modified areas whenever it executes. If a composite load module is to be serially reusable, all of its components must be reenterable or serially reusable.

11.4 AUTOMATIC MODULE REPLACEMENT

You can replace one or more object modules in a composite load module without recreating the load module. The new object modules must have the same names as the object modules they replace and must be included for linkage editor processing before the composite load module.

In the following example, we will show the JCL and linkage editor control statements necessary to create a composite load module. We will then show how you would replace one of the object modules.

```
//CREATE    JOB   (accounting info)
//STEP01    EXEC  PGM=IEWL,PARM='AMODE=31,RMODE=ANY,REUS'
```

```
//SYSLMOD    DD      DISP=SHR,DSN=load library
//OBJLIB     DD      DISP=SHR,DSN=object module library
//SYSUT1     DD      UNIT=SYSDA,SPACE=(1024,(100,20))
//SYSPRINT   DD      SYSOUT=A
//SYSLIN     DD      *
    INCLUDE OBJLIB(A)
    INCLUDE OBJLIB(B)
    INCLUDE OBJLIB(C)
    NAME ABC(R)
//
```

We have now created a load module with the name of ABC. It is composed of object modules A, B, and C. The program attributes we have given this module state that program ABC expects to receive control in 31-bit addressing mode, can be loaded anywhere, and is serially reusable.

If you wanted to replace object module A, you could use the following linkage editor control statements. The preceding JCL could be used.

```
INCLUDE OBJLIB(A)
INCLUDE SYSLMOD(ABC)
NAME ABC(R)
```

12

Executing Your Programs

There are a number of operating environments in which your program can execute. In this chapter, we will describe how you would execute a program under the Time Sharing Option (TSO) and in batch. If your program is to execute in another operating environment, such as Customer Information Control System (CICS), or use database or data communication facilities, you may have to use other methods to compile and execute your program.

12.1 RUN-TIME OPTIONS

The run-time options allow you to specify the size and location of the heap and initial storage area (ISA) and produce a report of your program's storage use. You may also enable or disable the C error handler and set the initial state of the C/370 debugger.

A brief description of some of the run-time options follow. For a detailed discussion of all the run-time options, please refer to the *C/370 User's Guide*.

HEAP(size,increment,location,status)

Storage requests via the `malloc`, `realloc`, and `calloc` functions are satisfied from the heap. This option specifies how the heap storage is managed. The size value determines the minimum initial size of the heap. The increment value specifies the minimum size of any increases to the initial heap size. The location value specifies where the heap can be allocated. In an XA or ESA environment, this storage can be located above or below the 16M line. The status value specifies when the storage allocated to heap increments will be released.

ISAINC(size)

The initial storage area (ISA) is used for program management and dynamic storage allocation. This option specifies the minimum size of increments to the ISA.

ISASIZE(size)

This option specifies the amount of storage initially allocated to the ISA.

REPORT

With this option you can produce a report showing how your program uses storage.

SPIE

This option specifies that the C error handler will be called when a program interrupt occurs.

STAE

This option specifies that the C error handler will be called when your program ends abnormally.

You may specify the run-time options a number of ways, depending on how you execute your program. When executing under TSO, the run-time options are specified as part of the options list on the CALL command. If you are using batch processing to run your program, you would specify the run-time options via the PARM keyword of the EXEC JCL statement. You can always use the *runopts* pragma in your program to specify run-time options. You may need to use the *runopts* pragma if you have installed C/370 to ignore run-time options on a CALL command or PARM keyword. To override this install option for your program's execution, you would specify the *runopts* pragma with the EXECOPS value.

12.2 PROGRAM EXECUTION UNDER TSO

To execute a program in the TSO environment, you would issue a CALL command. The C/370 library and the PL/I-C common library must be allocated to the STEPLIB DD name. All of the data sets used in your TSO session are normally defined in your logon procedure. Consult the systems programmer who has the responsibility for creating and maintaining these procedures, to ensure that the required data sets are available. The format of the CALL command is:

> CALL load [parms] where load is the partitioned data set (PDS) containing the program to be executed. Parms is made of two parts—run-time options and program input. The format is: 'run-time options/program input'.

If you wanted to execute the program TEST1 contained in PDS 'Z5964WF.C.LOAD' and provide this program with an input of 'wednesday', the following command might be used.

```
CALL 'z5964wf.c.load(test1)' '/wednesday'
```

The default run-time options will be used. The data following the slash(/) will be passed to the main function. Please refer to the *TSO/E Command Language Reference Manual* for a detailed explanation of the CALL command.

12.3 PROGRAM EXECUTION WITH JCL

The following JCL stream will execute the program TEST1 and provide it with the input of 'wednesday'. The run-time options specified will bypass the trapping of program abends and will produce a report of this program's storage use.

```
//RUNJOB     JOB    (accounting info)
//STEP1      EXEC   PGM=TEST1,PARM='NOSTAE,REPORT/WEDNESDAY'
//STEPLIB    DD     DSN=Z5964WF.C.LOAD,DISP=SHR
//OUTPUT01   DD     SYSOUT=A
//CEEDUMP    DD     SYSOUT=A
```

The data set specified on the STEPLIB DD statement will be searched for the program TEST1. The output from this program will be directed to the file specified by the OUTPUT01 DD statement. The REPORT output will be written to the file specified by the CEEDUMP DD statement.

12.4 REDIRECTING STANDARD STREAMS

Every C program has three standard streams available to it: stdin, stdout, and stderr. The streams stdin and stdout are the input and output for your program. The stream stderr is where your program will write any error or warning messages. At some time, you may want to use a standard stream, but have the associated file be one of your choosing. This is called redirection. There are three ways to accomplish redirection:

1. *freopen* function.
2. Redirection symbols.
3. DD name association.

12.4.1 *freopen* Function

This function closes the file associated with the stream and associates a new file with the stream.

```
freopen("my.input", "r", stdin);
```

After the preceding statement is executed, your program would get its input from a file called 'my.input'. We have provided a complete description of the *freopen* function in Chapter 20. For a comprehensive overview, please refer to that description.

12.4.2 Redirection Symbols

There are two redirection symbols—'<' redirects input and '>' redirects output. If your program is executing under TSO and you want to redirect `stdin`, you might use the following format:

```
reporter < 'monday.file'
```

The program, reporter, would get its input from the file called 'monday.file'. If the same program was executing in batch mode, the following JCL might be used to redirect `stdin`.

```
//REPORTER    JOB     (accounting info)
//STEP01      EXEC    PGM=REPORTER,PARM='< TUESDAY.FILE'
//STEPLIB     DD      DSN=load library name
```

In this case, the program gets its input from a file called 'TUESDAY.FILE'.

12.4.3 Data Definition (DD) Name Association

You can associate a particular file to the standard streams by specifying the file name on a DD statement. The file is made available when your program executes.

The standard streams have associated DD names:

1. `stdin` is associated with DD name SYSIN. If SYSIN is not defined, data cannot be read from `stdin`.
2. `stdout` is associated with DD names SYSPRINT, SYSTERM, and SYSERR, in that order. This means that if the first DD name is not defined, C/370 will use the next.
3. `stderr` is associated with DD names SYSERR and SYSPRINT. The following JCL shows how you can use the associated DD names to perform redirection.

```
//REPORTER    JOB     (accounting info)
//STEP01      EXEC    PGM=REPORTER
//STEPLIB     DD      DSN=load library name
//SYSIN       DD      DSN=WEDSDAY.FILE,DISP=SHR
//SYSPRINT    DD      DSN=WEDSDAY.OUTPUT,DISP=MOD
//SYSERR      DD      SYSOUT=A
```

In the above example, the input will be read from 'WEDSDAY.FILE' and the output will be added to 'WEDSDAY.OUTPUT'. Any error messages will be written to the file specified by the SYSERR DD name. You can also use the TSO ALLOCATE command to associate a file with a particular standard stream:

```
ALLOCATE FI(sysin) DA('friday.file') SHR
```

With the preceding allocation in effect, your C program will read its input from 'friday.file'. If this DD name was used in a prior allocation, a FREE command should be issued to release the DD name. The format of the FREE command is:

```
FREE FI(sysin).
```

For a complete description of the ALLOCATE and FREE commands, please refer to the *TSO/E Command Language Reference Manual*.

12.5 ERROR HANDLING

With the more robust programming languages, you can define and activate error handling routines. These routines can be active for the life of your program and are able to handle specific or general exception conditions. Also, you may be able to deactivate and reactivate these error handlers at any time in your program's processing. In Assembler, the SPIE/ESPIE and STAE/ESTAE macros activate and deactivate abnormal condition handling routines. In PL/I, the on-unit defines and activates exceptional condition routines. In C, the `signal` function activates an error handling routine.

In general, error handlers are invoked when the operating system or hardware detect conditions that will cause your program to end abnormally. Conditions such as attempting to access a memory location outside the boundaries for your program or trying to divide by zero will be detected by the operating system, the hardware, or both. If routines have been defined and activated to handle these situations, they will be given control.

12.5.1 *signal* Function

To activate an error handler, you issue the `signal` function:

```
signal(signal, error_handler);
```

The value of the argument signal is one of the compiler-defined values or a user-defined value. The value of error_handler is the name of a C function that will handle the specific error situation. The following signal values are defined by the American National Standards Institute (ANSI) standard:

1. SIGABRT—Abnormal end; this might be caused by issuing the `abort` function.
2. SIGFPE—Erroneous arithmetic operation; dividing by zero would raise this condition.
3. SIGILL—An invalid instruction would raise this condition.
4. SIGINT—Interactive attention signal was received.
5. SIGSEGV—Invalid memory access would raise this condition.
6. SIGTERM—termination request was sent to the program.

C/370 extends this list by adding two user values—SIGUSR1 and SIGUSR2.

The error handler function must be written in C and must use the default linkage convention. When the signal is detected, it is reset to execute the system default action. This is done to prevent recursive calls to the error handler in case it fails. The error handling function remains active until:

1. A new error handler is activated for the same error condition or signal.
2. The signal is reset to the system default by the issuing signal(signal, SIG_DFL).
3. The signal is reset to the system default when the signal is detected.
4. The error handler is in a load module that is deleted.

If the error handler terminates by issuing a return statement, your program will resume execution at the point it was interrupted. There may be some implementation-defined restrictions in this area; you should consult the manuals for your particular compiler for the details.

12.5.2 raise Function

To send a signal to an error handler in your program, you would issue the raise function:

```
raise(signal);
```

This function can be used to test error handlers. Also, you can use it to terminate your program if an unexpected situation occurs—the should-never-happen situation.

12.5.3 Examples

In this example, a user-defined signal is detected and reported.

```
#include <signal.h>
#include <stdio.h>
#include <stdlib.h>

void error_handler(); /*prototype for error handler */

main()
{
    int sig_value;
    sig_value = signal(SIGUSR1, error_handler);
     if sig_value == SIG_ERR /* error handler activated ?*/
    {
    printf("Error handler could not be activated\n");
                        abort();   /*abend the program */
    }
    raise(SIGUSR1);                /* invoke error handler */
    printf("Return from error handler\n');
}

void error_handler()
{
printf("Error handler invoked\n");
}
```

13

MVS Files

In this chapter we will describe commonly used MVS file formats, file creation, and how to connect a file to your program, and show, through examples, how to access different file formats. We will discuss both Virtual Storage Access Method (VSAM) files, as well as non-VSAM files. The focus will be on record processing, not stream processing. We have described stream I/O in Chapter 6; please refer to it for a detailed discussion on that topic.

We emphasize record processing because that is how the various access methods in an MVS environment read and write data. A record is not a string of bytes but a well-defined structure. The underlying I/O routines that support the different access methods have been designed and optimized to process records.

An access method is a group of routines that perform the actual storing and retrieving of data. They are part of the operating system—MVS in this case. They are also responsible for detecting and possibly correcting a bad data transfer. Also, if used properly, you can process data in an effective, efficient, and secure manner.

13.1 NON-VSAM FILES

Non-VSAM files can be organized in four different ways, but we will discuss only the following three organizations:

1. Sequential—Records are stored in physical sequence, one after the other.
2. Direct—Records may be organized in any manner and are stored and retrieved directly. There is no index space allocated, and all space in the file is available to store data.
3. Partitioned—Groups of sequentially organized records are stored in members. Each member is identified in a directory that is part of the

file. The directory contains the names of all members, their locations within the file, and any user data.

13.1.1 Record Formats

A record is the basic unit of information that can be read or written by a program. It can be one character or many thousands of characters. Records can be grouped in blocks to conserve space on storage devices and increase processing efficiency by reducing the number of real I/Os necessary to access those records.

We will discuss the following record formats: fixed-length records, variable-length records, and undefined records.

When selecting a record format for a file, the following items should be considered:

1. What type of data will the program be processing?
2. What type of storage device will hold the data?
3. What access method will be used to read and write the data?

13.1.1.1 Fixed-Length Records

The length of all records in this type of file is the same. The number of records in a block is the same for every block in the file, unless short (truncated) blocks exist. If the file is unblocked, each record constitutes a block.

The record size or length is set when the file is defined. Other file attributes, such as block size and file organization, are also set at file definition. Please refer to the discussion on non-VSAM file creation later in this chapter for an overview of attributes that can be given to a file when it is created.

13.1.1.2 Variable-Length Records

The lengths of records and blocks vary in this type of file. The first 4 bytes of each record and every block contain length information. A program must provide space for the 4-byte length field and space for a record of the maximum size in its buffers when processing a file containing variable-length records.

13.1.1.3 Undefined Records

These records do not conform to either the fixed or variable formats. Each block is treated as a record. If multiple logical records exist within a physical block, a program processing this file must break down each block to gain access to the individual records.

13.2 VSAM FILES

Record management is a component of VSAM, and file organization is part of record management. The organizations we will discuss are key sequenced (KSDS), entry sequenced (ESDS), and relative record (RRDS).

13.2.1 KSDS

Records are stored in ascending, collated sequence by key. The key must be in the same position in each record, and the key data must be contiguous. Each key must be unique and cannot be changed. A KSDS file has a prime index that relates key values to record locations in the file. This index is used to locate the correct position for writing a record to the file and to locate records for retrieval.

In any discussion about KSDS files, you will often hear the terms index component and data component. These terms describe the two parts of a KSDS file. The data component contains the file's records. The index component sets the sequence of records within the file. It is used to locate records with the data component.

13.2.2 ESDS

Records are stored in the order they are presented. New records are added to the end of the file. Records cannot be deleted physically from the file, but can be marked as deleted or inactive by a processing program. Records can be updated but cannot be lengthened.

Random record retrieval can be performed if the relative byte address (RBA) of the record is known. The RBA is the offset of a record from the beginning of a file. The first record in a file has an RBA of 0.

13.2.3 RRDS

This file type consists of a number of fixed-length slots or variable-length records. In a fixed-length RRDS, each slot has a unique relative record number (RRN). The slots are in ascending RRN order. One record occupies one slot. The record is stored and retrieved by the RRN of that slot. The position of the record is fixed—that is, the RRN cannot change.

A RRDS containing variable-length records is much the same as the fixed-length data set. Each record has a unique RRN and are in ascending RRN order. Each record is stored and retrieved by its RRN, which cannot change. The difference is that this file format contains variable-length records rather than slots.

13.2.4 Alternate Index

An alternate index provides a way to access records in a VSAM file, using more than one key field. The key used in an alternate index does not have to be unique—that is, it may point to more than one record in the base VSAM file. It performs the same functions as a prime index of a KSDS file.

An alternate index is a KSDS file. The records in the data component contain the alternate key and one or more pointers to records in the base VSAM file. When the base file is an entry sequenced data set (ESDS), the pointers are RBA values. For a key sequenced data set (KSDS), the pointers are prime keys.

The key used in an alternate index can be any record field in the base file. This field must be fixed-length and in the same position in each record.

13.2.5 Selecting a File Type

You should consider the following items when selecting a VSAM file type:

1. Record access—Will the file be processed sequentially, randomly, or both? If processing is mainly sequential, use the entry sequenced format. If record keys are to be used, implying random access, then the key sequence format is preferable. If the file is accessed by record number, use the relative record format.
2. Will the record length change during processing?
3. Are records to be deleted?
4. Will more than one access key per record be necessary? Will you need an alternate index?
5. Are all required operations supported by the file type selected?

13.3 VSAM FILE FUNCTIONS

Vendors whose compilers support VSAM have provided altered or new functions to process these files. The functions of C/370 that provide file access, file positioning, and direct I/O will be discussed.

13.3.1 File Access

Opening a VSAM file differs from opening a non-VSAM file. The VSAM file can be processed either forwards or backwards, and in stream or record mode. The general format of the `fopen` function is:

```
FILE *fopen(const char *filename, constant char *mode);
```

This function opens the file pointed to by `filename`. The `mode` is a character string specifying the type of access and other keyword parameters.

13.3.1.1 Access Mode

The following is a list of parameters that specify the access mode on the `fopen` function.

rb	Read.
wb	Write. Not initial load, and the file must be reusable.
ab	Read, write, update.
rb+/r+b	Update.
wb+/w+b	Read, write, update. If the file is reusable and it is not being loaded initially, the contents may be destroyed.
ab+/a+b	Read anywhere in the file, writing at file end.

You must use the binary form of the access mode when processing a VSAM file.

13.3.1.2 Access Direction

You may access VSAM files in a forward or backward direction. The value of the *acc* keyword states in what direction the currently opened file is going to be processed.

> *acc=FWD*—The file is processed in the forward direction. When you open this file, the file pointer is positioned at the first physical record. Subsequent reads will set the file position to the start of the next record.
>
> *acc=BWD*—The file is processed in the backward direction. When opened, the file is positioned at the last record. Subsequent read operations will set the file position to the start of the preceding record.

13.3.1.3 Record Format

All three types of VSAM files may be processed in either stream or record modes. ESDS files may be written to in stream mode only. You use the *type* keyword to specify the processing mode. If you want to open a file for record processing, you would specify 'type=RECORD'. If you want to open a file for stream processing, you would omit the *type* keyword.

13.3.1.4 OPEN Example

The following example shows how to open a VSAM file for input (read), using record mode processing and in the forward direction:

```
FILE *rdfile;
rdfile = fopen("vsam.cluster", "rb, acc=FWD, type=RECORD");
```

13.3.2 File Positioning

When processing VSAM files in stream mode, you can use the fgetpos and fsetpos functions to determine and establish a position within a file. If you are processing a VSAM file in record mode, you must use the flocate function. With this function, you can set a record pointer, given the record key, RBA or RRN.

The general format of the flocate function is:

```
int flocate(FILE *filename, const void *key, size_t key_len, int options);
```

The above function positions the file using the value pointed to by key with a length of key_len within the file pointed to by filename. The options that can affect the positioning are:

	_KEY_FIRST	Positions to the first record in the file, regardless of the key value.
	_KEY_LAST	Positions to the last record in the file,

regardless of the key value. Subsequent reads are in the backward direction.

_KEY_EQ	Positions to the first record with a key equal to the specified key.
_KEY_EQ_BWD	Positions to the first record with a key equal to the specified key. Subsequent record access is in the backward direction.
_KEY_GE	Positions to the first record with a key equal to or greater than the specified key. If the file is an RRDS, the pointer may be positioned at an empty slot. If the key, a RRN, is greater than any existing RRN, an EOF indicator is returned.
_RBA_EQ	Positions to the record with the specified RBA.
_RBA_EQ_BWD	Same as above, but subsequent reads as in the backward direction.

If you want to use this function to perform a generic search on a file, specify a `key_len` value less than the actual key length. The key length is defined when the file is created.

13.3.3 Direct I/O

Records in all three types of VSAM files can be updated. Records in KSDS and RRDS files can be deleted as well. Two functions have been provided to delete and update records in a VSAM file.

The general format of the `fdelrec` function is:

```
int fdelrec(FILE *filename);
```

This function deletes the record in the file pointed to by `filename`, using the current position indicator. The file must have been opened with `type=RECORD`. The `fread` function must have been used to set the file position, and no other positioning functions can be issued between the `fread` and `fdelrec` functions.

The general format of the `fupdate` function is:

```
size_t fupdate(const void *buffer, size_t size, FILE *filename);
```

This function updates a previously read record from the file pointed to by `filename` with the contents of `buffer` for a length of *size*. When updating a KSDS file, the record can be lengthened or shortened.

This is a bit of an oddity, from an MVS point of view. When this function executes successfully, the size of the record is returned. When it is unsuccessful, zero is returned. In an MVS environment, a zero return code generally indicates a successful operation.

13.4 FILE CREATION

In an MVS environment, you can create a file either via batch processing or under TSO. The following sections will describe creating both non-VSAM and VSAM files. References will be provided to enable you to acquire more details.

13.4.1 Non-VSAM File Creation

Non-VSAM files can be created in batch mode or using TSO.

13.4.1.1 Batch File Creation

You can create a non-VSAM file by executing a program called IEFBR14. This is a do-nothing program. You supply the necessary JCL statements to define the file. The following example will demonstrate this.

```
//CREATE1    JOB    (accounting info)
//STEP1     EXEC   PGM=IEFBR14
//DD1        DD    DSN=NEW.FILE,DISP=(NEW,CATLG),UNIT=3380,
//                 DCB=(LRECL=80,BLKSIZE=3200,RECFM=FB,DSORG=PS),
//                 SPACE=(TRK,(1,1))
```

The keywords and their values are explained below. For a complete description of all available keywords and their values, refer to the *MVS JCL Reference Manual*.

DD1	is the DD (data definition) name. In this case, it can be any value, as long as that value follows the rules for DD names.
DSN	is the data set or file name.
DISP	is the disposition for the file. It is used to describe the file status to MVS and what action MVS should take on the file when the job or job step ends.
DCB	is the data control block. It is the physical description of the file. How the data is organized, the length of each record, whether the records are blocked, and, if so, the size of each block.
SPACE	is the file size as well as the units of allocation.
UNIT	is the device or device type or group where the file will reside.

13.4.1.2 TSO File Creation

Non-VSAM files can be created by using two TSO commands, ATTRIB and ALLOCATE. The ATTRIB command is used to create the file description in the same way that the DCB keyword is used in batch. The ALLOCATE command provides the rest of the information necessary for file definition. Refer to the *MVS TSO/E Command Language Reference Manual* for a complete description of these commands. The following example shows the use of the ATTRIB and ALLOCATE commands. The keywords of the command syntax are in uppercase.

```
ATTRIB attrlst BLKSIZE(3200) LRECL(80) RECFM(fb) DSORG(ps)

ALLOCATE USING(attrlst) DSNAME('new.file') NEW CATALOG
    UNIT(3380) SPACE(TRACKS,(1,1))
```

The preceding ATTRIB command would create an attribute list with a name of `attrlst`. The keywords and their values provide the physical description of the file. The ALLOCATE command will create a file called NEW.FILE, using the characteristics from the ATTRIB command. The DISPosition, SPACE, and UNIT keywords have the same meaning as in batch file creation.

13.4.2 VSAM File Creation

You use Access Method Services (AMS) commands to create and maintain VSAM files. You can also use JCL or TSO to create VSAM files in much the same way as non-VSAM files.

13.4.2.1 Using AMS Commands

You would use the DEFINE CLUSTER or ALLOCATE commands to create a VSAM file, using AMS. Please refer to the *MVS Access Methods Services Manual* for a complete description of all of the commands.

```
//DEFVSAM   JOB    (accounting info)
//STEP1     EXEC   PGM=IDCAMS
//SYSPRINT  DD     SYSOUT=A
//SYSIN     DD     *
                  DEFINE CLUSTER                    -
                       (NAME(NEW.VSAM.CLUSTER)      -
                       VOLUME(ABC123)               -
                       TRACKS(10,5))                -
                   DATA                             -
                       (NAME(NEW.VSAM.DATA)         -
```

```
                RECORDSIZE(80 80)              -
                KEYS(4 0))                     -
                INDEX                          -
                (NAME(NEW.VSAM.INDEX))
```

In the above example, a VSAM key sequenced (KSDS) file is created. As mentioned earlier, a KSDS file is composed of a data component and an index component. The file name is NEW.VSAM.CLUSTER. It will reside on a volume with a serial number of ABC123 and will have a primary space allocation of ten tracks and a secondary space allocation of five tracks. The data component of this file is named NEW.VSAM.DATA. The records are fixed length and are 80 bytes long. The record keys are four bytes in length and start at the first byte of the record. The index component is called NEW.VSAM.INDEX.

At this point we have only defined the file; it does not have any data in it. The file can be loaded using the REPRO command or you may write a program. If an alternate index is to be used, the DEFINE ALTERNATEINDEX command defines the file. It is related to the base VSAM file via the DEFINE PATH command and built using the BLDINDEX command. The reference manual provides a complete description of these commands.

Access Method Services can be invoked from TSO or a user-written program. The reference manual describes how this can be accomplished and provides further references.

13.4.2.2 Using JCL

As previously mentioned, creating a VSAM file using JCL is much like using JCL to create a non-VSAM file. There are some restrictions when using JCL to define VSAM data sets. You should contact the system programmer responsible for VSAM before you attempt to use this method.

```
//DD1     DD      DSN=NEW.VSAM.DATA,DISP=(NEW,KEEP),
//                SPACE=(80,(100,25)),AVGREC=U,
//                RECORG=KS,KEYLEN=4,KEYOFF=0,LRECL=80
```

We will describe only those keywords and values that have a different meaning in this context or have not been fully described in our non-VSAM example.

	AVGREC	specifies that records are the units of allocation and a multiplier for the primary and secondary space quantity specified on the SPACE keyword.
	KEYLEN	specifies the record key length.
	KEYOFF	specifies the position of the key within the record.
	RECORG	specifies the file organization.

SPACE   the first value specifies the record length. The next two values are the primary and secondary space. The primary value specifies the initial number of records in the data set. The secondary value specifies how many records will be in each file extension. In the example the record length is 80 bytes. The initial data set will contain 100 records, and each extension will be 25 records. The value in the AVGREC keyword indicates a multiplier of 1.

13.5 FILE ALLOCATION

In this context, allocation is making a file available to a program. This availability may mean creating a new file or connecting a program to an existing file.

File allocation can be performed in one of three ways:

1. JCL (Job Control Language).
2. Dynamic allocation.
3. TSO ALLOCATE command.

13.5.1 JCL File Allocation

When allocation means creating a new file, the JCL statements used would be the same as that described in the section on Batch File Creation. Please refer to that section for the discussion on creating a file.

When allocating an existing file, the file name and disposition are provided on a DD statement:

```
//INPUT01 DD DSN=MASTER.FILE,DISP=OLD
```

A program would have a control block defined for this file, a DCB (data control block) for a non-VSAM file or an ACB (access control block) for a VSAM file. The file is connected to the program through this control block. The control block is connected to the file via the DD name.

Specifying a DISPosition of OLD means that this file already exists and, once it is allocated, no other program can use it until it is deallocated. Refer to the *MVS JCL Reference Manual* for a complete description of this method of file allocation.

13.5.2 Dynamic Allocation

A file can be connected to a program when the program is executing, rather than at the start of a job or job step or at the logon of a TSO user. This type of file allocation is accomplished via a supervisor call or SVC. You would issue SVC 99 to perform dynamic allocation. With this SVC, you can allocate files by data set name or DD name. You can refer to Chapter 15 on "Advanced Programming Techniques" for an explanation of dynamic allocation and an example using C/370. Additionally, you can refer to the *MVS/ESA System Programming Li-*

brary: Application Development Guide or *MVS/XA System Programming Library: System Macros and Facilities* for a complete description of this SVC.

Performing the allocation by filename is equivalent to file allocation at the start of a job or job step. The parameter list that is passed to SVC 99 is equivalent to a DD statement. Many of the keywords used on a DD statement can be passed, such as DISP, DCB, DSN, UNIT, SPACE, and VOLUME.

13.5.3. TSO ALLOCATE Command

The ALLOCATE command can be used to create a new file or connect a program to an existing file. We have described its use in creating new files in an earlier section of this chapter.

```
ALLOCATE FILE(input01) DSN('master.file') DISP(old)
```

Issuing the above command would allocate MASTER.FILE to the TSO session. A DISPosition of OLD would not allow any other TSO user or batch program to access this file. TSO commands or programs executing under TSO would access this file, using the DD name INPUT01.

13.6 EXAMPLES

The following examples will demonstrate how to access fixed-length files, variable-length files, and VSAM files. JCL to compile, link-edit, and run the programs will be included.

13.6.1 Fixed-Length File

```
/* Program: NVSAMP1
   This program will read the first 10 records of a fixed-length,
   unblocked file and print them. */

#include <stdio.h>

#include <stdlib.h>

#include <errno.h>

main()
{
    FILE *fixlen;
    int  counter;

/* buffer will contain the record when it is read in. it is 1
   byte longer than the record so there will be a null character
   for string processing when we print the record. */

    char buffer[101];

/* we use the DD name form to specify the file we want to pro-
   cess. more general than specifying the file name. */
```

```
    fixlen=fopen("DD:input01", "rb, lrecl=100, recfm=f, \
type= record");
        if(fixlen==NULL)
        {
           printf"Open failed on file input01\n");
           exit(EXIT_FAILURE);
        }
        for(counter=0; counter<10; counter++)
        {
/* the C reference manual states that when using fread for re-
cord input, set size to 1 and count to the expected record
length. */
        fread(buffer, 1, sizeof(buffer), fixlen);
        if(ferror(fixlen))
        {
           printf("Read error on file input01\n");
           fclose(fixlen);
           exit(EXIT_FAILURE);
        }
printf("%s\n", buffer);
}
fclose(fixlen);
      exit(EXIT_SUCCESS);
}
```

The following JCL to compile and link-edit this program assumes that the shipped IBM procedures have been installed and modified to meet installation standards and naming conventions.

```
//CMPLLINK    JOB  (accounting info)
//STEP1       EXEC EDCCL,INPUT='SOURCE.C(NVSAMP1)',
//            OUTPUT='LOAD.C(NVSAMP1)'
```

SOURCE.C is a PDS containing the sample source statements. The executable load module produced from the link-edit step will be placed in a PDS called LOAD.C. The name of the source program and the load module is NVSAMP1. The installation default compiler options have been selected, refer to the *C/370 User's Guide* for an explanation of the options and how they may be of benefit to you.

To run the program, the following JCL might be used:

```
//NVSAMP1   JOB    (accounting info)
//STEP1     EXEC   PGM=NVSAMP1
//STEPLIB   DD     DSN=LOAD.C,DISP=SHR
//INPUT01   DD     DSN=FIXED.LEN,DISP=SHR
//SYSPRINT  DD     SYSOUT=A
```

13.6.2 Variable-Length File

```
/* Program: NVSAMP2
   This program will write 10 variable-length records
   to a file and print them. */
#include <stdio.h>
#include <stdlib.h>
#include <errno.h>

main()
{
    FILE *varlen;
    int counter;
    int recnum;
    int reclen[]={20,25,30,35,40,45,50,55,60,65};
    char buffer[101];

    varlen=fopen("DD:output01", "wb, lrecl=100, recfm=v,
    type=record");
    if(varlen==NULL)
    {
       printf"Open failed on file output01\n");
       exit(EXIT_FAILURE);
    }
    for(recnum=0; recnum<10; recnum++)
    {
       for(counter=0; counter<reclen[recnum]; counter++)
       {
           buffer[counter] = 'a';
       }
       fwrite(buffer, reclen[recnum], 1, varlen);
       if(ferror(varlen))
       {
         printf("Write error on file output01\n");
         fclose(varlen);
         exit(EXIT_FAILURE);
       }
    }
    fclose(varlen);
    exit(EXIT_SUCCESS);
}
```

The JCL used in the previous example to compile and execute program NVSAMP1 may be used here. The program name must be changed to NVSAMP2. To run the program, the following JCL might be used:

```
//NVSAMP2    JOB    (accounting info)
//STEP1      EXEC   PGM=NVSAMP2
//STEPLIB    DD     DSN=LOAD.C,DISP=SHR
//OUTPUT01   DD     DSN=VARY.LEN,DISP=SHR
```

```
//SYSPRINT      DD      SYSOUT=A
```

To print the output file, the following JCL might be used:

```
//PRINT         JOB     (accounting info)
//STEP1         EXEC    PGM=IEBGENER
//SYSIN         DD      DUMMY
//SYSUT1        DD      DSN=VARY.LEN,DISP=SHR
//SYSUT2        DD      SYSOUT=A
//SYSPRINT      DD      SYSOUT=A
```

The output from the job should be ten lines of lower case a's. The first line should have 20 a's in it. Every subsequent line should have 5 more a's.

13.6.3 VSAM File Processing

We have described the IBM functions used to process VSAM files earlier in this chapter. Now we will show you how to use those functions to find a particular record in a VSAM KSDS file, and update it. We will also demonstrate how you would delete a record from a KSDS file. If you are unfamiliar with VSAM file creation, we will walk you through the entire process. If you are comfortable with this material already, you can go to the programs directly.

You can load a VSAM file with the contents of a physical sequential file. You can use different methods to create the physical sequential file. If you are familiar with ISPF (Interactive System Productivity Facility), you know that it has a panel to allow you to create new files. If you do not know how to use ISPF or do not have access to it, you can use JCL to allocate the new file.

```
//NEWFILE       JOB     (accounting info)
//STEP1         EXEC    PGM=IEFBR14
//DD1           DD      DSN=NEW.FILE,DISP=(NEW,CATLG),
//                      SPACE=(TRK,(5,5)),DCB=(LRECL=80,RECFM=F,BLKSIZE=80),
//                      UNIT=3380
```

Once you have allocated the file, you should use the editor of your choice to add records to it or write a program to do this. The following JCL and commands will allocate, load, and print the VSAM KSDS file used in the example programs.

```
//VSAMFILE      JOB     (accounting info)
//STEP1         EXEC    PGM=IDCAMS
//SYSPRINT      DD      SYSOUT=A
//INPUT         DD      DSN=NEW.FILE,DISP=SHR
//SYSIN         DD      *
```

```
              DEFINE CLUSTER -
                      (NAME(VSAM.KSDS)     -
                      INDEXED              -
                      IMBED        -
                      KEYS(4 0)            -
                      TRK(5 0)             -
                      RECORDSIZE(80 80)    -
                      VOLUME(ABC123)       -
                      SHR( 2 ) )

                      REPRO INFILE(INPUT) ODS(VSAM.KSDS)
                      PRINT IDS(VSAM.KSDS)
//
```

The preceding program, IDCAMS, and the commands DEFINE CLUSTER, REPRO, and PRINT are described in the *MVS Access Method Services Manual*. Please refer to it for a complete description of the program and all related commands. Briefly, the above commands will create a VSAM KSDS file. The records are all 80 bytes long, with the key in the first 4 bytes. The physical sequential file is loaded into the VSAM file, and the VSAM file is printed.

```
/* Program NVSAMP3
   This program will locate a record in a VSAM KSDS file,
   read it and update it. */
#include <stdio.h>
#include <stdlib.h>
#include <errno.h>
main()
{
            FILE *vsamfle;
            int   reg_15;
    __amrc_type    return_codes;
    char ksds_record_key[4]="0013";
    char buffer[81]="This is for initialization";
    char new_record[76]="This is record thirteen";

    vsamfle=fopen("DD:input01", "rb+, type=record");
    if(vsamfle==NULL)
    {
       return_codes = *__amrc;
       printf("Open failed on file input01\n");
       printf("Return code = %8d\n",
       return_codes.__codes.__feedback.__rc);
```

```c
      printf("Reason code =%8d\n",
      return_codes.__code.__feedback.__fdbk);
      exit(EXIT_FAILURE);
   }

   reg_15=flocate(vsamfle, ksds_record_key, 4, __KEY_EQ);
   if(reg_15 != 0)

   {
      return_codes = *__amrc;
      printf("Locate error\n");
      printf("register 15 = %8d\n", reg_15);
      printf("Return code = %8d\n",
      return_codes.__code.__feedback.__rc);
      printf("Reason code = %8d\n",
      return_codes.__code.__feedback.__fdbk);
      fclose(vsamfle);
      exit(EXIT_FAILURE);
   }
/* the C reference manual states that when using fread
   for record input, set size to 1 and count to the expected
   record length. */

   fread(buffer, 1, sizeof(buffer), vsamfle);
   if(ferror(vsamfle))

   {

      return_codes = *__amrc;
      printf("Read error\n");
      printf("Return code = %8d\n",
      return_codes.__code.__feedback.__rc);
      printf("Reason code = %8d\n",
      return_codes.__code.__feedback.__fdbk);
      fclose(vsamfle);
      exit(EXIT_FAILURE);
   }

   printf("record content is %s\n", buffer);
   memcpy(buffer+4, new_record, sizeof(new_record));
   printf("new record content is %s\n", buffer);

   fupdate(buffer, sizeof(buffer)-1, vsamfle);
   if(ferror(vsamfle))

   {
      return_codes = *__amrc;
      printf("Update error\n");
      printf("Return code = %8d\n",
      return_codes.__code.__feedback.__rc);
      printf("Reason code = %8d\n",
      return_codes.__code.__feedback.__fdbk);
      fclose(vsamfle);
```

```
            exit(EXIT_FAILURE);
    }
    fclose(vsamfle);
    exit(EXIT_SUCCESS);
}
```

You can reuse the JCL from the previous examples to compile the above program. Remember to change the program name. The following JCL may be used to execute the program.

```
//NVSAMP3     JOB     (accounting info)
//STEP1       EXEC    PGM=NVSAMP3
//STEPLIB     DD      DSN=LOAD.C,DISP=SHR
//INPUT01     DD      DSN=VSAM.KSDS,DISP=SHR
//SYSPRINT    DD      SYSOUT=A
```

If each record in the input VSAM file had the following format—0001THIS IS RECORD ONE OF FOURTEEN—the output from the above sample program would be:

```
record content is 0013THIS IS RECORD THIRTEEN OF FOURTEEN
new record content is 0013This is record thirteen.
```

```
/*  Program NVSAMP4
        This program will delete a record in a VSAM KSDS file. */

#include <stdio.h>
#include <stdlib.h>
#include <errno.h>

main()
{
            FILE    *vsamfle;
            int     reg_15;
    __amrc_type return_codes;
    char ksds_record_key[4] = "0014";
    char buffer[81] = "This is for initialization";

    vsamfle=fopen("DD:input01", "rb+, type=record");
    if(vsamfle==NULL)
    {
        return_codes = *__amrc;
        printf"Open failed on file input01\n");
        printf("Return code = %8d\n",
        return_codes.__code.__feedback.__rc);
        printf("Reason code = %8d\n",
        return_codes.__code.__feedback.__fdbk);
        exit(EXIT_FAILURE);
    }

    reg_15=flocate(vsamfle, ksds_record_key, 4, __KEY_EQ);
```

```c
            if(reg_15 != 0)
            {
               return_codes = *__amrc;
               printf("Locate error\n");
               printf("register 15 = %8d\n", reg_15);
               printf("Return code = %8d\n",
                  return_codes.__code.__feedback.__rc);
               printf("Reason code = %8d\n",
                  return_codes.__code.__feedback.__fdbk);
               fclose(vsamfle);
               exit(EXIT_FAILURE);
            }

            fread(buffer, 1, sizeof(buffer), vsamfle);
            if(ferror(vsamfle))
            {
               printf("Read error\n");
               printf("Return code = %8d\n",
                  return_codes.__code.__feedback.__rc);
               printf("Reason code = %8d\n",
                  return_codes.__code.__feedback.__fdbk);
               fclose(vsamfle);
               exit(EXIT_FAILURE);
            }
            printf("record content is %s\n", buffer);
            reg_15=fdelrec(vsamfle);
            if(reg_15 != 0)
            {
               printf("Delete error\n");
               printf("Return code = %8d\n",
                  return_codes.__code.__feedback.-_rc);
               printf("Reason code = %8d\n",
                  return_codes.__code.__feedback.__fdbk);
               fclose(vsamfle);
               exit(EXIT_FAILURE);
            }

            fclose(vsamfle);
            exit(EXIT_SUCCESS);
}
```

Reuse the JCL from previous examples to compile and execute this program. If the VSAM file from the previous example were used, the output from this sample program would be:

```
record content is 0014THIS IS RECORD FOURTEEN OF FOURTEEN.
```

14

Interlanguage Communication

In this chapter, we will describe the C/370 implementation of interlanguage communication. Our discussion will cover communications between C/370 and 370 assembler, COBOL, FORTRAN, and PL/1. We will describe the environment that must exist to perform interlanguage communication and provide examples that outline what you must do to be CALLed by or CALL a C/370 function.

14.1 EXCHANGING DATA

Programs pass data to one another by parameter-lists. A parameter-list contains data or pointers to data. Additionally, each programming language expects the parameter-list to be in its own language-specific format.

There are two ways programs can exchange data. A copy of the data can be passed to the called program. This is known as passing data 'by-value'. The calling program will be unaware of any changes made to this data by the called program. With the second method, pointers to the data are passed to the called program. This is known as passing data 'by-reference'. In this situation, the calling program will be sensitive to any modifications made to the passed data by the called program. The various programming languages use either or both methods to pass data. C/370 passes data 'by-value'. 370 assembler and FORTRAN pass data 'by-reference'. COBOL and PL/1 can use either method.

Pointers are handled differently from other data types when used in a parameter-list. Instead of placing the address of the pointer in the list, the value of the pointer, itself an address, is placed in the parameter-list.

C/370 does not support all of the data types available in other languages. Tables will show the compatible data types in the sections that describe the details of interlanguage communication between C/370 and other programming languages.

14.2 THE *linkage* PRAGMA

The linkage conventions define how data is passed to a called program and how a called program returns values to its caller. In C/370, the linkage pragma tells the compiler how to write and read the parameter-list.

The format of the linkage pragma is:

```
#pragma linkage(identifier,type)
```

where identifier is the name of the called function or a name of a function pointer, and type is one of OS, PL/I, FORTRAN, or COBOL and causes the compiler to use the appropriate linkage conventions.

14.3 C AND 370 ASSEMBLER

There is full two-way communication between C and assembler language programs. This means that a program written in C can call or be called by a program written in assembler. The linkage pragma handles the communication in both directions. The format of the linkage pragma is:

```
#pragma linkage(identifier,OS)
```

If the value of identifier is longer than eight characters, only the first eight characters are used.

Assembler routines must preserve the C environment for proper communication. This means that various general purpose registers and particular storage areas must have their contents maintained. A number of macros have been provided as part of C/370. These macros generate the prolog and epilog code that guarantee the maintenance of the C environment when an assembler routine is called, and allow the routine to access automatic storage.

14.3.1 Registers at Routine Entry

The general purpose registers have the following values when C/370 and 370 assembler language routines are communicating.

Register	Value
R0	unpredictable
R1	parameter-list address
R2–R11	unpredictable
R12	control block address
R13	Dynamic Storage Area (DSA) address
R14	return address
R15	called routine address

14.3.2 Registers at Routine Exit

At the exit point of a routine using the OS linkage convention, the general purpose and floating point registers have the following values:

R0–R1	values not defined by convention
R2–R13	restored to values at entry
R14	value not defined
R15	return value for integer or pointer types
FP0	return value for float or double
FP0&FP2	return value for long double

14.3.3 Managing the C Environment

A C function may be called several times from an assembler routine, or many different C functions may be called. It is more efficient to create the C environment once, perform all of the functions, and then remove the C environment. The overhead of creating and deleting the environment is incurred only once. Vendors of the various compilers have come up with different solutions, but they are similar conceptually. There is a way to initialize or create the C environment. Once created, the C functions can be executed. When all processing has been completed, the C environment can be deleted or terminated.

14.3.4 Compatible Data Types

This is not an issue when communicating with assembler language routines, since assembler can operate on any data type available to C programs. However, it is possible to define a data type in assembler that is not available to C, such as packed decimal. Some vendors have provided functions to transform packed decimal data into a data type available to C programs.

14.3.5 Examples

The following examples will show how to call an assembler routine from a C/370 function, passing data to the called routine and an assembler routine calling a C/370 function.

As we have mentioned earlier, in the C/370 implementation, the C environment must be established before a C/370 function can be called. That is the reason why the second example starts with a simple C/370 function. Also, because we are using the Queued Sequential Access Method (QSAM) to print the data returned from the C/370 function, all of the programs in the second example must execute below the 16M line. Please refer to the section on Addressing and Residency modes in Chapter 11 for more information on how you can ensure that your programs execute below the 16M line.

```
/*This C program calls an Assembler routine to issue a WTO */
#pragma linkage(callwto,OS)
#include <stdio.h>
int callwto(size_t void *);
main()
{
    char buffer[]= "Hello universe";
    callwto(sizeof(buffer), buffer);
}
R1              EQU 1
R2              EQU 2
R4              EQU 4
R5              EQU 5
R6              EQU 6
R15     EQU 15
CALLWTO         CSECT
                EDCPRLG
                LR      R2,R1 R2        PARM LIST ADDRESS
                L       R6,0(,R2)
                L       R6,0(,R6)       DATA LENGTH
                L       R4,4(,R2)       DATA ADDRESS
                LA      R15,16          ERROR RETURN CODE
                CH      R6,=H'125'      TOO MUCH DATA?
                BH      CALLEXIT        YES - EXIT
                BCTR    R6,0            PREPARE FOR EX INST
                LA      R5,WTODATA
                EX      R6,MVC1
                WTO     MF=(E,WTOLIST)
                SR      R15, R15
CALLEXIT        DS      0H
                EDCEPIL
WTOLIST         '                                                        X
                                                                         X
                ',ROUTCDE=(11),DESC=(7),MF=L
                ORG     WTOLIST+4
WTODATA         DS      CL125
                ORG     ,
MVC1            MVC     0(0,R5),0(R4)
                END     ,
```

```
/*Exists only to create the C environment */
#pragma linkage(asm370,OS)
main()
{
    asm370();
}
```

```
R1              EQU 1
R14     EQU 14
R15     EQU 15
* CALL C ROUTINE TO GET FORMATTED MONTH, DAY, YEAR AND
* TIME OF DAY
ASM370 CSECT
            EDCPRLG
            LA      R1,OUTPUT1          POINT TO PARM LIST
            L       R15,=V(DATETME)     ADDR OF C ROUTINE
            BASR    R14,R15             CALL IT
            SPACE ,
            OPEN    (OUTDCB,OUTPUT)
            SPACE ,
            PUT     (OUTDCB,PRINTLNE)
            SPACE ,
            CLOSE   (OUTDCB)
            SPACE ,
            EDCEPIL
OUTPUT1     DC      A(OUTAREA)          ADDR OF DATA
            ORG     OUTPUT1
            DC      AL1(X'80')          END OF PARM LIST
            ORG     ,
PRINTLNE    DC      133C ' '
            ORG     PRINTLNE
            DC      C '1'               NEW PAGE
            DC      C 'DATE/TIME ARE:   '
OUTAREA     DS      CL117
            ORG     ,
OUTDCB      DCB     BLKSIZE=133,DDNAME=PRNTLINE,DSORG=PS,LRECL=133, X
                          MACRF=PM,RECFM=FA
            LTORG ,
            END   ,
```

```
*C routine for getting formatted date/time */
#pragma linkage(datetme,OS)
#include <stdio.h>
#include <time.h>
int datetme(char *dest)
{
    struct tm *date_time;
        time_t time_value;
```

```
        time(&time_value);
        date_time=localtime(&time_value);
        strcpy(dest,asctime(date_time));
}
```

14.3.6 Special Considerations and Limitations

Following are some special considerations and limitations:
1. You must establish the C environment before you call any assembler routines. You can do this in one of two ways:
   a. Call the assembler routine from your C main program.
   b. Initialize the C environment from your assembler program, using the preinitialization method as described in the *C/370 User's Guide*.
2. If the C environment was initialized from an assembler routine, the return value from a C program will not be in register 15. You must pass the address of a field to contain the return value in the parameter-list when calling the C program.

14.4 C AND COBOL

A C function can receive and pass data to a COBOL routine. A linkage pragma allows the C compiler to read and write the parameter-list in the appropriate format. Only compatible data types—those common to both languages—can be used.

The format of the linkage pragma is:

```
#pragma linkage(identifier,COBOL)
```

If the value of identifier is longer than eight characters, only the first eight characters are used.

14.4.1 Creating the COBOL Environment

Prior to executing a COBOL routine, the COBOL initialization routines must be invoked. Once the COBOL environment has been created, it will remain active until the function that created it ends.

When a C function calls a COBOL routine, a function must be used to perform the call. An example of a call to a COBOL routine is shown following. The COBOL routine must be declared with a type of void, a return value cannot be passed from the COBOL routine.

```
#pragma linkage(testcob1,COBOL)
#include <stdio.h>
main()
{
    int pass_value;
    void testcob1(int *);
    pass_value = 1000;
```

```
        testcob1(&pass_value);
        printf("pass value is: %d\n", pass_value);
}
IDENTIFICATION DIVISION.
PROGRAM-ID. TESTCOB1.
ENVIRONMENT DIVISION.
DATA DIVISION.
LINKAGE SECTION.
            01 LS-INT          PIC S9(9) COMP.
PROCEDURE DIVISION USING LS-INT.
    MULTIPLY 2 BY LS-INT.
    DISPLAY LS-INT.
    GOBACK.
```

You must compile both of the above programs and link-edit them to form a composite load module. The output from executing the composite load should resemble the following lines.

```
pass value is: 1000
000002000
```

14.4.2 Compatible Data Types

As mentioned previously, only those data types common to both COBOL and C can be passed in the parameter-list. Table 14.1 identifies the compatible data types.

14.4.3 COBOL to C

Parameters passed to a C program are considered to be passed by-reference. However, parameters can be received by-value by the appropriate declarations in the C program. C/370 will produce the necessary code to access the values of the parameters.

If a C/370 program is receiving parameters passed by-reference from a COBOL program, the C routine may use the parameters as if received by-value. However, if the value of a parameter is altered, the effect on the variable in the calling

TABLE 14.1 Compatible COBOL-C Data Types

COBOL	C
COMP S9 (9)	signed int
COMP-2	double
01	structure
05	
05	
01	
05 OCCURS	array

Reprinted by permission from *IBM C/370 User's Guide*. © 1988, 1990 by International Business Machines Corporation.

COBOL routine is unpredictable. To receive and properly handle parameters passed by-reference, the prototype statement must be declared as a pointer to the correct type. For example, when you pass a PIC S9(9) COMP value to a C routine, the function prototype might look like int CRTN(int *).

An example of a call from COBOL to C is shown below.

```
IDENTIFICATION DIVISION.
PROGRAM-ID. TESTCOB.
ENVIRONMENT DIVISION.
DATA DIVISION.
WORKING-STORAGE SECTION.
    01 WS-PRINT-RECORD.
    05 WS-PRINT-RECORD-TITLE       PIC X(15)
            VALUE   'DATE/TIME ARE:'.
    05 WS-PRINT-RECORD-DATA        PIC X(117).
PROCEDURE DIVISION.
      CALL 'DATETME' USING WS-PRINT-RECORD-DATA.
      DISPLAY WS-PRINT-RECORD.
      GOBACK.
/*C routine for getting formatted date/time */
#pragma linkage(datetme,COBOL)
#include <stdio.h>
#include <time.h>
int datetme(char *dest)
{
    struct tm *date_time;
    time_t time_value;
    time(&time_value);
    date_time=localtime(&time_value);
    strcpy(dest,asctime(date_time));
}
```

You must compile both of the above programs and link-edit them to form a composite load module. The output from executing the composite load should resemble the following line.

```
DATE/TIME ARE: Tue Apr 16 19:40:47 1991
```

14.4.4 Special Considerations and Limitations

Following are some special considerations and limitations:

1. Unpredictable results can occur if the COBOL initialization routines are reinvoked after the environment has been terminated. To avoid this situation, these suggestions should be followed:
    a. Develop a simple COBOL routine to be called to invoke the COBOL initialization routines.
    b. Call this simple routine from the C main function.
2. A composite load module of C functions and COBOL routines cannot be reentrant, even though the C functions are reentrant. The reentrant compile-time option should not be used when compiling the C programs.

3. All routines called by a C function or that call a C function must be part of a single composite load module.
4. A COBOL routine must use a static call to call a C function. This is accomplished by placing the name of the C function in single quotes on the CALL statement.
5. A GOBACK statement should be used to terminate a COBOL routine. A STOP RUN statement should not be used in the following situations:
    a. When the main program is not written in COBOL.
    b. If a C environment is still active.
6. A `return` statement or the physical end should be used to terminate a C function. An *exit* or *abort* function should not be issued when:
    a. The main program is not written in C.
    b. If a COBOL environment is still active.
7. Nonlocal goto's accomplished via the `setjmp` and `longjmp` functions cannot be used beyond one call to a COBOL routine or to cross environment boundaries.
8. When passing structures between C and COBOL routines (see Table 14.1), it is your responsibility to ensure that the elements in the structure have the same byte alignment. Table 14.2 shows C/370's data alignment characteristics.

Use the MAP option on the COBOL compile and the AGGREGATE option on the C compile to list the layout and offsets of any structures.

14.5 C AND PL/I

There is full two-way communication between programs written in C and those written in PL/I. A `linkage` pragma allows the C compiler to read and write the parameter-list in the appropriate format. Those data types common to both languages can be passed in the parameter-list.

TABLE 14.2 Data Types and Their Alignments

Data Type	Alignment
char	byte
short int	halfword
int	fullword
long int	fullword
pointer	fullword
float	doubleword
double	doubleword
long double	doubleword

Reprinted by permission from *IBM C/370 User's Guide*. © 1988, 1990 by International Business Machines Corporation.

14.5.1 Creating the PL/I Environment

If you are using C/370 with PL/I, you do not need to establish a PL/I environment, since C/370 and PL/I share a common operating environment. However, if you are using another C compiler, you must use the routines or macros supplied to create a PL/I environment. The linkage pragma for PL/I is:

```
#pragma linkage(identifier,PLI)
```

where identifier is the name of a function or a pointer to a function. C/370 uses only the first eight characters. If the value of the identifier is longer than eight characters, characters after the eighth are ignored.

14.5.2 Compatible Data Types

C/370 and PL/I can pass data by-value and by-reference. Table 14.3 defines the compatible data types for when data is passed by-value.

Pointers are passed by-reference. The compiler puts the value of the pointer, an address, in the parameter-list. Table 14.4 list compatible data types for when data is passed by-reference.

14.5.3 Special Considerations and Limitations

Following are some special considerations and limitations:
1. A clear distinction should be made when passing data. If the data is being passed by-reference, the called routine should indicate that it is receiving a reference parameter. Unpredictable results occur if parameters are not used in the proper context.
2. PL/I transfer of control, either by the GOTO statement or by an on-unit, should not cross load module boundaries if the called program contains both C and PL/I routines.
3. A C function cannot be loaded by a PL/I FETCH statement.
4. C and PL/I routines in the same load module cannot read or write to the same DD name.
5. NULL in C/370 is hex zeroes, x'00000000', whereas in PL/I NULL is x 'FF000000'.
6. Parameters pass from PL/I to C/370 should be defined with the ALIGNED attribute.

14.6 C and FORTRAN

A linkage pragma allows the C compiler to read and write the parameter-list in the appropriate format. Only compatible data types, those common to both languages, can be used.

TABLE 14.3 Compatible PL/I-C Data Types

PL/I	C
FIXED BIN(31,0)	signed int
	signed long int
FLOAT BIN(53)	double
FLOAT DEC(16)	
FLOAT BIN(109)	long double
FLOAT DEC(33)	

Reprinted by permission from *IBM C/370 User's Guide.* © 1988, 1990 by International Business Machines Corporation.

14.6.1 Creating the FORTRAN Environment

Before a FORTRAN routine can be called, a FORTRAN environment must be created. Once created, it will remain active until the function that created it ends. The linkage pragma for C-to-FORTRAN communication is:

```
#pragma linkage(identifier,Fortran)
```

where identifier is the name of the routine or a typedef used to define the name. The value of identifier can be up to seven characters in length. If it is more than seven characters, the first four characters and the last three characters are used to create the name.

14.6.2 Compatible Data Types

As mentioned previously, only those data types common to both FORTRAN and C can be passed. Table 14.5 identifies those data types.

TABLE 14.4 Compatible PL/I-C Data Types

PL/I	C
FIXED BIN(15,0)	signed short
FIXED BIN(31,0)	signed int
	signed long int
FLOAT BIN(21)	float
FLOAT DEC(06)	
FLOAT BIN(53)	double
FLOAT DEC(16)	
FLOAT BIN(109)	long double
FLOAT DEC(33)	
POINTER	pointer to...

Reprinted by permission from *IBM C/370 User's Guide.* © 1988, 1990 by International Business Machines Corporation.

TABLE 14.5 Compatible FORTRAN-C Data Types

FORTRAN	C
INTEGER*4	int
REAL*8	double
REAL*16	long double
type array (size)	type array[size]

Reprinted by permission from *IBM C/370 User's Guide*. © 1988, 1990 by International Business Machines Corporation.

14.6.3 Special Considerations and Limitations

Following are some special considerations and limitations:

1. Unpredictable results can occur if the FORTRAN initialization routines are reinvoked after the environment has been terminated. To avoid this situation, these suggestions should be followed:
   a. Develop a simple FORTRAN routine to be called to invoke the FORTRAN initialization routines.
   b. Call this simple routine from the C main function.
2. By-value parameters cannot be passed from FORTRAN to C.
3. Parameters passed by-reference from FORTRAN to C cannot be modified. The effect on the FORTRAN variable is undefined.
4. A composite load module of C and FORTRAN routines cannot be reentrant, even though the C routines are reentrant. The reentrant compile-time option should not be used when compiling the C program(s).
5. All routines called by a C function or that call a C function must be part of a single composite load module.
6. A STOP statement should be used to terminate a FORTRAN routine in the following situations:
   a. when the main program is not written in FORTRAN.
   b. if a C environment is still active.
7. A return statement or the physical end should be used to terminate a C function. An exit or abort function should not be issued when:
   a. The main program is not written in C.
   b. If a FORTRAN environment is still active.
8. Nonlocal goto's accomplished via the setjmp and longjmp functions cannot be used beyond one call to a FORTRAN routine or to cross environment boundaries.
9. To avoid name conflicts for a range of functions, you should include the math.h and stdlib.h header files in any C routines.

15

Advanced Programming Techniques

A number of programming techniques have been available to 370 assembler language programmers, but are recent additions to the programming arsenal of high-level language users. Three of these techniques are reentrancy, multitasking, and dynamic file allocation.

Simply put, reentrant programs are not self-modifying. The same physical copy of a program can be executed by several different users at the same time. Multitasking allows applications to be divided into several independent functions that can execute concurrently. Dynamic file allocation enables you to acquire a file when needed and release it when all processing has completed.

Until recently, high-level languages have not provided the necessary framework to support these programming techniques. It follows that programmers who use these high-level languages have not had the opportunity to develop the conceptual skills necessary to solve problems by using these techniques. This has all changed.

All of the C compilers we have discussed allow you to develop reentrant programs. You can develop multitasking applications, using C/370. Dynamic file allocation is supported in both C/370 and Waterloo C. In the following sections, we will outline why these techniques are valuable to you, the application developer, and how to use them with C/370.

15.1 REENTRANCY

You know that several users can share a single copy of a reentrant program. If this were not the case, just imagine the performance of a computer that, for every I/O request, brought a new copy of the service routine into the user's memory to execute. The programs used to load these routines would themselves have to be loaded into the user's memory. In the early days of computing, a single user consumed the resources of an entire computer system. Designing reentrant system software allows multiple users to share heavily used service routines. If you are involved in designing and developing high-use programs or utilities, you should consider reentrancy. There could be significant improvements in system performance.

To create a reentrant program, you must have a single copy of the executable code and any constants. A separate copy of modifiable variables exists for each user. The following discussion will describe reentrancy in a C/370 context.

The portion of a program that can be updated is called the 'writable static'. It is composed of three elements:
1. Variables defined as static.
2. Variables defined as external.
3. Strings that may be modified.

To separate the executable code and constants from the 'writable static', you would compile your programs with the reentrant option and use the supplied pre-link utility to create an object module. This object module is then processed by the linkage editor to create an executable load module.

If your program does not contain 'writable static', there is no need to specify the reentrant compile-time option or use the pre-link utility. Refer to Chapter 10 for a description of the CLISTs and JCL procedures available to create reentrant programs.

There may be cases where external variables and character strings are not updated. Each user would not need a separate copy of these variables and strings. To force an external variable to be part of the executable code and constants, you would use the `variable` pragma, which has the following format:

```
#pragma variable(name,NORENT)
```

The use of this pragma is shown in the following program stub:

```
#pragma variable(ext_values,NORENT)
extern ext_values[]={1,2,3,4,5};
extern ext_fields[10];
int main()
{
    program code
}
```

The program would have been compiled with the reentrant option or with the `options` pragma. The array `ext_fields` will be part of the 'writable static'. The array `ext_values` will be part of the executable code and constants.

You should be aware of the following points when using the `variable` pragma:
1. Variables with a type `static` are always part of the 'writable static'; you cannot use this pragma on these variables.
2. Modifying variables that have been identified with this pragma may cause your program to terminate abnormally or produce unpredictable behavior.

3. This pragma must be included in every source file using the identified variable.

To force a character string to be part of the executable code and constants, you would use the `strings` pragma:

```
#pragma strings(readonly)
```

In the following program, the string "C - the new wave" would be part of the executable code. If, in your program, you modified a read only string, your program may end abnormally or exhibit unpredictable behavior.

```
#pragma strings(readonly)
#include <stdio.h>
int main()
{
    printf("C - the new wave" \n);
}
```

15.2 MULTITASKING

You can develop applications that run as multiple independent tasks, using MVS facilities. These facilities have always been available to the 370 assembler language programmer. They allow for the creation and deletion of a subtask by a main task and the synchronization of work of all the tasks. Also, a main task can handle the abnormal termination of a subtask as part of its error recovery.

One common use of multitasking in an MVS environment is I/O processing. Whenever a read or write request is issued, the main task will pass the request to a subtask, which performs the operation. The main task can continue processing and be informed about the I/O completion by the subtask. Without subtasking, the program issuing the I/O request would have to wait for the request to complete before it could continue processing. The terms commonly used for these two situations are asynchronous and synchronous processing. Multitasking provides asynchronous processing; the main task can do other work while the subtask performs a related function.

Many existing products make use of multitasking to maximize their throughput—the amount of useful work they perform. Customer Information Control System (CICS), which is a multitasking environment itself, can use a subtask to satisfy an I/O request from application programs.

The Multitasking Facility (MTF) of C/370 is dependent on MVS multitasking facilities. It is interesting to note that SAS/C offers coprocessing and not multitasking. Coprocessing enables you to implement your application as independent processes; however, it is operating-system independent. In an MVS environment, it would not make use of existing multitasking facilities to perform its functions. With coprocessing, only one of the cooperative processes, or coprocesses, may be active at a time. On the other hand, with multitasking, any one or all of the tasks may be active at any time.

The following diagram shows the structure of an application using multitasking.

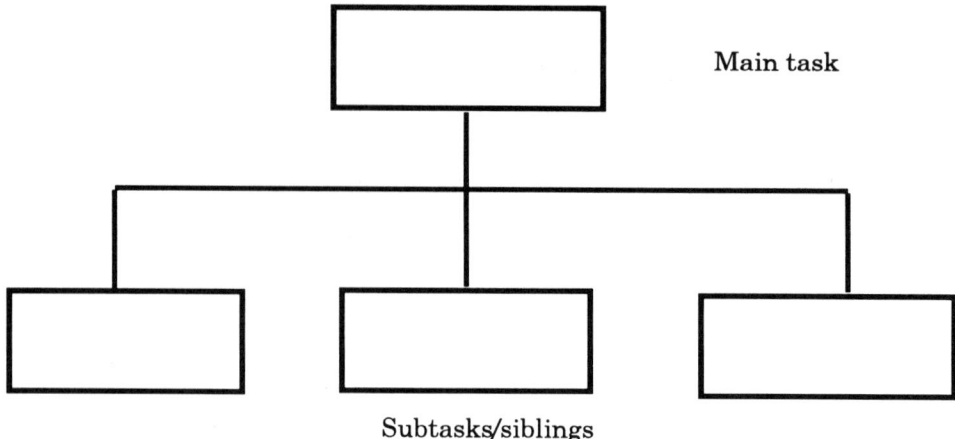

FIGURE 15.1 Multitasking structure.

The main task creates the subtasks and schedules their execution. Data can be exchanged between tasks. Execution of all or any the tasks can be synchronized, and the main task can be informed of the termination of a subtask.

MTF provides a subset of the MVS multitasking functions. With MTF, functions are provided to initialize the environment, schedule a subtask function, wait on a function's completion, and terminate the environment.

If you are familiar with multitasking in an MVS environment, there are some differences you must be aware of when using MTF. In an MTF environment, there are only two load modules. The main task is in one load module, and all the subtask functions are in a separate load module. The subtasks cannot invoke MTF functions. This means that a subtask cannot create subtasks of its own.

15.2.1 Storage Allocation

All the tasks have their own run-time storage environment. This environment consists of the Initial Storage Area(ISA), residual storage, and heap. The ISA contains automatic variables and storage for program management. The residual storage contains I/O buffers and dynamically loaded routines, acts as an overflow for the ISA, and contains the heap. The heap is created in the residual area if your program uses `calloc`, `malloc`, or `realloc` functions. The heap also contains storage used by C/370. Each task has its own 'writable static', its own run-time library storage, and separate abnormal condition and signalling environments.

From the previous discussion, you can see that any task acquiring storage must be the task that releases it. Also, any task that opens a file must process and close that file.

15.2.2 Input/Output

Only one task should process a file at any one time. Data corruption may occur if one task updates a file that is being read or updated by another task. This restriction includes memory files. This special file type cannot be shared by multiple tasks.

15.2.3 Passing Data

You can pass data between the tasks by passing a pointer to a data area. It is your responsibility to ensure that the area is not released or altered while it is being accessed by other tasks.

With C, the value of a *static* variable is maintained between function calls. This is true in an MTF environment, but only if you schedule the function on the same task ID as it was initially scheduled. Refer to the discussion of the MTF functions (section 15.2.8) for a description of the task ID.

15.2.4 Exceptional Condition Handling

Each task has its own exceptional condition handling environment. The subtask functions execute with the STAE and SPIE run-time options. These options allow C/370 to trap abnormal terminations and invoke the C/370 error handler to raise a signal.

The signals for the subtask functions are set to their default values when the task is first scheduled. These values can be changed only by a subtask function executing on that subtask. Of course, the operating system, MVS, can raise any signal during the execution of a task.

If a signal is raised within a subtask function and a routine has not been established to handle that signal, MTF will consider that subtask to have ended abnormally. This may cause your main task to abend as well. When using MTF, you should establish routines to handle all signals. This will ensure that all subtask functions terminate normally.

15.2.5 Redirecting Standard Streams

If you wish to redirect the standard streams in an MTF environment, you must supply unique DD names for each subtask. The format of the DD names are:

STDINtsk#

STDOUTtsk#

STDERRtsk#.

The value of tsk# is the two digit task identification number. Refer to the discussion of the MTF functions (section 15.2.8) for a description of the task ID number.

15.2.6 Subtask Load Module

There is one load module that contains all the subtask functions used in your multitasking application. It must not contain any C main programs. A C/370 routine, EDCMTFS, is the main function for all subtasks. This routine controls the scheduling of all functions contained in the load module. If you are using the IBM-supplied procedure to create the load module, you must include the following linkage editor control statements.

```
INCLUDE SYSLIB(EDCMTFS)
ENTRY CEESTART
```

If your installation has modified the supplied procedure or created one of its own, the DD name on the INCLUDE statement may be different.

The reasons for these statements are to include the EDCMTFS routine as part of the subtask load module and to ensure that the load module entry point name is CEESTART.

15.2.7 Special Considerations and Limitations

Following are some special considerations and limitations:

1. Subtask functions cannot return a value; they should be defined with a type of void.
2. Subtask functions must be written in C; however, they can call functions written in C, PL/1, or assembler.
3. The load module containing the subtasks must not be link-edited with the not editable attribute. If a program has been initially created with this attribute, it cannot be reprocessed by the linkage editor. The module must be recreated if reprocessing is necessary. If the subtask load module has this attribute, the main task may abend when attempting to schedule a subtask. You may also get a non-zero return code from the tsched function.
4. Do not use the following products if you are using MTF:

   CICS—Customer Information Control System

   DB2—DATABASE 2

   IMS—Information Management System.

   MTF may not be used with other IBM products; we mention only those products discussed in our text.
5. ISPF (Interactive System Productivity Facility) and GDDM (Graphical Data Display Manager) may be used from the main task only. Other products may have restricted use under MTF. As previously indicated, we mention only those products discussed in our text.
6. exit, abort, and atexit functions should not be issued from the subtask functions.

7. `setjmp/longjmp` functions can be used in any task, but cannot be used to cross task boundaries—you cannot use these functions to transfer control from one task to another.
8. Each task has its own locale information.
9. The `tmpnam` function may create the same temporary file name if you use it in more than one task.
10. A fetch'd module must be release'd by the same task. The `fetch` and `release` functions are used to bring a load module into storage and subsequently free the storage it occupied.

15.2.8 MTF Functions

The MTF header file contains the functions you would use to create a multitasking application. We will describe each function and provide a simple example showing their use.

Refer to the section on special considerations and limitations for any restrictions using the MTF functions. Refer to the *C/370 User's Guide* for a list of return codes for these functions and their meaning.

15.2.8.1 Task Attach

In 370 assembler, a main task would issue an ATTACH macro to start the execution of a subtask. The comparable C/370 function is `tinit`.

```
int tinit(const char *load_module_name, int max_num_tasks);
```

The first parameter is the name of the load module that contains all subtask functions. The second parameter is the maximum number of subtasks that can be scheduled.

We mentioned earlier that all subtask functions must be in one load module. The library containing this load module must be associated with the STEPLIB DD statement when you execute your application.

The `tinit` function is issued in the main task. It should be issued only once. Any subsequent calls to this function will return a value indicating that the MTF environment is already active. If the MTF environment is terminated, via the `tterm` function, `tinit` can be reissued, specifying the same or different parameters.

15.2.8.2 Task Scheduling

The `tinit` function does not start the execution of a subtask function. The `tsched` function does this:

```
int tsched(int task_id, const char *func_name, [parms]);
```

The first parameter is the task identification. Its value can range from 1 to the value specified as the maximum number of tasks on the `tinit` function call. A generic value, MTF_ANY, may be used to indicate that this subtask function can execute on any available subtask.

The second parameter is the function name. It can be up to eight characters long. If it is longer, only the first eight characters will be used. Any other parameters are optional and are specific to the subtask being invoked.

You can issue tsched as many times as necessary from the main task program. However, if you have already scheduled the maximum number of subtasks, any new requests wait until an appropriate subtask becomes available.

15.2.8.3 Task Synchronization

Once the subtask functions have been scheduled, the main task will want to wait until their work is complete. This is accomplished using the tsyncro function:

```
int tsyncro(int MTF_ANY|MTF_ALL|nn);
```

The only parameter specifies the subtask that the main task is waiting on. The main task can wait until any one of its subtasks have completed. In this case, the task ID of the terminating task is returned. If all subtasks have completed, a value indicating this is returned. The main task can wait until all of its subtasks have completed or until a specific subtask has finished. In the latter case, the specified task ID is returned to the main task.

15.2.8.4 Task Detach

When your application has completed its processing, you must issue the tterm function:

```
int tterm(void);
```

This function will terminate the MTF environment, but only after all scheduled subtasks have completed.

15.2.9 Example

In this example, we will show a main task performing all the functions necessary to implement multitasking. The subtask functions will print a message indicating that they have executed.

```
/*This program will demonstrate the use of MTF. It is the
    main function. PROGRAM NAME MAINTASK*/
#include <stdio.h>
#include <stdlib.h>
#include <mtf.h>

main()
{
 int rcode;
 int ctr;
```

```c
rcode=tinit("subtsks",3);   /* load module name */
if(rcode != MTF_OK)
    {
     printf("task initialization failed - RC = %d\n",
        rcode);
     exit(EXIT_FAILURE);
    }

ctr = 3;
rcode=tsched(3,"print3",ctr);    /*function name */
if(rcode != MTF_OK)
    {
     printf("Task scheduling failed - RC = %d\n",
         rcode);
    }

ctr = 1;
rcode=tsched(1,"print1",ctr);    /*function name */
if(rcode != MTF_OK)
    {
     printf("Task scheduling failed - RC = %d\n",
         rcode);
    }
ctr = 2;
rcode=tsched(2,"print2",ctr);    /* function name */
if(rcode != MTF_OK)
    {
     printf("Task scheduling failed - RC = %d\n",
         rcode);
    }
rcode=tterm();
if(rcode != MTF_OK)
    {
     printf("Task termination failed - RC = %d\n",
         rcode);
    }
 exit(EXIT_SUCCESS);
}
```

```c
/* This program will demonstrate the use of MTF. It is a subtask
   function. */
#include <stdio.h>
#include <stdlib.h>
void print1(int ctr)
{
    printf("Function print1 value is %d\n", ctr);
}
/* This program will demonstrate the use of MTF. It is a
   subtask function. */
#include <stdio.h>
#include <stdlib.h>
void print2(int ctr)
{
    printf("Function print2 value is %d\n", ctr);
}


/* This program will demonstrate the use of MTF. It is
   a subtask function. */
#include <stdio.h>
#include <stdlib.h>
void print3(int ctr)
{
   printf("Function print3 value %d\n", ctr);
}
```

You may use the supplied catalogued procedures to compile the programs. The main task can be compiled and link-edited in the same job. The subtask functions may be compiled separately and then combined by the linkage editor to form a composite load module. If you do this, the following JCL might be used to create the load module.

```
//LINKEDIT    JOB     (accounting info)
//STEP01      EXEC    PGM=HEWL
//SYSLIN      DD      DDNAME=SYSIN
//SYSLIB      DD      DISP=SHR,DSN=SEDCBASE
//            DD      DISP=SHR,DSN=SIBMBASE
//            DD      DISP=SHR,DSN=C.LOAD
//SYSLMOD     DD      DISP=SHR,DSN=C.LOAD
//COBJLIB     DD      DISP=SHR,DSN=C.OBJ
//SYSUT1      DD      UNIT=SYSDA,SPACE=(1024,(100,20))
//SYSPRINT    DD      SYSOUT=A
//SYSIN       DD      *
   INCLUDE COBJLIB(PRINT1)
   INCLUDE COBJLIB(PRINT2)
```

```
         INCLUDE COBJLIB(PRINT3)
         INCLUDE SYSLIB(EDCMTFS)
         ENTRY CEESTART
         NAME SUBTSKS(R)
//
```

After you have successfully created the subtask load module, you may use the following JCL to execute our sample.

```
//RUNJOB     JOB     (accounting info)
//STEP01     EXEC    PGM=MAINTASK
//STEPLIB    DD      DISP=SHR,DSN=C.LOAD
//SYSPRINT   DD      SYSOUT=A
//STDOUT     DD      SYSOUT=A
//STDOUT01   DD      SYSOUT=A
//STDOUT02   DD      SYSOUT=A
//STDOUT03   DD      SYSOUT=A
```

The standard output, STDOUT01, should contain the line "Function print1 value is 1". The output for the other subtask functions should contain similar messages.

15.3 DYNAMIC FILE ALLOCATION

In a batch job, the files specified in the JCL are allocated when a job step begins its execution and are released when that step ends. For TSO users, files are allocated at logon and kept for the life of the session, unless explicitly freed. In a situation where a job or TSO user may not always need a particular file, or when a file must be shared among users, you might better acquire it only when needed. Dynamic allocation via supervisor call (SVC) 99 allows you to perform the following functions:

1. Allocate/acquire a file.
2. Unallocate/release a file.
3. Concatenation of acquired files.
4. Deconcatenation of a group of concatenated files.
5. Retrieve information about acquired files.

To invoke the services of SVC 99, you set up a parameter-list that contains the request information. One important field is the verb code, which identifies the function you wish to perform. Another field, the text unit, provides the details for the requested function. A number of text units may be required to satisfy a particular request. For example, if you are allocating a file, the text units will contain the file name, file attributes, disposition, and any other information necessary to satisfy the allocation request.

15.3.1 Allocate/Acquire a File

Files can be allocated via data set name or DD name. We will discuss allocation by data set name only. File allocation by DD name requires a knowledge of file allocation that is beyond the scope of this book. Dynamic allocation by data set name is equivalent to JCL allocation in a job step or allocation in a TSO logon CLIST. You use verb code X '01' to request this function. You can acquire an existing data set or use this function to allocate a new data set. You use the text units to specify data set name, status, disposition, space, volume, unit, and other necessary attributes.

There are some parameters that cannot be specified via SVC 99 that can be specified on a JCL DD statement and some SVC 99 text units that do not have a JCL equivalent. Please refer to *MVS/ESA System Programming Library: Application Development Guide* or *MVS/XA System Programming Library: System Macros and Facilities* for a complete description of SVC 99.

15.3.2 Unallocate/Release a File

To release a data set, you use verb code X '02'. You can use text units to specify a DD name, a data set name, a PDS member name, an overriding data set disposition, plus other attributes. When you release a data set, the following processing takes place:

1. The DD name is disassociated from the data set.
2. The data set disposition takes affect.
3. The data set is available to other users.
4. The data set's unit(s) are freed.
5. The data set's volume is released.

A few restrictions exist when releasing a data set:

1. If the data set is opened, it will not be released.
2. If you release a SYSOUT data set, it will be available for output immediately, unless you specify an overriding disposition.
3. If you specify a data set name but do not specify a DD name, and the data set is associated with more than one DD name, then all DD name/data set name pairs are released
4. If you specify a member name and a data set name, only the matching allocations are released.

15.3.3 Concatenation

Concatenation is connecting a number of data sets to a single DD name. This technique is useful during program execution. A DD name, such as STEPLIB or JOBLIB, can have several load libraries associated with it, and all of them will be searched for the program. You specify verb code X '03' to request this function. The data sets to be concatenated must be already allocated. You use the DD name of the allocated data set in the concatenation text units. The data sets are concatenated in the order specified. This is important, as this is the search order and, if you have more than one program with the same name, the first one found satisfies the search.

15.3.4 Deconcatenation

You specify verb code X '04' and provide the DD name in the text units to request this function. You cannot deconcatenate the group if it is open.

15.3.5 File Information Retrieval

You use verb code X '07' to request information about your current file allocations. You can request the DD name, data set name, member name, status, data set disposition, and other allocation information.

15.3.6 Example

```
/* This program will allocate an existing file and
print the DD name associated with the file. */

#include <stdio.h>
#include <string.h>
#include <stdlib.h>

main()
{
    /* SVC 99 requires a parameter-list. The structure
    defines that list. */

    struct_S99struc SVC99_parmlst;
    int SVC99_rc;


    struct
    {
    short unsigned   SVC99_tu_key;
    short unsigned   SVC99_tu_nmbr;
    short unsigned   SVC99_tu_len;
    char             SVC99_tu_parm[21];
    } SVC99_tul_struct; /* working structure */
    struct
    {
    short unsigned   SVC99_tukey;
    short unsigned   SVC99_tunmbr;
    short unsigned   SVC99_tulen;
    char             SVC99_tuparm[8];
    } SVC99_tu_struct; /* working structure */

    #define hi_order_bit_on 0x80000000

    /* What follows are the text units required by SVC 99. The
    first one specifies the type of allocation and what is being
```

allocated. The second one specifies the dataset disposition, in this case OLD. The third specifies that the associated DD name be returned and leaves 8 blanks for it. */

```
char *SVC99_tu_ptr[3] =
{
"\0\x02\0\x01\0\x15""PS1234.TEST01.INPUT01",
"\0\x04\0\x01\0\x01\x01",
"\0\x55\0\x01\0\x08""        "
};
/* Set the SVC 99 parameter-list to zeroes. */
memset(&SVC99_parmlst,0,sizeof(SVC99_parmlst));

/* The last address in the text unit pointer list must have
the high-order bit turned on, set to X '80'. This is the
standard method in MVS for indicating the end of a parameter-
list. This instruction says that the value is a long, 4 bytes,
unsigned pointer to a character. And it is being OR 'ed
with X'80'. */

SVC99_tu_ptr[2] =
(char *) ((long unsigned) (SVC99_tu_ptr[2] | hi_order_bit_on);

/* the request block length is fixed at 20 bytes. */
SVC99_parmlst._S99RBLN = 20;

/* dataset name allocation verb */
SVC99_parmlst._S99VERB = 1;

/* pointer to text units in request block */
SVC99_parmlst._S99TXTPP = SVC99_tu_ptr;

/* invoke SVC 99 by passing address of parameter-list */
SVC99_rc = svc99(&SVC99_parmlst);

if (SVC99_rc != 0)
{
printf("SVC99_rc = %d S99ERROR in hex = %X S99INFO     \
in hex %X\n", SVC99_rc, SVC99_parmlst._S99ERROR,
SVC99_parmlst._S99INFO);
memcpy(&SVC99_tu1_struct,SVC99_tu_ptr[0],
sizeof(SVC99_tu1_struct));
printf("DSN = %s\n", SVC99_tu1_struct.SVC99_tu_parm);
exit(EXIT_FAILURE);
}

memcpy(&SVC99_tu_struct,SVC99_tu_ptr[2],
sizeof(SVC99_tu_struct));
printf("The returned DD name is: %s\n",
SVC99_tu_struct.SVC99_tuparm);
```

When this program is compiled and executed, the output should be similar to the following line.

```
The returned DD name is: SYS00001
```

If you have errors in the parameter-list or if SVC 99 is not available in your installation, the return code, error code, and data set name are printed to aid in problem resolution. Refer to the manuals mentioned previously for a complete description of dynamic allocation, as well as the return codes and their meanings.

16

C and Database and Data Communication Products

When you write programs in C, they can execute in different environments and access the facilities of a number of existing MVS database and data communication products. Programs can be written to execute under TSO, CICS, or IMS. Full-screen applications can be developed using ISPF, CICS-BMS, or IMS-MFS. A DB2 database can be accessed using SQL statements in your C program.

You must be aware of the details of the C interface in the various environments. There may be restrictions on your use of certain environment-specific facilities, or your C program may require processing by an environment-specific language processor.

In this chapter we will discuss some of the constraints placed on you when developing C programs that interface with CICS, IMS, and DB2. The material presented here assumes you have a basic knowledge of these products. If you are new to the MVS environment or unfamiliar with any of the products, please refer to the bibliography for a list of reference manuals. In subsequent chapters, we will discuss using C to develop full screen application programs and database access programs.

16.1 C AND CICS

If you want to use C to develop programs for the CICS environment, you must use CICS/ESA Version 3 Release 1 or a later release.

16.1.1 EXED CICS ADDRESS Command

If you are an experienced CICS user, you know that the addresses of Exec Interface Block (EIB) and the inter-program communication area are passed or made available to your program by CICS. The address of the EIB is provided automatically by CICS when using languages such as assembler or COBOL. However, when writing C programs for the CICS environment, you must get the address of the EIB explicitly. You do this by issuing the EXEC CICS ADDRESS command, specifying the EIB option.

The inter-program communication area or COMMAREA address is passed to the called program via a field in the Exec Interface storage in assembler programs or via the linkage area in COBOL programs. C programs must issue the EXEC CICS ADDRESS command, specifying the COMMAREA option to obtain the address of this area.

16.1.2 Exception Handling

The C compiler will flag the following commands as errors if you use them in your program:

1. HANDLE CONDITION
2. HANDLE ABEND label
3. IGNORE CONDITION
4. HANDLE AID
5. PUSH/POP HANDLE

You would use these commands in your application program to:

1. Trap exception conditions and pass control to routines to handle those conditions.
2. Turn off exception handling for a particular error.
3. Pass control to a routine, depending on what key the user pressed.
4. Save and restore the existing exception handling environment in order to establish a temporary environment in a particular routine.

Both the C signal handler and the CICS abnormal condition program are active in C programs that execute under CICS. The C signal handler will process all program exceptions. Other abnormal terminations, such as the EXEC CICS ABEND command, will be processed by the CICS abnormal condition program. The raise function will cause only the corresponding C signal handler to be invoked. If a C signal handler, established via the signal function, and a CICS abend handler, established via the HANDLE ABEND PROGRAM command, were to process the same condition, the CICS abend handler would take precedence. If the NOSPIE and NOSTAE run-time options were specified in your program, only the CICS abend handlers can be activated.

Since you cannot issue many of the CICS commands to handle exception conditions in C programs, the default actions are not taken when a command fails. After a CICS command is executed, control will be returned to the instruction following the command. It is your responsibility to test for the success or failure of any CICS command.

16.1.3 Storage Management

There are CICS commands to acquire and release storage used by your program. You can use the equivalent C storage management functions, but there are differences. Storage acquired by a C function exists until explicitly freed or until the acquiring program terminates. This storage is taken from the heap area. Storage acquired via the EXEC CICS GETMAIN command exists for the life of the task, unless explicitly freed.

If you use C functions to request more storage than is currently available, your task will be suspended until the storage becomes available. If you use the EXEC CICS GETMAIN command, you can specify an option that will cause control to be returned to your program if the storage is not available. If a C storage request function asks for less than 1 byte of storage or for more than the amount available to CICS, a null pointer is returned. The EXEC CICS GETMAIN command will fail in this case.

CICS will allow you to specify the area used to satisfy storage requests. Either the Extended Dynamic Storage Area (EDSA), which resides above the 16M line, or the Dynamic Storage Area (DSA), which resides below the 16M line. All the storage for C programs comes from the EDSA unless otherwise specified through the HEAP and STACK run-time options.

When your program invokes a C function, that function may need storage to perform its task. The C run-time environment will acquire and release storage on behalf of your program.

16.1.4 File Access

CICS provides an application program interface to access files. VSAM, BDAM, and QSAM files may all be accessed through this interface.

C/370 allows you to specify a memory file. This is a temporary file that resides in memory acquired from the EDSA. If you use large memory files, you run the risk of reducing through-put for your CICS region. The EDSA and DSA are used by all CICS tasks to satisfy their explicit or implicit storage requests.

When using C under MVS, there are a number of ways to redirect the standard streams. Under CICS, however, standard streams may be redirected to memory files only. If `stdin` has not been redirected and you attempt to read from it, you will get an end-of-file indication from the read operation.

The output of `stdout` and `stderr` is sent to transient data destinations under CICS. A transient data destination can be a file available to programs outside the CICS region, an extrapartition destination. Or a destination can be available only to programs running with the CICS region, an intrapartition destination. If you want to know the type of destination used for these standard streams and the name of the file where the data will be written, you must consult the system programmer responsible for maintaining the CICS tables. In this case, the Destination Control Table (DCT) is the table of interest to you.

16.1.5 Unavailable C Functions

A number of C functions are unavailable to you when developing a program to run under CICS. In many cases, a CICS command is available that provides the same functionality. Table 16.1 lists the unavailable C functions, the value returned if the function is invoked, and the equivalent CICS command, if available.

In a CICS environment, the locale information must be defined in the Processing Program Table (PPT). When you issue the `setlocale` function, the locale information is loaded from the PPT. If the locales are not defined, the function returns a NULL value.

16.1.6 Program Termination

A program executing under CICS can end in a number of different ways. The program can return control to its caller by issuing an EXEC CICS RETURN command. It can transfer control to another program by issuing an EXEC CICS XCTL command. Or it can abend without having an abend handler active. Additionally, a C program can terminate normally via the `exit` function or `return` statement, or abnormally via the `abort` function.

A C program can return a value to a calling program via the `exit` function or `return` statement. If executing under CICS, the return value is stored in the EIBRESP2 field in the Exec Interface Block (EIB).

TABLE 16.1 Unavailable C Functions and Cics Equivalents

C function	RC	EXEC CICS command
clock	(time_t)-1	
ctdli	-1	DLI
fetch	NULL	LOAD PROGRAM
release	nonzero	RELEASE
svc99	0/nonzero	
system	0/nonzero	
_ctrace		SET TRACE
_csnap		DUMP TRANSACTION
_cdump		DUMP TRANSACTION
_ctest		
tinit	EWRONGOS	
tsched		START TRANSACTION
tsyncro		WAIT/POST
tterm		

16.1.7 Preparing C Programs for CICS Execution

CICS provides a preprocessor to translate the CICS commands into appropriate C language function calls. All of your C-for-CICS programs must be processed by this language translator before they are used as input to the C compiler.

If the reentrant option was specified on the compile step, you must use the pre-link utility to generate separate executable code and constants and the 'writable static'. You should make all of your CICS programs reentrant, as this is a good programming practice. If you have not asked CICS to get a fresh copy of your program for every execution, an existing copy will be used if one is in storage. A self-modifying program may not execute in the same manner each time.

CICS provides a catalogued procedure to translate, compile, pre-link, and link-edit your C programs. Refer to the CICS manuals for the name of this procedure and the options available. Also, consult the systems programmer responsible for CICS, as the procedure may have been modified to meet installation standards.

16.1.8 Run-time Options

If you want to specify run-time options in a C-for-CICS program, you must use the `runopts` pragma directive. Experienced CICS programmers know that there is no way to pass this parameter data to the execution environment of a CICS program. This is not the only difference between CICS and non-CICS C programs. Certain run-time options are ignored when executing under CICS. Parsing arguments, providing operating environment information, passing run-time options on the command line, and redirecting the standard streams are some of the options ignored when executing in a CICS environment. If you specify the SPIE/STAE options to enable the C run-time abend handler, C/370 will not issue these macros in a CICS environment. Other options related to storage acquisition have different defaults and may operate in a different manner in a CICS environment. Refer to the appropriate user manual for the details.

16.1.9 Accessing CICS Resources and Facilities

If you want to access CICS-owned resources or use CICS facilities, you must use CICS commands in your C/370 program. The format of the CICS commands is described in the CICS/ESA manuals listed in the bibliography. With these commands, you can access VSAM files and IMS databases, send and receive data, or use a scratch pad facility. Also, you can use task management functions to retrieve the current time of day or schedule another task.

One oddity you will encounter, from a C perspective, is that the commands must be in uppercase. Other CICS-defined values must also be in uppercase.

Once you have written your C/370-CICS program, you must process it with the CICS language translator before compiling it. This program will convert the commands and CICS-defined values to a format acceptable to the C compiler.

16.1.10 Special Considerations and Limitations

Following are some special considerations and limitations:
1. When link-editing a C-for-CICS program, you must specify an addressing mode of 31, AMODE(31). For a complete description of addressing mode, refer to the *MVS System Programming Library: 31-Bit Addressing Manual.*
2. If you wish to call C or non-C programs, the CICS program control facilities should be used. You can CALL existing C and assembler language programs, but you should be aware that CICS will not know of the storage being used by the called program, reducing the effectiveness of CICS storage management. These called programs should not issue any CICS commands.
3. Since C does not support the packed decimal data format, no arithmetic operations can be performed on this data. However, you can access packed decimal data using the character string data type.
4. The CICS keywords on the `pragma` directive statement must be in uppercase; all other keywords may be in mixed case.
5. You should specify the appropriate length keyword and provide the correct value with all commands that have a length keyword.
6. There is a maximum length for the names of programs, files, maps, and so on. If you use a name shorter than the maximum, you must pad the value with blanks so that it is equal to the maximum length. Refer to the appropriate CICS/ESA manual listed in the bibliography for the details.
7. Normally, two values, `argc` and `argv`, are passed to the `main` function in a C program. The first value, `argc`, is the number of variables passed. The second value, `argv`, is an array of pointers to strings. When executing under CICS, the value of `argc` is 1, `argv[0]` points to the transaction code initiating the execution of the program, and `argv[1]` is NULL.

16.2 C AND IMS

Information Management System (IMS) was one of the first IBM products to have a C interface. Both the Whitesmith's and IBM's C compilers have functions that enable you to develop C programs for the IMS environment. Our discussion will focus on the C/370 implementation of the IMS interface.

16.2.1 Accessing IMS Facilities

You gain access to all IMS facilities via a single function, `ctdli`. The format of the function is:

```
int ctdli(int parmcount, const char *function, parms);
```

The first argument is the count of all parameters in the function call and is optional. The second argument is the function you wish to perform. The parameters that follow depend on the requested function. Please refer to the various IMS manuals found in the bibliography to get a complete list of functions and their related operands.

16.2.2 Extended Addressing

C/370 allows you to write programs, making use of the extended addressing capabilities of MVS. You can address areas above the 16M line in your programs. There is a restriction in the IMS/VS-MVS/XA environment. With the exception of the optional parameter count field, all arguments passed to IMS/VS must reside below the 16M line. Various portions of a program's run-time environment may be above or below the line. You can specify where the heap and stack will reside via run-time options. If you use the defaults, you should consider the following items:

1. The Initial Storage Area (ISA) is normally allocated below the 16M line. This is where automatic variables are stored; they can be passed to IMS.
2. The heap is normally allocated above the line. Storage acquired via calls to the `malloc`, `calloc`, or `realloc` functions cannot be used as parameters to an IMS call. The 'writable static' is part of the heap; variables that can be updated in a reentrant program cannot be passed to IMS.
3. If you load a program with a residency mode of ANY, this program may be loaded above the line. If this occurs, you cannot pass program constants to IMS.

In an IMS/ESA-MVS/ESA environment, the above restrictions and considerations do not apply. Variables located above the line can be passed to IMS/ESA. For a complete description of extended addressing, refer to the *MVS System Programming Library: 31-Bit Addressing Manual*.

16.2.3 Exception Handling

If you are an experienced IMS user, you know of its database protection capabilities. If your transaction terminates abnormally, IMS will backout any uncommitted updates to your database(s) and stop the abending program. C/370 provides run-time options and functions that enable you to trap and possibly correct conditions that may cause your program to abend. When writing C-for-IMS programs, you should follow these rules of thumb:

1. The STAE and SPIE run-time options should be specified.
2. The `ctdli` function should be used to invoke IMS services.
   This function will know where an abend has occurred, in IMS or the C program. If the failure is in IMS, the C error handler will issue an abend so that IMS error processing can ensure database integrity. If the failure is in the C program, you must perform one of the following:

a. Fix the error so that the program can continue processing normally.
b. Issue a rollback call so that IMS can backout uncommitted database updates and then end the program.
c. ensure that the program abends, and provide an exit that will turn all program failures into operating system abends so that IMS will initiate rollback on your databases. The system programmer responsible for IMS would write this exit. You may not want to use this method when other approaches provide the same function, but do not require involvement from your IMS support group.

3. If you do not use the ctdli function to invoke IMS services, you should not use the SPIE and STAE options and you are responsible for issuing a rollback call to IMS before your program ends.

16.2.4 Program Termination

C-for-IMS programs can terminate in a number of ways:

1. The physical end of the main function, there is no return statement.
2. The return statement is executed from the main function.
3. An exit or abort function is issued in any function.
4. You can longjmp back to the main function and have that function end.

16.2.5 Run-time Options

You must specify the env and plist options in your C-for-IMS program. The env option specifies your program's operating environment. The plist option specifies the format of the parameter-list received by your program when it is invoked. These options can be specified using the runopts pragma directive.

16.2.6 Special Considerations and Limitations

Following are some special considerations and limitations:

1. Normally, two values, argc and argv, are passed to your C program when it is invoked. These values are not passed to your C-for-IMS program. Instead, the value of argc is 1 and the value of argv[0] is equal to NULL.
2. You can transfer control to another C program by using the system function. The argc and argv values can be used to pass information to the called program.
3. Your program accesses the IMS parameter-list by receiving a list of PCB addresses. Your get the address via the ___pcblist macro. The address of the I/O PCB must be converted, or casted, to the proper type.

   (IO_PCB_TYPE *)(_pcblist)[0]

   The type and macro are defined in the IMS header file.

4. You can define an integer to contain the DL/I status code returned from the `ctdli` function call. The two-character return code is in the lower two bytes of the integer. If both characters are blanks, indicating that the called function was successful, the integer is set to 0.

16.3 C AND DATABASE 2

Database 2 (DB2) is a relational database that can be accessed by programs running in batch, under TSO, IMS, or CICS. Any restrictions placed on your C programs while executing within these environments still hold for your C-DB2 programs.

16.3.1 DB2 Access

You would use Structure Query Language (SQL) statements in your C program to access a DB2 database. These statements enable you to retrieve, update, replace, and delete data from the database. SQL statements are used to perform other database functions as well. Please refer to Chapter 18 and to the manuals listed in the bibliography.

16.3.2 Preparing C Programs to Access DB2

Your C programs must be processed by a language translator/preprocessor if they contain any SQL statements. This program replaces the SQL statements with the appropriate C function call. This preprocessor also performs syntax checking on the SQL statements.

If you are developing C programs for the CICS environment that will also access DB2 databases, your programs must be processed by the CICS language translator as well as the DB2 preprocessor. You may run the language translator before or after the DB2 preprocessor. However, if your program is first processed by the CICS language translator you will receive a warning message for every SQL statement. This should not affect the programs's execution.

There are supplied JCL procedures, CLISTs, and ISPF interfaces to prepare your programs to access DB2 databases. Please refer to the DB2 manuals and the DB2 support in your organization for the names of those procedures.

17

Full-Screen Application Development

The ability to provide end users with a 'friendly' interface to software products is a prerequisite into today's marketplace. Interactive, full-screen applications enable you to become familiar with a software product quickly and efficiently. The screens can walk you through all the features a product has to offer or allow you to select specific areas of interest. If used in a data entry situation, an interface can control the quality of data entered by passing it through an application-specific verification process. It also ensures the integrity of existing data by controlling the update and recovery processes. If you are considering using C to develop in-house or commercial software, the compiler should allow you to develop full-screen, interactive interfaces to your applications with ease.

If you are using C/370, you can develop programs to run in a CICS, IMS, or ISPF environment. In all three environments, facilities exist to create full-screen application interfaces. Also, you can access the graphic capabilities of GDDM in any of the above environments.

Whitesmith's C for System/370 has an IMS interface, and through it you can develop applications that have full-screen interfaces. If you are using SAS/C, you have access to the Full-Screen Support Library (FSSL) functions. With FSSL, you can develop applications for the TSO environment. Waterloo C provides users with a Panel Library. These functions enable you to develop full-screen applications for the TSO environment.

In the following sections, we will provide descriptions of all of the full-screen application development facilities mentioned above. A detailed explanation of the use of these products or features is available in the various product manuals. We refer you to the bibliography for a complete documentation list.

17.1 IBM PRODUCTS

CICS, IMS, ISPF, and GDDM enable you to develop text mode or graphic full-screen applications. Each product allows you to develop applications specific to its environment.

A single product has been developed that enables you to design and generate screens for all of these environments. Screen Definition Facility (SDF) II provides you, the developer, with a single tool for producing on-line applications screens for commonly used IBM transaction management products. We will not describe SDF II further. Please refer to the bibliography for a list of SDF II manuals.

17.1.1 Customer Information Control System (CICS)

With Basic Mapping Support (BMS), you can develop full-screen interfaces for your CICS applications. With BMS, you can format the input entered by users, as well as the output produced by your programs.

You create the 'maps' or screen definitions using BMS macros. These macros are used to define the screen layout. Constants, such as titles or screen IDs, can be defined, as can input and output areas. The input areas allow users of your application to enter data. The output areas are used by your application programs to send responses to the user's terminal. As part of the map definition process, you state the terminal types on which the map will be displayed, the programming language of your application programs, and other environmental information. This allows BMS to generate the correct map attributes for the terminals you use and the appropriate copy code for your programming language.

When you define the maps, BMS generates a physical version and a symbolic version of the map. The physical map is a load module containing the device-specific attributes and any constants. The symbolic version is used by your application program to access the input and output areas. This separation of the physical and symbolic versions of the maps means that you can generate maps for different terminal types without having to modify your application program.

The types of application interface you can develop using BMS range from simple item list selections to pull-down and pop-up windows, much like personal computer applications. The simpler applications do not require much knowledge of CICS terminal processing or screen management. However, if you are interested in developing applications that have the look and feel of PC-based software, you must acquire an in-depth knowledge of terminal processing in a CICS environment, develop techniques to save and restore the map areas overlaid by pull-down or pop-up windows, and be able to maintain the background screen attributes.

You can view the interaction between the terminal user and your CICS application program as a conversation. Initially, the user enters a transaction code. The appropriate program is invoked and sends a map to the terminal. The program can wait until the user enters data or presses a program function key or program attention key. This technique, where the program waits for a user response, is called *conversational programming*. The program or programs remain active until the user is finished with the application. The preferred method is to develop a *pseudo-conversational* application. With this approach, the initial program sends the map to the terminal and requests that any input from the terminal start another transaction to process that input. The initial transaction ends. This approach is preferred because all the resources held by the initial transaction and its programs are released when the transaction ends. For example, if the terminal user had to think about how to respond to a particular screen, the conversational program would hold on to all of its storage, any records it had read for update, and other potentially scarce resources. Using the pseudo-conversational approach, all resources are released when the map is sent to the terminal.

In the following program stub, we will show you the CICS commands used to send and receive a map, how to determine if any data was entered, and what key the user pressed, all in one example. Not all of the functions involved in the stub are shown. The point of the example is to show you the CICS command format and how to test the various returned values to control your program's processing.

Figure 17.1 shows a sample map that could be used by our sample program stub.

```
#include <dfhbmsca.h>      /* CICS supplied header files */
#include <dfhaid.h>
#include <mapgrp.h>         /* contains mapset - user file */
DFHEIBLK *eib_ptr;          /* pointer to EIB */

main()
{
    long int cics_resp;   /* return code from CICS command */

   EXEC CICS ADDRESS EIB(eib_ptr);/* get EIB address */

   maplst1.maplst1o.1stval1 = -1; /* set cursor position */
EXEC CICS SEND MAP ('maplst1')   /* sends map to the screen */
              MAPSET ('MAPGRP ')
              ERASE
              CURSOR
              FREEKB
              RESP(cics_resp);

if(cics_resp != DFHRESP(NORMAL))
{
error_rpt(cics_resp);
EXEC CICS RETURN;
}
EXEC CICS RECEIVE MAP('maplst1') /* receives user input */
              MAPSET('MAPGRP ')
              RESP(cics_resp);
switch(cics_resp)
{
case DFHRESP(NORMAL) : process_input(); /* data was entered */
              break;
```

```
                case DFHRESP(MAPFAIL) : what_key();      /* no data, PF key? */
                                       break;
                default : error_rpt(cics_resp);  /* unexpected response */
                }
                EXEC CICS RETURN;
                }
                void what_key()
                {
                switch(EIBAID)
                {
                case DFHPF1 : help_lst1();
                              break;
                case DFHPF3 : break;
                case DFHPF12 : break;
                case DFHENTER : break;
                case DFHCLEAR : break;
                default : bad_key();
                    }
                }
```

17.1.2 Information Management System (IMS)

Message Format Services (MFS) provides you with an environment to develop full-screen interfaces for your IMS application programs. With MFS, you can define the layout of the screen the user receives. Also, MFS provides 'data mapping' between the terminal display and the application program. That is, when a user enters data into the application screen, MFS puts it into a format expected by the processing program. And when the program sends a response to the terminal, MFS formats the output based on the application screen definition.

```
LSTOO1                        Application Display Menu

To select a particular list of applications records, enter the appropriate
number and press enter.

                Selection           Applications

                                    1. Local Applications.
                   —                2. Remote Applications.
                                    3. Control Applications.


F1=Help     F3=Exit     F12=Cancel
```

Figure 17.1. CICS map MAPLST1.

You or the MFS administrator use macros to generate the control blocks that define the screen layout and the device type on which the map will be displayed. This allows you to write programs that are device-independent. You do not need to know the specifics of the data that is transmitted to the terminal. That type of information is contained in the screen definition control blocks.

Certain application functions can be performed by MFS without an application program being invoked. In our discussion of CICS-BMS, the example showed that the program function (PF) keys were being handled by the application program. If you pressed PF1 to request help, the program detected this and invoked a function to handle this situation. In an MFS environment, displaying a help panel would not require invoking any of your application programs. MFS would detect that PF1 was pressed, and if you had defined a /FORMAT command to be executed when PF1 was pressed, that command would be executed. With the /FORMAT command you can display a predefined help screen.

You may also page up or down with the PF keys, or you may request that a specific page be displayed. Decisions such as these must be made during the application design process. The program attention (PA) keys have special meaning and are reserved by MFS.

To start an IMS-MFS interactive session, you would enter the IMS /FORMAT command. The parameter on this command would be the application screen you wanted displayed. For example, the command /FORMAT HRMSYS might display the screen shown in Figure 17.2. Once the screen has been displayed, you may enter the necessary data. In this example, the data you would enter are the employee number and surname. The following is a brief description of the processing that occurs once you have entered data and pressed the enter key. A message is placed on the message queue associated with the program that will process the screen. When this application program requests a message, the formatted message is put into the program's input/output area by IMS. It is now in a format that the program expects.

Once the program has processed the message, it inserts a message on a queue for the terminal that initiated the original transaction. The output from the processing is shown in Figure 17.3.

Human Resource Mgmt System

Employee number:
Employee name:

Figure 17.2. /FORMAT command output.

Human Resource Mgmt System

Employee number: 123456
Employee name: Smith
Job title: Supervisor
Grade level: 6
Rating: B+

Figure 17.3. Output from program.

In the following example, we will show how a C/370 program can receive a message, perform a database access, and send the output back to the terminal that initiated the transaction.

```
#pragma runopts(env(IMS),plist(IMS))
#include     <ims.h>
#include     <string.h>

/* input message format */

struct
{
short int    inmsg_lng;
short int    inmsg_zz;     /* reserved for IMS */
char         inmsg_txn[8];
char         inmsg_enmbr[6];
char         inmsg_ename[15];
} input_msg;

/* output message format */
struct
{
short int    outmsg_lng;
short int    outmsg_zz;
char         outmsg_enmbr[6];
char         outmsg_ename[15];
char         outmsg_etitle[10];
char         outmsg_elevel[2];
char         outmsg_erate[2];
} output_msg;

/* database record format */
struct
{
char dbr_enmbr[6];
char dbr_ename[15];
```

```c
       char dbr_etitle[10];
       char dbr_elevel[2];
       char dbr_erate[2];
       } dbr_area;

       IO_PCB_TYPE     *io_pcb_ptr; /*types defined in IMS header */
       PCB_STRUCT_8_TYPE    *dbase_pcb_ptr;

       char GU_func[]='GU  ';      /* IMS function names */
       char ISRT_func[]='ISRT';

       SSA_key[]='000000';

       int rcode;

       main()
       {
           /* set pointers to PCBs */
       io_pcb_ptr = (IO_PCB_TYPE *)(_pcblist) [0];
       dbase_pcb_ptr = (_pcblist)[1];

       /* get input from message queue */
       rcode = ctdli (GU_func,io_pcb_ptr,&input_msg);
       if(rcode != 0)
       {
              error processing
       }
       /* set database key */
       SSA_key[]=input_msg.inmsg_enmbr;

       /* get the record from the database */
       rcode = ctdli(GU_func,dbase_pcb_ptr,&dbr_area,SSA_key);
       if(rcode != 0)
         {
            error processing
         }

       /* move the data to the output area */
       strncopy(output_msg.outmsg_enmbr, dbr_area.dbr_enmbr,
              sizeof(dbr_area.dbr_enmbr));

       /* you may issue the above function for each field
       that should be moved to the output area */

       /* send the output message to the terminal */
       rcode = ctdli(ISRT_func,io_pcb_ptr,&outmsg_msg);
       if(rcode != 0)
         {
            error processing
         }
       }
```

If you have read the section on CICS-BMS or if you are familiar with other full-screen application environments, you may ask yourself where, in the above example, MFS services are invoked. The answer is that they aren't. MFS is outside your application. The services it provides are entirely transparent to your program. Once the various screen formats, transactions, and terminal definitions have been installed, you only have to write a program directly related to the application. The data mapping services of MFS manage the formatting of data between your application program and the terminal.

17.1.3 Graphical Data Display Manager (GDDM)

You can use GDDM to create and display graphic images on a terminal capable of displaying graphics. These images can be stored in standard MVS files. With GDDM, you can create the following types of images:

1. Graphs and charts that can be printed or plotted.
2. Presentation graphics with logos and multiple letter design.
3. Color slides or prints.
4. Paper documents that can be scanned, with their images stored and processed at any time.

GDDM provides three programming interfaces: An interface used by non-reentrant programs, suitable for most applications, an interface used by reentrant programs, and a systems programmer interface for those users who intend to develop their own graphics system.

From a C perspective, you must include a linkage pragma directive for every GDDM routine used in your program. GDDM uses OS style linkages, so the format of the pragma would be:

```
#pragma linkage(name,OS);.
```

The GDDM routines also must be declared as external functions. You can do this by using the following declaration:

```
extern name(parameters);.
```

It is interesting to note that GDDM routines can be invoked from programs executing in an IMS, CICS, or ISPF environment. All of these products have a C interface.

17.1.4 Interactive System Productivity Facility (ISPF)

ISPF manages the "dialog" or conversation between a user at a terminal and an executing program. A dialog is composed of a number of elements. They are:

1. Function—A function controls the processing within a dialog. It can be a CLIST or a program written in a any one of a variety of languages.
2. Panel definition—Panels are the user interface for the dialog. Panels can be developed for list processing, data entry, data display, and displaying application-specific information.

3. Messages—Messages are used to inform the user of the result of the request or to indicate errors in input data.
4. Tables—Tables store various data captured during the dialog. They can be of a temporary or permanent nature.
5. File tailoring—This is used to make displaying output easier by controlling the formatting of dialog variables when they are written to the terminal.
6. Display variables—These are used to pass information between dialog functions and services provided by ISPF.

The basic dialog management services provided by ISPF are:

1. Display services, which allow your program to display panels, windows, messages, and so on, and receive input from the user.
2. Select services, which allow your program to display a particular panel or execute a particular function.
3. Table services, which allow your program to store values from dialog variables.
4. File tailoring services, which allow a function to open, close, update, and delete files.
5. Variable services, which allow your program to define and use dialog variables.

The portion of a dialog that we are concerned with is the function. It is this element that can be implemented by using C. It is within the function that you control panel display and process user input. This is accomplished with calls to ISPF, using the isplink function. With this function you can invoke all the dialog management services.

Within your C program, you must define the parameter-list format for communicating with ISPF. This is done with the linkage pragma. In this case, the OS parameter-list format is used. The pragma statement would be:

```
#pragma linkage(isplink,OS);.
```

The isplink function is an external function and should be defined in your program in the following manner:

```
extern int isplink();.
```

You would invoke ISPF services in the following manner:

```
ret_code=isplink("service name", parm1, parm2,…);.
```

All of the arguments in the isplink function must be in uppercase. If the argument is a literal value, such as the service name, it must be enclosed in double quotes. If it is less than eight characters long, it should be padded with blanks. For example, if you wanted to display a panel named PANEL1, the following C/370 statement would be used:

```
ret_code=isplink("DISPLAY ", "PANEL1 ");.
```

The various services and their required parameters are defined in the *ISPF*

Dialog Management Guide and Reference Manual. The return codes from the services are fully described as well.

A simple list processing example will describe how you would develop an ISPF application using C/370. Two panels, Figures 17.4 and 17.5, and a portion of a program are provided. The main panel definitions' Figure 17.6, is included so that you will see how selecting an option invokes the appropriate function.

```
/* Program ADDFUNC - displays panel DISCADD so information
   on a new compact disc can be added to the library.  */

#include <stdio.h>
#pragma linkage(isplink,OS);

main()
{
    extern int isplink();

    char    TITLE[20],
        ARTIST[35],
        LABEL[15],
        CATEGORY[15],
        PLAYTIME[3];

    int     L_TITLE,
        L_ARTIST,
        L_LABEL,
        L_CATEGORY,
        L_PLAYTIME;

    int ret_code;

    /* initialize variables */
        L_TITLE = sizeof(TITLE);
        L_ARTIST = sizeof(ARTIST);
        L_LABEL = sizeof(LABEL);
        L_CATEGORY = sizeof(CATEGORY);
        L_PLAYTIME = sizeof(PLAYTIME);

    /* define variables to ISPF */
        ret_code = isplink("VDEFINE ", "TITLE   ", TITLE, "CHAR    ",
            L_TITLE);
        ret_code = isplink("VDEFINE ", "ARTIST  ", ARTIST, "CHAR    ",
            L_ARTIST);
        ret_code = isplink("VDEFINE ", "LABEL   ", LABEL, "CHAR    ",
            L_LABEL);
        ret_code = isplink("VDEFINE ", "CATEGORY", CATEGORY,
            "CHAR    ", L_CATEGORY);
        ret_code = isplink("VDEFINE ", "PLAYTIME", PLAYTIME,
            "CHAR    ", L_PLAYTIME);
```

```
/* Use existing variables table or create new table */
    ret_code = isplink("TBOPEN  ", "DISCTBLE");
    if(ret_code == 8)
       {
       ret_code = isplink("TBCREATE", "DISCTBLE",
          "(TITLE, ARTIST)", "(LABEL, CATEGORY, PLAYTIME)");
       }
/* display DISCADD panel, position cursor at TITLE */
    ret_code = isplink("DISPLAT ", "DISCADD ",, "TITLE   ");
```

17.2 FULL-SCREEN APPLICATIONS USING WATERLOO C

You can develop full-screen applications for a TSO environment, using the Waterloo C Panel Library. The functions contained in the library enable you to develop nongraphic, text mode applications that run on 3270-type terminals.

With products such as CICS, IMS, and ISPF, you create the application screens outside of the application programs. You would use macros or panel definition

―― Compact Disc Library ――

SELECT AN OPTION ===>

1 Add new entry
2 Update existing entry
3 Delete entry
X Exit

Figure 17.4. Main Panel.

―― Add new Disc Entry ――

Title:
Artist:
Label:
Category:
Playing Time:

Figure 17.5. Panel DISCADD.

```
%                  —— Compact Disc Library ——
+
%          SELECT AN OPTION ===>_ZCMD
%
%          1    +Add new entry
%          2    +Update existing entry
%          3    +Delete entry
%          X    +Exit
+
  )PROC
  &ZSEL = TRANS( TRUNC (&ZCMD, '.')
                 1,      'PGM(ADDFUNC)'
                 2,      'PGM(UPDFUNC)'
                 3,      'PGM(DELFUNC)'
                 X,      'EXIT')
  )END
```

Figure 17.6. Panel definition.

statements, which may need further processing. However, if you are using the Waterloo C Panel Library to develop applications, you would create the screen by issuing functions calls from within your program.

Functions are available that allow your program to create the screen layout, send data to the terminal, and receive any data a user has entered. When creating a screen layout, you can add emphasis such as highlighting, color, and outlining, to direct a user's attention to important portions of the screen. This makes for a more useful and informative interface, especially for new users. Fields may also be non-display if you want to use the screen to contain function control information, but do not want the user to know this. You can define fields as constants; a user cannot edit a constant field. The fields where you want the user to enter data will be defined with the edit usage attribute. Other attributes exists that allow the user to tab from field to field, that define a field to be light pen detectable, or that will allow only numerics or alphanumerics to be entered into a particular field.

An interesting feature of this product is that a single function writes to the screen and receives the user input. Another function allows you to write to the screen, but does not return the user's input. When you read the screen, you may receive the user's data or the response may be a program function (PF) key. If your application allows the user to enter a PF key, you must determine if one of these keys was pressed before attempting to process the input.

Functions exist to manage the screen storage or the storage of any field within the screen. This allows you to use only as much storage as you need—not all of the screens that an application uses have to be in storage at all times.

As you would expect, the Waterloo C Panel Library contains functions that support windowing. A screen can contain a number of different windows, which may overlap. With these functions, you can create the pull-down and pop-up windows available in many personal computer applications.

17.3 FULL-SCREEN APPLICATIONS USING SAS/C

With SAS/C and its Full-Screen Support Library (FSSL), you can develop interactive applications in a TSO environment. These applications must run on 3270-type terminals. With FSSL, you can dynamically create the screens. This gives you maximum control over the user interface.

The functions contained in the FSSL can be divided into three classes. One class performs the full-screen environment initialization and termination. They also provide access to the terminal attributes. You may want to add emphasis in the form of color to your screens to make them more interesting and to direct the user to a particular portion of the screen. If your application is executing at a terminal that does not support color, you can determine this and set the field attributes appropriately. Color, along with a number of other features, is an extended attribute, and some 3270-type terminals do not support these features. Another class of functions deals with screen creation. You can define the entire physical screen as a single entity, or you can split the physical screen horizontally. This group of functions also allows you to define fields within a screen or a portion of a screen. The final class of functions sends and receives data. Your program can receive user input, process it, and return the results to a user at a terminal.

The types of interactive applications you can develop depends on your knowledge of SAS/C and FSSL. You can develop simple data entry and verification applications, or you can employ the techniques used by many personal computer software products.

18

Databases

A database is a collection of interrelated data stored together. There are a number of different types of databases; we will discuss hierarchical and relational databases. The two database management systems (DBMS) we will discuss are Information Management System/Database (IMS/DB), which is a hierarchical database, and Database 2 (DB2), which is a relational database.

A hierarchical database is organized in the form of a tree. Each record or segment has only one owner who represents how the records or segments are related and who determines the path to the stored data.

A relational database is organized and accessed according to relationships between data items. These relationships are expressed by means of tables, where rows represent entries and columns represent entry attributes. The interdependencies among the tables are expressed by data values, rather than by pointers or location. Data items are accessed by matching values of attributes and not by following a predefined path. This means that the path to any data item is established when the item is accessed. This allows a high degree of data independence.

18.1 IMS/DB

IMS/DB uses a hierarchical structure to store and access data. With a hierarchy, you can show how one piece of data relates to other pieces of data. All of these related data items refer to the same subject.

Figure 18.1 shows a hierarchical database structure. The data being stored are various weather measurements for a day of the week. The highest level is the week number; this is the subject. Beneath this level are the days of the week; only one day is shown. And for each day of the week, the high and low temperature for the day is stored, as is the total amount of precipitation.

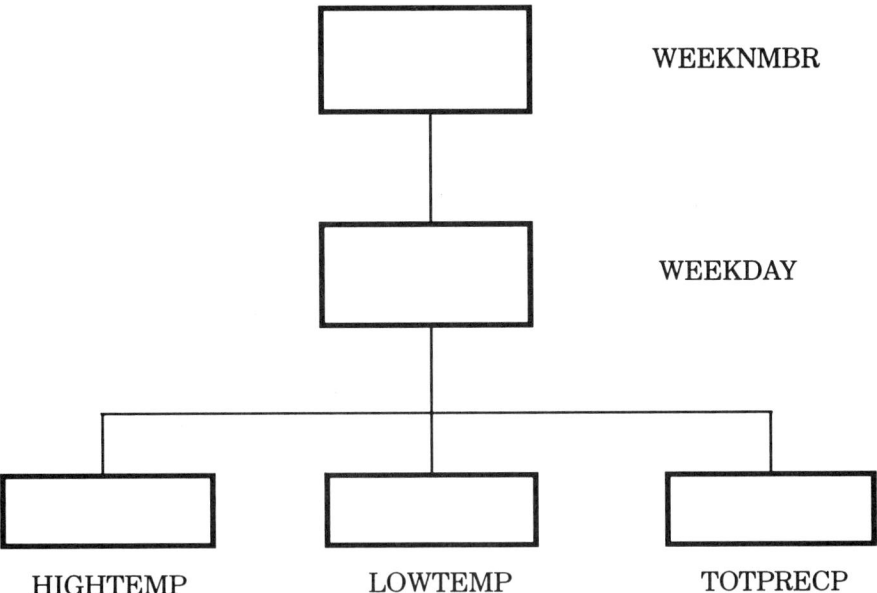

Figure 18.1. Hierarchical database.

The smallest piece of data that a program can retrieve from IMS/DB is a *segment*. A segment contains one or more items, or *fields*. In the above structure, the week number would be one segment. All the information to identify that week would be stored in this segment. This high-level segment is called the *root segment*. All the segments below the root are children or dependents of the root segment. This would include the weekday segments plus the segments for each day. The weekday segments are called *direct dependents* of the root segment, since they are at the level immediately below the root segment. A record in an IMS database is a root segment along with all of its dependent segments. In the above example, there would one record for each week. There can be only one root segment in a record. However, you can have several levels of dependent segments.

Using IMS/DB makes it possible for your program to be insensitive or independent of the way data is stored in the database. To provide this independence, IMS uses two control blocks—one that defines the physical structure of the database, and another that defines your program's view of the database. We will not discuss the physical structure definition. If you wish more information, please refer to the IMS manuals listed in the bibliography.

A database program communication block (DB PCB) defines your application program's view of the database. Your program may need to access only a few segments in a record. The PCB defines what segments your program can access. The processing for each segment may vary as well. Your program may need to update some segments and only read others. The PCB contains this information. Please refer to the IMS manuals for a complete description of PCBs.

18.1.1 Database Types

IMS has two types of databases—full function and fast path. The full function databases offer a wide range of access methods. They are:

HDAM	Hierarchical Direct Access Method
HIDAM	Hierarchical Indexed Direct Access Method
HSAM	Hierarchical Sequential Access Method
HISAM	Hierarchical Indexed Sequential Access Method
SHSAM	Simple Hierarchical Sequential Access Method
SHISAM	Simple Hierarchical Indexed Sequential Access Method.

The fast path databases are the Main Storage Database (MSDB) and the Data Entry Database (DEDB). They offer quick access and high availability.

18.1.2 Accessing an IMS Database

Your program must issue DL/I calls to access an IMS database. For C programs using either C/370 or C for System/370, the `ctdli` function is used. The parameters in this function are the database function, the DB PCB, the input/output area, and the segment search argument (SSA).

You can retrieve, delete, update, or insert a segment. All of these requests are specified by the database function parameter. You can also perform other functions that are not directly related to segment processing. As we mentioned earlier, the DB PCB defines your application program's view of the database. IMS places the results of each DL/I call in a field of the PCB.

The input/output (I/O) area is used to pass segments to and from the database. When you retrieve a segment, IMS places the segment in the specified I/O area. Your program may update this segment and replace the existing one with the updated version. IMS will take the modified segment from the I/O area.

The segment search argument (SSA) is a way to qualify your DL/I call. Within an SSA you can specify the name of a segment. In our example, the segment name for the days of the week is WEEKDAY. You can further qualify the SSA by providing a specific description of the segment. Specifying WEEKDAY=MONDAY tells IMS exactly which segment you wish to access. You can provide more information in an SSA to further extend the DL/I call. Please refer to the IMS manuals for a complete discussion on using SSAs.

For an example showing you how to access an IMS database using an SSA, please refer to Chapter 17, "Full Screen Application Development." In the example, a message processing program receives a message from a user, retrieves a database segment based on the message, and sends a reply back to the user.

18.2 DATABASE 2

Database 2 is a relational database. Data is made available to your application program in the form of tables. A table is rows and columns of related data.

As with other databases, DB2 provides great flexibility in how your application program sees data. With DB2, you can define views of the data. A view is a set of rows and columns that limits a program's access to the database. Using the sample table shown in Table 18.1, if you wanted to know only where the flowers were planted and what their color is, the view that would be defined would only allow access to three columns—FLOWER, WHPLNT, and COLOR. Our example does not contain data of any real importance, but if you have confidential data to protect, defining and using views can limit an application program's access to that data.

Views can also be used to combine data from two or more tables, or to have DB2 perform various calculations on the data and return the result to your application program.

18.2.1 Accessing DB2

DB2 databases can be accessed by programs executing in batch mode or under TSO. Programs running in a CICS or IMS environment can also access a DB2 database. In all environments, you would use Structured Query Language (SQL) to access and manipulate the data. With SQL statements, you can operate on data in a single row, or process all rows with a data item that has a particular value.

The basic SQL statements enable you to retrieve, update, insert, and delete data in tables or views. To determine the success or failure of the execution of any SQL statement, you must check the SQL communication area (SQLCA). This area must be defined in all applications programs accessing a DB2 database. A number of fields in the SQLCA are of particular importance in determining the result of a statement's execution. The SQLCODE field contains the return code from DB2. If the value of this field is non-zero, an error condition exists. The SQLERRD field provides further information on the execution of the SQL statement. One valuable piece of information in this field is the number of rows processed by an insert, update, or delete statement. The SQLWARNO field will contain blanks if your SQL statement executed without any warnings. Otherwise, there are positional values that define the condition that caused the warning to be raised.

18.2.2 Example

In the following program stub, we will create a view of our sample database table, shown in Table 18.1. We will select a row based on a value of one column and then print the results.

TABLE 18.1. Relation Database

FLOWER	WHPLNT	DTPLNT	DTBLMSD	CNDTN	COLOR
Rose bush	D3	05/23/1990	07/10/1990	Aphids	Red
Tulips	A1	11/01/1989	05/01/1990	Thrived	Yellow
Trillium	B2	08/10/1989	05/01/1990	Thrived	White

```
#include <stdio.h>
#include <string.h>
EXEC SQL INCLUDE SQLCA;
main()
{
 char flower_name[15];
 char where_planted[2];
 char condition[10];

/* this SQL statement creates the limited view */
EXEC SQL CREATE VIEW FLWRDATA
  AS SELECT FLOWER, WHPLNT, CNDTN
  FROM DSN9999.FLOWER;

/*test the return code from the SQL call */
if(sqlca.sqlcode !=0)
{
    printf("Create View failed, return code = %d/n",
            sqlca.sqlcode);
    exit(EXIT_FAILURE);
}

/*  this SQL statement SELECTS all the rows where the
    condition value is not thrived */
EXEC SQL SELECT *
FROM FLWRDATA
INTO :flower_name, :where_planted, :condition
WHERE NOT CNDTN = 'Thrived';
/*test the return code from SQL call */
if(sqlca.sqlcode != 0)
}
    printf("Select failed, return code = %d\n",
            sqlca.sqlcode);
    exit(EXIT_FAILURE);
}

printf("Flower name is %s, where planted is %s,
        condition is %s\n", flower_name, where_planted,
        condition);
```

```
/*this SQL statement will delete the view */
EXEC SQL DROP VIEW FLWRDATA;

/*test the return code from SQL call */
if(sqlca.sqlcode != 0)
{
    printf("Drop failed, return code = %d\n",
            sqlca.sqlcode);
    exit(EXIT_FAILURE);
}
}
```

19

Library Function Summary

This chapter provides a summary of all library functions, as well as definitions of some of the structures, macros, constants, and data objects found in the include files.

For more details on the functions, refer to Chapter 20. The notation conventions of a function are shown in Figure 19.1.

Floating-point and integer limits as well as buffer size for the setjmp and

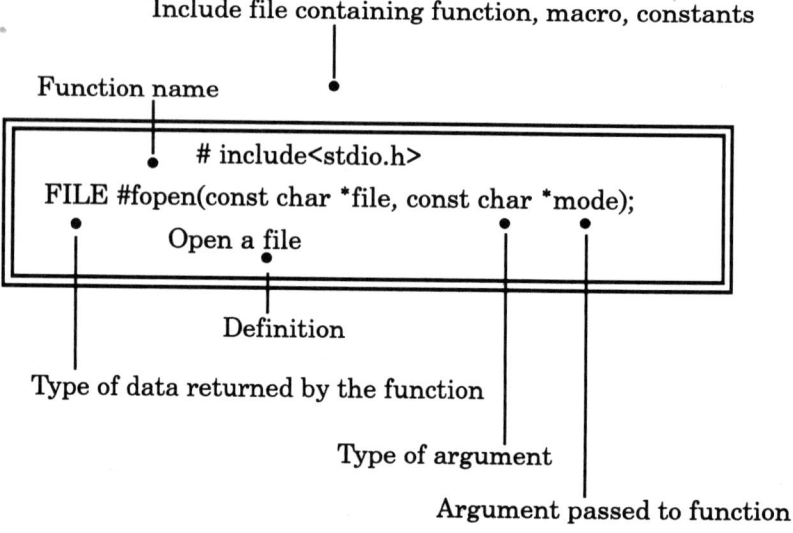

Figure 19.1. The notation conventions of function.

longjmp functions listed in this chapter are from the include files of IBM C/370 version 1.2.

19.1 DIAGNOSTICS   #include <assert.h>

```
void assert( int expression );
```

Add diagnostics to program

19.2 CHARACTER HANDLING   #include <ctype.h>

```
int isalnum( int c );
```
Test for alphanumeric character
```
int isalpha( int c );
```
Test for alphabetic character
```
int iscntrl( int c );
```
Test for control character
```
int isdigit( int c );
```
Test for a numeric character
```
int isgraph( int c );
```
Test for printable character excluding space
```
int islower( int c );
```
Test for lower case character
```
int isprint( int c );
```
Test for printable character including space
```
int ispunct( int c );
```
Test for punctuation character
```
int isspace( int c );
```
Test for white space character
```
int isupper( int c );
```
Test for upper case character
```
int isxdigit( int c );
```
Test for hexadecimal character
```
int tolower( int c );
```
Convert upper case to lower case
```
int toupper( int c );
```
Convert lower case to upper case

19.3 ERRORS   #include <errno.h>

This include file contains the following macros: EDOM and ERANGE. Both macros expand to different, non-zero integral constants. EDOM is used to indicate a domain error. ERANGE is used to indicate a range error. Both macros are used by various functions to set the value of errno. Your program should test the value of errno when the returned value indicates an unsuccessful operation and that function is described as using errno to provide more detail on the failed operation.

19.4 FLOATING-POINT LIMITS   #include <float.h>

Various floating-point characteristics and limits are defined in this include file. Some of the identifiers are defined as follows.

Identifier	Defined as
DBL_MAX	7.237006E+75
FLT_MAX	7.237005E+75
LDBL_MAX	7.237006E+75
DBL_MIN	5.397605E-79
FLT_MIN	5.397605E-79
LDBL_MIN	5.397605E-79
DBL_EPSILON	2.220446E-16
FLT_EPSILON	2.220446E-16
LDBL-EPSILON	3.081488E-33

19.5 INTEGER LIMITS   #include <limits.h>

Various integral characteristics and limits are defined in this include file. Some of the identifiers are defined as follows.

Identifier	Defined as	Description
CHAR_BIT	8	Number of bits in a byte
CHAR_MAX	255	Maximum value for char type
CHAR_MIN	0	Minimum value for char type
SHRT_MAX	32767	Maximum value for short int type
SHRT_MIN	-32768	Minimum value for short int type
INT_MAX	2147483647	Maximum value for int type
INT_MIN	-2147483648	Minimum value for int type

19.6 LOCALIZATION #include <locale.h>

In this include file, lconv structure is defined.

```
struct lconv {
            char *decimal_point;
            char *thousands_sep;
            char *grouping;
            char *int_curr_symbol;
            char *currency_symbol;
            char *mon_decimal_point;
            char *mon_thousands_sep;
            char *mon_grouping;
            char *positive_sign;
            char *negative_sign;
            char int_frac_digits;
            char frac_digits;
            char p_cs_precedes;
            char p_sep_by_space;
            char n_cs_precedes;
            char n_sep_by_space;
            char p_sign_posn;
            char n_sign_posn;
```

Also, the values and scope of the argument category, used in the setlocale function, are defined as follows.

Category	Affects
LC_ALL	Names the program's entire locale
LC_COLLATE	Affects behavior of strcoll and strxfrm functions
LC_CTYPE	Affects behavior of character handling functions
LC_NUMERIC	Affects decimal-point character for formatted input/output functions, string conversion functions, and non-monetary formatting information returned by localeconv function
LC_MONETARY	Affects monetary formatting information returned by localeconv function
LC_TIME	Affects behavior of strftime function

```
struct lconv *localeconv( void );
    Get locale settings

char *setlocale(int category, const char *locale);
    Set current locale
```

19.7 MATHEMATICS #include <math.h>

This include file contains the macro HUGE_VAL, which expands to a positive double expression.

A *domain error* occurs when a mathematical function is called with an argument outside the range of values allowed for that function. In this case, `errno` is set to EDOM.

A *range error* occurs when a return value of a mathematical function cannot be represented in a *double*. If the return value is too large (overflow), HUGE_VAL is passed to the caller; if it is too small (underflow), then -1 is returned. In case of an overflow, `errno` is set to ERANGE.

```
double acos( double x );
```
Calculate arc cosine

```
double asin( double x );
```
Calculate arc sine

```
double atan( double x );
```
Calculate arc tangent of x

```
double atan2( double y, double x);
```
Calculate arc tangent of y/x

```
double ceil( double x );
```
Get integer greater or equal to floating-point value

```
double cos( double x );
```
Calculate cosine

```
double cosh( double x );
```
Calculate hyperbolic cosine

```
double exp( x );
```
Exponential function

```
double fabs( double x );
```
Absolute value of floating-point

```
double floor( double x );
```
Get integer less than or equal to floating-point value

```
double fmod( double x, double y );
```
Floating-point remainder

```
double frexp( double y, int *exp );
```
Decompose of floating-point value

```
double ldexp( double x, int exp );
```
Multiply a value by power of 2

```
double log( double x );
```
Calculate the natural log

```
double log10( double x );
```
Calculate the log base10

```
double modf(double value, double *iptr)
```
Break down floating-point value

```
double pow( double x, double y );
```
Calculate power

```
double sin( double x );
```
Trigonometric sine
```
double sinh( double x );
```
Hyperbolic sine
```
double sqrt( double x );
```
Compute square root
```
double tan( double x );
```
Trigonometric tangent
```
double tanh( double x );
```
Hyperbolic tangent

19.8 NONLOCAL JUMP   #include <setjmp.h>

The buffer of type `jmp_buf` is defined as:
```
type long jmp_buf[72];
void longjmp( jmp_buf env, int val );
```
Restore calling environment
```
int setjmp( jmp_buf env );
```
Save calling environment

19.9 SIGNAL HANDLING   #include <signal.h>

In this include file the following signal values are defined.

Signal	Description
SIGABRT	Abnormal termination; may be initiated by the `abort` function
SIGFPE	Invalid arithmetic operation, for example, divide by 0
SIGILL	Invalid function image, for example, an illegal instruction
SIGINT	Interactive attention signal, caused by attention (ATTN) or program attention 1 (PA1) key
SIGSEGV	Invalid memory access
SIGTERM	Termination request sent to program

```
int raise(int sig);
```
Send a signal
```
void (*signal(int sig, void (*func)(int)))(int);
```
Signal handling

19.10 VARIABLE ARGUMENTS   #include <stdarg.h>

```
void va_start(va_list ap, parmN);
```
Initialize argument pointer

```
type va_arg(va_list ap, type);
```
Get next argument

```
void va_end(va_list ap);
```
End argument processing

19.11 COMMON DEFINITIONS   #include <stddef.h>

In this include file some data types and macros are defined that are commonly used in various functions.

```
typedef unsigned short wchar_t;

typedef int ptrdiff_t;

typedef unsigned size_t;

#define NULL ((void *)0);

#define offsetof(x, y)((size_t) &(((x*) 0) -> y))
```

19.12 INPUT/OUTPUT   #include <stdio.h>

```
void clearerr( FILE *stream );
```
Clear error indicators

```
int fclose( FILE *stream );
```
Close a stream

```
int feof( FILE *stream );
```
Test for end of file

```
int ferror( FILE *stream );
```
Test read/write error

```
int fflush( FILE *stream );
```
Clear data buffer

```
int fgetc( FILE *stream );
```
Get a character

```
int fgetpos( FILE *stream, fpos_t *pos );
```
Get file-position indicator

```
char *fgets( char *s, int n, FILE *stream );
```

Get a string

    FILE *fopen(const char *filename, const char *mode);
Open a file

    int fprintf(FILE *stream, const char *format,argument-list);
Write formatted string to file

    int fputc(int c, FILE *stream);
Write a character to file

    int fputs(const char *s, FILE *stream);
Write string to file

    size_t fread(void *ptr, size_t size, size_t nmemb,
        FILE *stream);
Read a block of data from file

    FILE *freopen(const char *filename, const char *mode,
        FILE *stream);
Redirect an open file

    int fscanf(FILE *stream, const char *format, argument-list);
Read formatted data from file

    int fseek(FILE *stream, long int offset, int whence);
Move file pointer indicator

    int fsetpos(FILE *stream, const fpos_t *pos);
Set file-position indicator

    long int ftell(FILE *stream);
Get file-position indicator

    size_t fwrite(const void *ptr, size_t size, size_t nmemb,
        FILE *stream);
Write block data to file

    int getc(FILE *stream);
Get a character from a file

    int getchar(void);
Get a character from standard stream

    char *gets(char *s);
Get a line from standard stream

    void perror(const char *s);
Print error message

    int printf(const char *format, argument-list);
Print formatted data

    int putc(int c, FILE *stream);
Print a character to specified stream

    int putchar(int c);
Print a character to standard output stream

```
int puts( const char *s );
```
Print a string to standard output stream

```
int remove( const char *filename );
```
Delete a file

```
int rename(const char *old, const char *new);
```
Rename a file

```
void rewind(FILE *stream);
```
Set file-position indicator

```
int scanf(const char *format,…);
```
Formatted read data

```
void setbuf(FILE *stream, char *buf);
```
Buffering control

```
int setvbuf(FILE *stream, char *buf, int mode, size_t size);
```
Buffering control

```
int sprintf (char *s, const char *format,…);
```
Formatted print to a buffer

```
int sscanf(const char *s, const char *format,…);
```
Read data from a string

```
FILE *tmpfile(void);
```
Create a temporary file

```
char *tmpnam(char *s);
```
Generate temporary file name

```
int ungetc(int c, FILE *stream);
```
Push character onto input stream

```
int vfprintf(FILE *stream, const char *format, va_list ap);
```
Write formatted argument to a file

```
int vprintf(const char *format, va_list ap);
```
Write formatted argument to *stdout*

```
int vsprintf(char *s, const char *format, va_list ap);
```
Write formatted argument to a string

19.13 GENERAL UTILITIES   #include <stdlib.h>

This include file contains the declarations for the types `size_t`, `wchar_t`, `div_t`, `ldiv_t`. The following macros are also defined:

NULL	null pointer value
EXIT_FAILURE	unsuccessful function termination
EXIT_SUCCESS	successful function termination
RAND_MAX	maximum value returned by `rand` function
MB_CUR_MAX	maximum number of bytes in multibyte character

```
void abort( void );
```
Terminate program abnormally

```
int abs ( int j );
```
Compute absolute value

```
int atexit( void (* func) (void) );
```
Register exit function

```
double atof( const char *nptr );
```
Convert character string to floating-point

```
int atoi( const char *nptr );
```
Convert character string to integer

```
long int atol( const char *nptr );
```
Convert a character string to long integer

```
void *bsearch( const void *key, const void *base,
        size_t nelement, size_t size,
        int( *compare ) ( const void *element1,
                         const void *element2 ));
```
Search an array

```
void *calloc( size_t nelement, size_t size );
```
Allocate memory for an array

```
div_t div( int number, int denom );
```
Division

```
void exit( int status );
```
Exit program

```
void free( void *ptr );
```
Deallocate memory

```
char *getenv( const char *name );
```
Get environment variables

```
long int labs( long int j );
```
Calculate long absolute value

```
div_t ldiv( long int numer, long int denom );
```
Division of long integer

```
void *malloc( size_t size );
```
Allocate memory

```
int mblen( const char *s, size_t n );
```
Get length of multibyte character string

```
size_t mbstowcs( wchar_t *pwcs, const char *s, size_t n );
```
Convert a multibyte character string

```
int mbtowc( wchart_t *pwc, const char *s, size_t n );
```
Convert a multibyte character

```
void qsort(void *base, size_t nelemt, sizt_t size,
      int (*compar) (const void *, const void*));
```
Sort array
```
int rand(void);
```
Generate random integer
```
void *realloc(void *ptr, size_t size);
```
Change storage size
```
void srand(unsigned int seed);
```
Seed for random integer generation
```
double strtod(const char *nptr, char **endptr);
```
Convert string to double
```
long int strtol(const char *nptr, char **endptr, int base);
```
Convert string to long
```
unsigned long int strtoul(const char *nptr, char **endptr,
      int base);
```
Convert a string to an unsigned long integer
```
int system(const char *string);
```
Execute command
```
size_t wcstombs(char *s, const wchar_t *pwcs, size_t n);
```
Convert a wide character string
```
int wctomb(char *s, wchar_t wchar);
```
Convert a wide character

19.14 STRING AND MEMORY   #include <string.h>

```
void *memchr( const void *s, int c, size_t n );
```
Search character in buffer
```
int memcmp( const void *s1, const void *s2, size_t n );
```
Compare two buffers
```
void *memcpy( void *s1, const void *s2, size_t n );
```
Copy buffer (without overlapping)
```
void *memmove( void *s1, const void *s2, size_t n );
```
Copy buffer (overlapping allowed)
```
void *memset( void *s, int c, size_t n );
```
Initialize buffer
```
char *strcat(char *s1, const char *s2);
```
Concatenate strings
```
char *strchr(const char *s, int c);
```
Find character within a string

```
int strcmp(const char *s1, const char *s2);
```
Compare strings
```
char *strcpy(char *s1, const char *s2);
```
Copy strings
```
size_t strcspn(const char *s1, const char *s2);
```
Find characters within a string
```
int strcoll(const char *s1, const char *s2);
```
Compare strings using collating sequence
```
char *strerror(int errnum);
```
Get error message
```
size_t strlen(const char *s);
```
Compute string length
```
char *strncat(char *s1, const char *s2, size_t n);
```
Append characters to a string
```
int strncmp(const char *s1, const char *s2, size_t n);
```
Compare characters in strings
```
char *strncpy(char *s1, const char *s2, size_t n);
```
Copy characters to a string
```
char *strpbrk(const char *s1, const char *s2);
```
Find character within a string
```
char *strchr(const char *s, int c);
```
Find last occurrence of a character within a string
```
size_t strspn(const char *s1, const char *s2);
```
Find characters outside of a string
```
char *strstr(const char *s1, const char *s2);
```
Find character string
```
char *strtok(char *s1, const char *s2);
```
Convert string to tokens
```
size_t strxfrm(char *s1, const char *s2, size_t n);
```
Transform strings

19.15 TIME AND DATE   #include <time.h>

```
char *asctime( const struct tm *timeptr );
```
Convert time to string
```
clock_t clock( void );
```
Get processor elapse time
```
char *ctime( const time_t *timer );
```
Convert calendar time to string

```
double difftime( time_t time1, time_t time0 );
```
Calculate the difference in two time

```
struct tm *gmtime( const time_t *timer );
```
Break down time

```
struct tm *localtime( const time_t *timer );
```
Break down local time

```
time_t mktime( struct tm *timeptr );
```
Convert to local time

```
size_t strftime(char *s, size_t maxsize, const char *format,
            const struct tm *timeptr);
```
Convert time to a string

```
time_t time(time_t *timer);
```
Determine current calendar time

20

Run-time Library Functions

In this chapter we describe the C run-time library functions. Each description contains the following:

- Include files that define the function.
- Function call statement.
- Function description.
- Return values.

Only those functions that are part of the ANSI standard are described. Where necessary, and appropriate, we have added information that pertains to the MVS environment only. The functions are listed in alphabetic order.

Please refer to Chapter 19, "Library Function Summary," for a description of the functions according to the task they perform.

abort—Terminate program abnormally.

```
#include <stdlib.h>

void abort( void );
```

- Description

The `abort` function causes a program to end abnormally. This function raises the signal SIGABRT, and control is passed to an exception handler function, if one has been defined. If one is not defined, control is returned to the host environment. Whether open files are closed and temporary files are deleted depends on the implementation.

- Return

This function does not return a value.

abs—Calculate absolute value.

```
#include <stdio.h>

int abs( int j );
```

- Description

The `abs` function calculates the absolute value of the integer argument j. The minimum and maximum integer values are specified in the <limits.h> header file. Any input that is outside this range or is not an integer will cause an undefined result.

- Return

The function returns the absolute value of an integer. It does not return an error value.

acos—Calculate arc cosine.

```
#include <math.h>

double acos( double x );
```

- Description

The `acos` function calculates the arc cosine of x, which must have a value between -1 and +1.

- Return

The function returns the arc cosine of x expressed in radians. The returned value will be between 0 and π(pi). If x is not between -1 and +1, `acos` will initialize `errno` to EDOM.

asctime—Convert time to string.

```
#include <time.h>

char *asctime( const struct tm *timeptr );
```

- Description

The `asctime` function converts a structured time value, pointed to by `timeptr`, to a character string. The conversion is in 24-hour format. The output has exactly 26 characters, including the newline character ('\n') and the end-of-string character ('\0'). The string has the form:

```
Sat Jul 13 13:04:19 1991\n\0
```

The structured time value may be retrieved by a call to either the `gmtime` or `localtime` function.

- Return

The function returns a pointer to the output string.

asin—Calculate arc sine.

```
#include <math.h>
double asin( double x );
```

- Description

The asin function calculates the arc sine of x. If x is not in the range of -1 and +1 `errno` is set to EDOM.

Return

The function returns the arc sin of x in the range $-\pi/2$ and $+\pi/2$ radians. If a domain error is detected, the return value is 0.

assert—Print diagnostic message.

```
#include <assert.h>
void assert( int expression );
```

- Description

The `assert` macro is used to debug a program or to verify that a program is executing as expected. When executed, `expression` is first evaluated; if it is false (0), the following message is written:

Assertion failed: `expression`, file `filename` line `linenumber` where `filename` is the name of the source file `linenumber` is the line number of the `assert` call in the source file.

If the `expression` is true (non-zero), no action is taken.

Once the program is executing correctly, set the identifier NDEBUG to any value, using the #define directive. This causes the compiler to produce harmless, ineffective code when expanding the `assert` macro.

- Return

This routine does not return a value.

atan—Calculate arc tangent of x.

```
#include <math.h>
double atan( double x );
```

- Description

The `atan` function calculates the arc tangent of x.

- Return

The function returns a value in the range $-\pi/2$ and $\pi/2$ radians.

atan2—Calculate arc tangent of y/x.

```
#include <math.h>
double atan2( double y, double x );
```

- Description

The `atan2` function calculates the arc tangent of y/x. If both x and y are 0s, the function sets `errno` to EDOM.

- Return

The function returns a value in the range $-\pi$ and π radians. A zero value is returned if the values x and y are 0s.

atexit—Register program termination function.

```
#include <stdlib.h>
int atexit( void (* func) (void) );
```

- Description

The `atexit` function stores the address of a function that is called during termination of a program. A number of `atexit` calls can be made in a program, and the functions are executed in "last in, first out" order. The number of registered functions cannot exceed 32. The function specified in an `atexit` call cannot have any arguments.

- Return

The function returns 0 if successful; otherwise, it returns a non-zero valve.

atof—Convert character string to floating-point value.

```
#include <stdlib.h>
double atof( const char *nptr );
```

- Description

The `atof` function converts a string pointed to by `nptr` to a double-precision floating-point value.

- Return

The function returns the converted floating-point value.

atoi—Convert character string to integer value.

```
#include <stdlib.h>
int atoi( const char *nptr );
```

- Description

The `atoi` function converts a string pointed to by `nptr` to an integer value.

- Return

The function returns the converted integer value.

atol—Convert a character string to long integer value.

```
#include <stdlib.h>
long int atol( const char *nptr );
```

- Description

The `atol` function converts a string pointed to by `nptr` to a long integer value.

- Return

The function returns a long integer value.

bsearch—Search an array.

```
#include <stdlib.h>
void *bsearch( const void *key, const void *base,
               size_t nelement, size_t size,
               int ( *compare ) ( const void *element1,
                                  const void *element2 ) );
```

- Description

The bsearch function searches for a value pointed to by key in an array whose first element is pointed to by base. The number of elements to search is nelement; each size bytes large.

Compare is a pointer to a user-supplied function that sorts the array and performs the comparison. The arguments, element1 and element2, point to the key object and to a member in the array.

The comparison function must return the following.

Value	Comparison
<0	element1 < element2
0	element1 = element2
>0	element1 > element2

- Return

The function returns the pointer to the element where a match is found; otherwise, it returns a NULL pointer.

calloc—Allocate memory for an array.

```
#include <stdlib.h>
void *calloc( size_t nelement, size_t size );
```

- Description

The calloc function allocates memory for an array of nelement elements, each of length size. All elements of the storage are initialized with 0s.

- Return

The function returns a pointer to the base of reserved memory. If enough space is not available, a NULL pointer is returned.

ceil—Get integer greater than or equal to floating-point value.

```
#include <math.h>
double ceil( double x );
```

- Description

The ceil function calculates the smallest integer value that is greater than or equal to x.

- Return

The function returns the integer as a double precision value.

clearerr—Clear error indicators.

```
#include <stdio.h>
void clearerr( FILE *stream );
```

- Description

The clearerr function clears the error and end-of-file indicators for the stream pointed to by stream.

- Return

    This function does not return a value.

clock—Get elapsed time.

```
#include <time.h>
clock_t clock( void );
```

- Description

    The `clock` function determines the processor time elapsed since a program was invoked. To calculate the elapsed time in seconds, divide the returned value by the value of the macro CLK_TCK.

- Return

    The function returns the elapsed processor time, or (`clock_t`) -1 if the processor time is not available.

cos—Calculate cosine.

```
#include <math.h>
double cos( double x );
```

- Description

    The `cos` function calculates the cosine of x, where x is measured in radians.

- Return

    The function returns the cosine value.

cosh—Calculate hyperbolic cosine.

```
#include <math.h>
double cosh( double x );
```

- Description

    The `cosh` function calculates the hyperbolic cosine of x. If x is too large, the function sets `errno` to ERANGE.

- Return

    The function returns the hyperbolic cosine. If x is too large, the value HUGE_VAL is returned.

ctime—Convert a time to a string.

```
#include <time.h>
char *ctime( const time_t *timer );
```

- Description

    The `ctime` function converts the time value pointed to by `timer` to local time in a character string format. The time value is usually obtained by calling the `localtime` function. The output string has exactly 26 characters, including newline ('\n') and end-of-string ('\0'), in the form:

    ```
    Tue Mar 12 17:55:12 1991\n\0
    ```

    This function uses a 24-hour clock format.

- Return

   The function returns a pointer to the output string.

difftime—Calculate time difference.

   #include <time.h>

   double difftime(time_t time1, time_t time0);

- Description

   The difftime function calculates the time elapsed between time0 and time1.

- Return

   The function returns the difference in seconds as a double precision value.

div—Division.

   #include <stdlib.h>

   div_t div(int number, int denom);

- Description

   The div function calculates the quotient and remainder when the numerator, number, is divided by the denominator, denom.

- Return

   The function returns the quotient and remainder in a structure of type

   div_t.

   struct div_t {
                int quot; /* quotient */
                int rem; /* remainder */
                };

exit—Terminate program.

   #include <stdlib.h>

   void exit(int status);

- Description

   The exit function terminates a program normally. Before control is returned to the host operating system, all functions registered by the atexit function are executed, all output streams are closed, and all temporary files, created by the tempfile function, are deleted. The value of the argument status can be EXIT_SUCCESS, to indicate a normal exit, EXIT_FAILURE, to indicate an error, or any value from 0 to 255.

- Return

   The function returns control to the host operating system.

exp—Exponential function.

   #include <math.h>

   double exp(x);

- Description

The `exp` function calculates the exponential function of x. If an overflow or an underflow occurs, `errno` is set to ERANGE, indicating a range error.

- Return

The function returns the exponential function of x. It returns HUGE_VAL if an overflow occurs, or 0 if an underflow occurs.

fabs—Convert floating-point value to absolute value.

```
#include <math.h>
double fabs( double x );
```

- Description

The `fabs` function calculates the absolute value of x, a floating-point number.

- Return

The function returns a double-precision absolute value.

fclose—Close a stream.

```
#include <stdio.h>
int fclose( FILE *stream );
```

- Description

The `fclose` function closes a stream, previously opened by the `fopen` function and pointed to by `stream`. Before closing, all buffers associated with the stream are flushed. Any allocated buffers for the stream are released. Finally, the `stream` is disassociated from the file.

- Return

The function returns 0 upon a succesful close; otherwise, it returns EOF.

feof—Test for end of file.

```
#include <stdio.h>
int feof( FILE *stream );
```

- Description

The `feof` function tests whether the EOF flag is set for the stream pointed to by `stream`.

- Return

The function returns a non-zero value if the EOF flag is set; otherwise, 0 is returned.

ferror—Test read/write error.

```
#include <stdio.h>
int ferror( FILE *stream );
```

- Description

The `ferror` function tests for a read or write error for a stream pointed to by `stream`.

- Return

The function returns a non-zero value if an error has occurred; otherwise it returns 0.

fflush—Clear data buffer.

```
#include <stdio.h>
int fflush( FILE *stream );
```

- Description

The fflush function causes the content of a buffer for a stream, pointed to by stream, to be written. The flushing of the data buffer occurs only for a stream opened for output.

- Return

The function returns a 0 if the flush was successful; otherwise, it returns EOF.

fgetc—Get a character.

```
#include <stdio.h>
int fget( FILE *stream );
```

- Description

The fgetc function gets the next character (if available) as an unsigned int from the input stream pointed to by stream. It also sets the file-position indicator to point to the next character.

- Return

The function returns the character read, or EOF if end-of-file or an error occurs.

fgetpos—Get file position.

```
#include <stdio.h>
int fgetpos( FILE *stream, fpos_t *pos );
```

- Description

The fgetpos function saves the current value of the file-position indicator in the buffer pointed to by pos. The value can be used in a subsequent fsetpos function call.

- Return

The function returns 0 if it was successful. If an error occurs, a non-zero value is returned and errno is set to non-zero value.

fgets—Get a string.

```
#include <stdio.h>
char *fgets( char *s, int n, FILE *stream );
```

- Description

The fgets function reads a string from a stream pointed to by stream and writes it to a buffer pointed to by s. It reads from the current file-position indicator until a newline character ('\n') is found, or end-of-file is reached, or n-1 characters are read. After storing the string in the buffer, a NULL character ('\0') is added.

- Return

The function returns a pointer to the buffer if the operation is successful. It returns a NULL pointer if end-of-file or an error occurs. The `feof` and `ferror` functions can be used to check whether end-of-file or an error has occurred.

floor—Get integer less than or equal to floating-point value.

```
#include <math.h>
double floor( double x );
```

- Description

The `floor` function calculates the largest integer value that is less than or equal to x.

- Return

The function returns the integer value expressed as a `double`.

fmod—Floating-point remainder.

```
#include <math.h>
double fmod( double x, double y );
```

- Description

The `fmod` function calculates the floating-point remainder of x/y.

- Return

The function returns the remainder of x/y, which is always less than the absolute value of y. If y is 0, it returns a 0 value.

fopen—Open a file.

```
#include <stdio.h>
FILE *fopen( const char *filename, const char *mode );
```

- Description

The `fopen` function associates a stream with a file. A successful execution of open is necessary before a subsequent operation on the stream can be done.

The `filename` is a pointer to a string of characters that contains a valid data set name (DSNAME) or data definition name (DDNAME).

The `mode` is a pointer to a string, containing the mandatory open status and, optionally, characteristics of the data set. The following lists the open status.

Type	Description
"r"	Open an existing text file for reading.
"w"	Create or open a text file for writing. If the file exists, its contents are deleted.
"a"	Open a text file to append at the end of the file. Create it if it does not exist.
"r+"	Open an existing text file for reading and writing.

Type	Description
"w+"	Create or open a text file for reading and writing. If the file exists, its contents are deleted.
"a+"	Open a text file to read or append at the end of the file. If the file does not exist, create it.
"rb"	Open an existing binary file for reading.
"wb"	Create or open a binary file for writing. If the file exists, its contents are deleted.
"ab"	Open a binary file to append at the end of the file. Create it if it does not exist.
"rb+" or "r+b"	Open an existing binary file for reading and writing.
"wb+" or "w+b"	Create or open a binary file for reading and writing. If the file exists, its contents are deleted.
"ab+" or "a+b"	Open a binary file to read or append at the end of the file. If the file does not exist, create it.

The following is a list of all the options that can be included as part of the mode parameter.

Options	Description
blksize	The maximum length in bytes of a physical block of records.
lrecl	The length in bytes of fixed-length records or variable-length records.
recfm	File format. The valid values are: F: Fixed-length, unblocked records. FB: Fixed-length, blocked records. V: Variable-length, unblocked records. VB: Variable-length, blocked records.
type	The type of the file to be opened. The valid types are: memory: The file is temporary and memory resident. record: The file is opened only for record I/O.

- Return

The function returns a pointer to the FILE structure associated with the stream, if the open operation is successful; otherwise, it returns a NULL pointer.

fprintf—Write formatted string to file.

```
#include <stdio.h>

int fprintf( FILE *stream, const char *format,argument-list );
```

- Description

The `fprintf` function writes formatted data to a stream. It takes an item from the argument list, if any, and converts it according to a corresponding type found in the format-control string pointed to by `format` before writing it to the `stream`. The format-control string of `fprintf` is the same as the `printf` function.

- Return

The function returns a positive number, indicating the number of characters written, or a negative number, if any output error occurs.

fputc-Write a character to file

```
#include <stdio.h>

int fputf( int c, FILE *stream );
```

- Description

The `fputc` function writes a character `c` to the stream pointed to by `stream`. The character is written at the current file position.

- Return

The function returns the character written. An error is indicated by a return value of EOF.

fputs—Write string to file.

```
#include <stdio.h>

int fputs( const char *s, FILE *stream );
```

- Description

The `fputs` function writes a string pointed to by `s` to a stream pointed to by `stream`. The end-of-string character ('\0') is not written to the output stream.

- Return

The function returns a nonnegative value if successful; otherwise, it returns EOF.

fread—Read a block of data from file.

```
#include <stdio.h>

size_t fread( void *ptr, size_t size, size_t nmemb,
                    FILE *stream );
```

- Description

The `fread` function reads up to `nmemb` items, each `size` bytes, from a stream pointed to by `stream` into a buffer specified by `ptr`.

The data is read from the file at the current file position, which is increased by the number of bytes successfully read.

In record mode (specified on the `fopen` function), if `size` is less than the actual length of the record being read, only `size` number of bytes will be in the buffer. A subsequent read operation will get the next record.

- Return

The function returns the number of bytes read, which may be less than `nmemb` if end-of-file occurs before reaching `nmemb` bytes or an error occurs. The `foef` or `ferror` function can be used to check if an end-of-file or an error condition has occurred.

free—Release memory.

```
#include <stdlib.h>
void free( void *ptr );
```

- Description

The `free` function releases the memory pointed to by `ptr`, previously allocated by calling the `calloc`, `malloc`, or `realloc` functions. The freed memory is available for allocation again.

- Return

This function does not return a value.

freopen—Redirect an open file.

```
#include <stdio.h>
FILE *freopen( const char *filename, const char *mode,
               FILE *stream );
```

- Description

The `freopen` function first closes the file pointed to by `stream`. Next, it opens the file pointed to by `filename`. The `mode` is a pointer to a string, containing the mandatory open status and, optionally, data set characteristics. Refer to the `fopen` function for a list of open statuses and file characteristics.

The `freopen` can be used:

1. To redirect streams `stdin`, `stdout`, and `stderr` to data sets.
2. To change the open status of a data set (e.g., from read to write).

- Return

The function returns a pointer to the `FILE` structure associated with the new file. If an error occurs, a NULL pointer is returned.

frexp—Decompose floating-point value.

```
#include <math.h>
double frexp( double y, int *exp );
```

- Description

The `frexp` function decomposes a floating-point value y into a mantissa m (.5 >= m > 1) and an exponent to the power of 2. The signs of both parts are the same as y.

- Return

The function returns the mantissa m as a double-precision floating-point value and places the exponent in the object pointed to by `exp`. When y is 0, both mantissa and exponent are 0.

fscanf—Read formatted data from file.

```
#include <stdio.h>
int fscanf( FILE *stream, const char *format,
                         argument-list );
```

- Description

The fscanf function reads data from a stream pointed to by stream into memory location specified in argument-list. The value of format is a pointer to a format-control string, which is the same as for the scanf function. The scanf function starts reading at the current file position; and converts data according to a corresponding type found in the format-control string.

- Return

The function returns the number of arguments that were successfully converted and assigned. This return value does not include any argument that was read but not assigned.

fseek—Move file pointer.

```
#include <stdio.h>
int fseek( FILE *stream, long int offset, int origin );
```

- Description

The fseek function moves the file-position indicator of a stream pointed to by stream to a new position. The offset is the number of bytes that the indicator has to be changed from origin.

The argument origin can have three constant values defined in the <stdio.h> include file.

Origin	Description
SEEK_SET	Beginning of a file
SEEK_CUR	Current file-position
SEEK_END	End of file

For streams opened in binary mode, the file-position indicator can be set beyond the end of the file; however, it will return an error if an attempt is made to set the position before the beginning of the file. The fseek function clears the end-of-file indicator. For streams opened in text mode, the result of a call to fseek may produce unexpected results because of the system-dependent character translations.

While using the fseek function, there are a few restrictions to remember:
1. Cannot be used for spanned text stream.
2. Some devices, such as printers and terminals, do not support seeking.
3. File-position indicator can be set for a tape file opened for reading (r or rb) only.

4. If a file is opened in write-only mode (w, wb, a, and ab), fseek is allowed to find positions:
   a. Beginning of the file, using fseek (fp, 01, SEEK_SET).
   b. Current position, using fseek (fp, 01, SEEK_CUR).
   c. End of file, using fseek (fp, 01, SEEK_END).

- Return

The function returns a 0 value upon a successful operation; otherwise, it returns a non-zero value.

fsetpos—Set file-position indicator.

```
#include <stdio.h>
int fsetpos( FILE *stream, const fpos_t *pos);
```

- Description

The fsetpos function sets the file-position indicator of the stream pointed to by stream to the value of the object pointed to by pos. A successful call to this function clears the end-of-file indicator.

- Return

The function returns a 0 value upon a successful repositioning; otherwise, a non-zero value is returned.

ftell—Get file position.

```
#include <stdio.h>
long int ftell( FILE *stream );
```

- Description

The ftell function gets the value of the file-position indicator of the stream pointed to by stream.

- Return

The function returns the current value of the file-position indicator when successfully executed. If the device does not support file positioning, such as terminals and printers, the return value is undefined. If an error occurs, the function returns -1L and sets errno to a non-zero value.

fwrite—Write data to file.

```
#include <stdio.h>
size_t fwrite( const void *ptr, size_t size, size_t nmemb,
               FILE *stream );
```

- Description

The fwrite function writes up to nmemb items of data to the stream pointed to by stream from the buffer pointed to by ptr. The length of each item is size bytes. The data is written to the file at the current file position, and the file-position indicator value is increased by the number of bytes successfully written.

For record mode processing, if the total number of bytes to be written is less than the minimum allowed for the file, the write operation fails. If the total output byte count is greater than the actual record size, the data is truncated to record size and only one record is written. For an update, the output byte count must be the same as the record length.

- Return

The function returns the number of bytes written, which can be less than the number of bytes specified if an error occurs. The `ferror` function can be used to check the error indicator.

getc—Get a character from a file.

```
#include <stdio.h>

int getc( FILE *stream );
```

- Description

The `getc` function reads one character from the stream pointed to by `stream`. If a file-position indicator exists for the associated file, it is increased, to point to the next character.

- Return

The function returns the character read or EOF if end-of-file or an error occurs. Calling `ferror` or `feof` can determine the cause of the returned EOF value.

getchar—Get a character from standard stream.

```
#include <stdio.h>

int getchar( void );
```

- Description

The `getchar` function reads one character from the standard input stream `stdin`. If a file-position indicator exists, it is incremented to point to the next character.

- Return

The function returns the character read or EOF if end-of-file or an error occurs. Calling `ferror` or `feof` can determine the cause of the returned EOF value.

getenv—Get environment variables.

```
#include <stdlib.h>

char *getenv( const char *name );
```

- Description

The `getenv` function searches the environment variables list for an entry corresponding to `name`.

- Return

The function returns a pointer to the environment list entry matching `name`. A null pointer is returned if the specified variable is not defined or the host environment does not support this function.

gets—Get a line from standard stream.

```
#include <stdio.h>

char *gets( char *s );
```

- Description

The `gets` function reads a line of data from the standard input stream `stdin`. A line consists of any character, ending with a newline character ('\n'). Upon a successful read, all the characters of the line are moved to the buffer pointed to by s, except that the newline character is converted to end-of-string character ('\0').

- Return

The function returns the pointer s if successful. A null pointer is returned if an end-of-file or an error occurs. Calling `ferror` or `feof` can determine the cause of the returned NULL pointer.

gmtime—Convert calendar time.

```
#include <time.h>

struct tm *gmtime( const time_t *timer );
```

- Description

The `gmtime` function converts a calendar time pointed to by `timer` into a structured representation of Greenwich Mean Time. The time value can be obtained via a call to the `time` function.

- Return

The function returns a pointer to a `tm` structure. The fields are as follows.

Fields	Description
tm_sec	seconds (0–60)
tm_min	minutes (0–59)
tm_hour	hours (0–23)
tm_mday	day of month (1–31)
tm_mon	month (0–11, January = 0)
tm_year	year (current year minus 1900)
tm_wday	day of week (0–6, Sunday = 0)
tm_yday	day of year (0–365, January 1= 0)
tm_isdst	zero if daylight saving time is not in effect, positive if daylight saving time is in effect, negative if the information is not available.

A NULL pointer is returned if Greenwich Mean Time is not available.

isalnum—Test for alphanumeric character.

```
#include <type.h>

int isalnum( int c );
```

- Description

    The isalnum function tests for upper or lower case characters ('A' to 'Z' or 'a' to 'z') or numeric characters ('0' to '9').

- Return

    The function returns non-zero if the test is true; otherwise, it returns 0.

isalpha—Test for alphabetic character.

```
#include <type.h>

int isalpha( int c );
```

- Description

    The isalpha function tests for upper or lower case alphabetical characters ('A' to 'Z' or 'a' to 'z').

- Return

    The function returns non-zero if the test is true; otherwise, it returns.

iscntrl—Test for control character.

```
#include <type.h>

int iscntrl( int c );
```

- Description

    The iscntrl function tests for a control character.

- Return

    The function returns non-zero if the test is true; otherwise, it returns 0.

isdigit—Test for a numeric character.

```
#include <type.h>

int isdigit( int c );
```

- Description

    The isdigit function tests for a numeric character ('0' to '9').

- Return

    The function returns non-zero if the test is true; otherwise, it returns 0.

isgraph—Test for printable character, excluding space.

```
#include <type.h>

int isgraph( int c );
```

- Description

    The isgraph function tests for a printable character, excluding space.

- Return

    The function returns non-zero if the test is true; otherwise, it returns 0.

islower—Test for lower case character.

```
#include <type.h>

int islower( int c );
```

- Description

  The `islower` function tests for a lower case character ('a' to 'z').

- Return

  The function returns non-zero if the test is true; otherwise, it returns 0.

isprint—Test for printable character, including space.

```
#include <type.h>
int isprint( int c );
```

- Description

  The `isprint` function tests for a printable character, including space.

- Return

  The function returns non-zero if the test is true; otherwise, it returns 0.

ispunct—Test for punctuation character.

```
#include <type.h>
int ispunct( int c );
```

- Description

  The `ispunct` function tests for a punctuation character.

- Return

  The function returns non-zero if the test is true; otherwise, it returns 0.

isspace—Test for white space character.

```
#include <type.h>
int isspace( int c );
```

- Description

  The `isspace` function tests for white space character.

- Return

  The function returns non-zero if the test is true; otherwise, it returns 0.

isupper—Test for upper case character.

```
#include <type.h>
int isupper( int c );
```

- Description

  The `isupper` function tests for an upper case character ('A' to 'Z').

- Return

  The function returns non-zero if the test is true; otherwise, it returns 0.

isxdigit—Test for hexadecimal character.

```
#include <type.h>
int isxdigit( int c );
```

- Description

  The `isxdigit` function tests for hexadecimal digits ('0' to '9', 'A' to 'F', 'a' to 'f').

- Return

  The function returns non-zero if the test is true; otherwise, it returns 0.

labs—Calculate long absolute value.

```
#include <stdlib.h>
long int labs( long int j );
```

- Description

  The `labs` function calculates the absolute value of the long integer j. The behavior of this function is undefined if the result cannot be calculated.

- Return

  The function returns the absolute value of j.

ldexp—Multiply a value by power of 2.

```
#include <math.h>
double ldexp( double x, int exp );
```

- Description

  The `ldexp` function calculates the value of x * (2^{exp}). If an overflow occurs, `errno` is set to ERANGE.

- Return

  The function returns the value of x * (2^{exp}) if successful; if overflow occurs, +HUGE_VAL or -HUGE_VAL is returned, depending on the sign of x.

ldiv—Division of long integer.

```
#include <stdlib.h>
div_t ldiv( long int numer, long int denom );
```

- Description

  The `ldiv` function divides the numerator `numer` by the denominator `denom` giving a quotient and a remainder. This function is the same as `div` function, except that the arguments and the returned values are long integers.

- Return

  The function returns the quotient and remainder in the structure of type `ldiv_t`.

```
struct ldiv_t {
            long int quot ; /* quotient */
            long int rem;   /* remainder */
            };
```

localeconv—Get locale settings.

```
#include <locale.h>
struct lconv *localeconv( void );
```

- Description

The localeconv function initializes the elements of a structure of type lconv with the appropriate values of the current locale settings.

- Return

The function returns a pointer to a structure of type lconv.

```
struct lconv {
            char *decimal_point;
            char *thousands_sep;
            char *grouping;
            char *int_curr_symbol;
            char *currency_symbol;
            char *mon_decimal_point;
            char *mon_thousands_sep;
            char *mon_grouping;
            char *positive_sign;
            char *negative_sign;
            char int_frac_digits;
            char frac_digits;
            char p_cs_precedes;
            char p_sep_by_space;
            char n_cs_precedes;
            char n_sep_by_space;
            char p_sign_posn;
            char n_sign_posn;
            };
```

localtime—Convert time.

```
#include <time.h>
```

```
struct tm *localtime( const time_t *timer );
```

- Description

The localtime converts a time value pointed to by timer into a structured representation of the local time. The time value returned is correct for the local time zone and daylight saving time. The time value can be obtained via a call to the time function.

- Return

The function returns a pointer to a tm structure. The fields are as follows.

Fields	Description
tm_sec	seconds (0–60)
tm_min	minutes (0–59)
tm_hour	hours (0–23)
tm_mday	day of month (1–31)
tm_mon	month (0–11, January = 0)
tm_year	year (current year minus 1900)
tm_wday	day of week (0–6, Sunday = 0)
tm_yday	day of year (0–365, January 1 = 0)

Fields	Description
tm_isdst	zero if daylight saving time is not in effect, positive if daylight saving time is in effect, negative if the information is not available.

log—Calculate the natural log.

```
#include <math.h>
double log( double x );
```

- Description

The `log` function calculates the natural logarithm of x. If x is zero, `errno` is set to ERANGE, and if x is negative, `errno` is set to EDOM.

- Return

The function returns the natural logarithm. If x is 0 or negative, -HUGE_VAL is returned.

log10—Calculate the log base10.

```
#include <math.h>
double log10( double x );
```

- Description

The `log10` function calculates the base 10 logarithm of x. If x is 0, `errno` is set to ERANGE, and if x is negative, `errno` is set to EDOM.

- Return

The function returns the base 10 logarithm. If x is 0 or negative, -HUGE_VAL is returned.

longjmp—Restore calling environment.

```
#include <setjmp.h>
void longjmp( jmp_buf env, int val );
```

- Description

The `longjmp`, function restores the stack environment previously saved in env by a routine that invoked the `setjmp` function. The object val is the value to be returned to the routine that issued the `setjmp` call. The `setjmp` and `longjmp` functions can be used to perform a nonlocal goto.

- Return

This function does not return a value.

malloc—Reserve memory.

```
#include <stdlib.h>
void *malloc( size_t size );
```

- Description

The `malloc` function reserves a block of memory of size bytes.

- Return

  The function returns a pointer to the reserved memory block. If the size argument is 0 or there is not enough space available, a NULL pointer is returned.

mblen—Get length of multibyte character string.

```
#include <stdlib.h>
int mblen( const char *s, size_t n );
```

- Description

  The mblen function determines the number of bytes of the multibyte character pointed to by s. The value specifies the maximum number of bytes in a multibyte character

- Return

  If s is not a NULL pointer, the function returns one of the following:

  - Number of bytes in the multibyte character pointed to by s.
  - 0, if s points to a NULL character.
  - -1, if s does not point to a valid multibyte character.

  If s is a NULL pointer, the function returns one of the following:

  - 0, if the current locale does not support state-dependent encodings. What this means is that, when a string is composed of both single-byte and double-byte characters, a method must exist to indicate the shift from single-to double-byte characters and back. This is known as state-dependent encoding. One implementation of this encoding is to have a shift-out character precede and a shift-in character follow the double-byte character sequence.
  - -1, if the current locale supports state-dependent encodings.

mbstowcs—Convert a multibyte character string.

```
#include <stdlib.h>
size_t mbstowcs( wchar_t *pwcs, const char *s, size_t n );
```

- Description

  The mbstowcs function converts the multibyte character string pointed to by s, into a series of wide characters and stores them in the object pointed to by pwcs. No more than n wide characters will be stored in the target array.

- Return

  The function returns the number of elements modified in the destination string pwcs, excluding the terminating NULL character. If the sequence of characters in the input string is invalid, (size t)-1 is returned.

mbtowc—Convert a multibyte character.

```
#include <stdlib.h>
int mbtowc( wchart_t *pwc, const char *s, size_t n );
```

- Description

The `mbtowc` function determines the number of bytes of the string pointed to by `s`. Then it converts the multibyte character to a wide character and stores it in the object pointed to by `pwc`.

- Return

If `s` is not a NULL pointer, the function returns one of the following:

> - Number of bytes in the multibyte character pointed to by `s`.
> - 0, if `s` points to a NULL character.
> - -1, if `s` does not point to a valid multibyte character.

If `s` is a NULL pointer, the function returns one of the following:

> - 0, if the current locale does not support state-dependent encodings. What this means is that, when a string is composed of both single-byte and double-byte characters, a method must exist to indicate the shift from single to double-byte characters and back. This is known as state-dependent encoding. One implementation of this encoding is to have a shift-out character precede and a shift-in character follow the double-byte character sequence.
> - -1, if the current locale supports state-dependent encodings.

memchr—Search for character in buffer.

```
#include <string.h>

void *memchr( const void *s, int c, size_t n );
```

- Description

The `memchr` function looks for the first occurrence of character `c` in the buffer pointed to by `s`. The search stops when `n` bytes in `s` have been examined or the character is found

- Return

The function returns a pointer to the location of `c` in `s`, if found within `n` bytes; otherwise, it returns a NULL pointer.

memcmp—Compare two buffers.

```
#include <string.h>

int memcmp( const void *s1, const void *s2, size_t n );
```

- Description

The `memcmp` function compares the first `n` bytes of two buffers pointed to by `s1` and `s2`.

- Return

The function returns a value that shows the result of the comparison, as follows.

Return	Relationship
< 0	s1 < s2
0	s1 = s2
> 0	s1 > s2

memcpy—Copy buffer.

```
#include <string.h>
void *memcpy( void *s1, const void *s2, size_t n );
```

- Description

The memcpy function copies n bytes from the buffer pointed to by s1 to the buffer pointed to by s2. If source and destination buffers overlap, the results are undefined. The memmove function allows buffers to overlap.

- Return

The function returns a pointer to the destination buffer s2.

memmove—Copy buffer.

```
#include <string.h>
void *memmove( void *s1, const void *s2, size_t n );
```

- Description

The memmove function copies n bytes from the buffer pointed to by s1 to the buffer pointed to by s2. Overlapping of source and destination buffers is allowed.

- Return

The function returns a pointer to the destination buffer s2.

memset—Initialize buffer.

```
#include <string.h>
void *memset( void *s, int c, size_t n );
```

- Description

The memset function sets the first n bytes of the buffer pointed to by s to the value c. The value of c is converted to a character.

- Return

The function returns the value of s.

mktime—Convert to local time.

```
#include <time.h>
time_t mktime( struct tm *timeptr );
```

- Description

The mktime function converts a local time stored in a tm structure pointed to by timeptr into a calendar time. The values of the structure pointed to by timeptr are not restricted to the ranges shown in the other functions of the <time_h> include file.

- Return

The function it returns the calendar time as a value of type `time_t`. If the calendar time cannot be represented, a value of (time_f) (-1) is returned.

modf—Break down floating-point value.

```
#include <math.h>

double modf( double value, double *iptr )
```

- Description

The `modf` function breaks down the floating-point value, `value`, into fractional and integral components. The integral part is stored in the object pointed to by `iptr`, and the fractional portion is returned to the caller. The sign of both fractional and integral portions are the same as `value`.

- Return

The function returns the fractional component of `value` as a double-precision value.

perror—Print error message.

```
#include <stdio.h>

void perror( const char *s )
```

- Description

The `perror` function prints a message that is mapped to the current value in `errno` to stream `stderr`. First, the string pointed to by `s` is printed, followed by a colon and a space. Second, an implementation-defined message corresponding to the value in `errno` is printed, followed by a newline character. To produce the appropriate message, `perror` should be called immediately after the library function that produced the error.

- Return

This function does not return a value.

pow—Calculate power.

```
#include <math.h>

double pow( double x, double y );
```

- Description

The `pow` function calculates `x` to the power of `y`. If `y` is 0, the result is 1. If the values of `x` and `y` cause a range or domain error, the results are as follows:

	Result	errno
x = 0, y > 0	0	EDOM
Large value overflow	+HUGE_VAL	ERANGE
Small value overflow	-HUGE_VAL	ERANGE

- Return

The function returns the value of `x` to the power of `y`.

printf—Print formatted data.

```
#include <stdio.h>

int printf( const char *format, argument list);
```

- Description

The `printf` function writes formatted data to the standard output stream `stdout`. It takes an item from the argument list, if any, and converts it according to a corresponding type found in the format-control string pointed to by `format`.

An argument list consists of constants and identifiers.

A format-control string consists of ordinary characters, escape sequences, and format specifications for each argument. The format-control string and the argument list are scanned from left to right, and each type is matched with an argument. If the number of arguments and type specifications do not match, the result is unpredictable.

The form of the format specification is:

```
%[flags] [width] [.precision] [h|l|L]type
```

In the format specification, the `type` and `%` are mandatory and the other fields are optional. The description of the fields are as follows.

Field	Description
flags	Justify output and print signs, blanks, decimal points, octal, and hexadecimal prefixes (see Table 20.1).
width	Specifies the minimum number of characters printed.
precision	Specifies the maximum number of characters to be printed for all or part of the output fields. Or it specifies the minimum number of digits to be printed for integer values.
h,l,L	The character h indicates that the argument is a short *integer*. The character l indicates that the argument is a long *integer*. The character L indicates that the argument is a *long double*.

Prefixes	Type
h	d,i,o,u,x, or X
l	d,i,o,u,x, or X
L	e,E,f,g, or G

The values for `type` and its effect on output is shown in Table 20.2.

- Return

The function returns the number of characters printed.

TABLE 20.1. Flag Characters for PRINTF

Flags	Description
-	Left-justify the output within a field.
+	Prefix the output of a signed conversion with plus and minus sign.
space	Prefix the output of a signed conversion with space or minus sign (plus overrides space when both are used).
#	When the # flag is used with 0, x, or X format, non-zero is prefixed with 0, 0x, or 0X, respectively. When the # flag is used with g or G format, the trailing 0s of the are not removed. When the # flag is used with f, e, or E format, the output always has a decimal point. The # flag should not be used with c, d, i, u, s, or p formats

TABLE 20.2. Conversion Character for PRINT

Conversion character	Argument printed as
d,i	decimal integer
c	character
u	unsigned decimal integer
x,X	unsigned hexadecimal integer
e	floating-point number, e.g., 8.450000e+00
E	floating-point number, e.g., 8.450000E+00
f	floating-point number, e.g., 8.450000
g	e-format or f-format
G	E-format or f-format
s	string
p	pointer to void in hexadecimal number
n	pointer to integer in which the number of characters written to the stream is printed

putc—Print a character.

```
#include <stdio.h>

int putc( int c, FILE *stream );
```

- Description

The `putc` function writes the character c to the output stream pointed to by stream. The character is first converted to an unsigned character.

- Return

The function returns the character written. If an error occurs, EOF is returned and the error indicator is set.

putchar—Print a character to standard output.

```
#include <stdio.h>
int putchar(int c);
```

- Description

The `putchar` function writes the character c to the standard output stream. It is equivalent to `putc(c,stdout)`.

- Return

The function returns the character written. If an error occurs, EOF is returned and the error indicator is set.

puts—Print a string.

```
#include <stdio.h>
int puts(const char *s);
```

- Description

The `puts` function writes the string pointed to by s to the standard output stream and appends a newline character to the output.

- Return

The function returns a nonnegative value unless an error occurs, in which case, EOF is returned.

qsort—Sort array.

```
#include <stdlib.h>
void qsort(void *base, size_t nelemt, sizt_t size,
      int (*compar)(const void *, const void *));
```

- Description

The `qsort` function sorts an array of `nelemt` elements. The size of each element in the array is given by `size`. The address of the first element to be sorted is specified by `base`.

The elements of the array are sorted by the comparison function pointed to by `compar`. You must provide this function. The values passed to this function are pointers to the array elements being compared. The values returned from this function must be:

< 0	first element less than second element
= 0	first element equal to second element
> 0	first element greater than second element

- Return

This function does not return a value.

raise—Send a signal.

```
#include <signal.h>
int raise(int sig);
```

- Description

The `raise` function sends the signal `sig` to the currently executing program.

- Return

This function returns 0 if the operation was successful, non-zero if the operation was unsuccessful.

rand—Generate random integer.

```
#include <stdlib.h>
int rand(void);
```

- Description

The `rand` function computes a sequence of pseudo-random integers. The range of these integers is 0 to RAND_MAX. RAND_MAX is a macro defined in the header file <stdlib.h> and should be at least 32767.

- Return

The function returns a pseudo-random integer.

realloc—Change storage size.

```
#include <stdlib.h>
void *realloc(void *ptr, size_t size);
```

- Description

The `realloc` function changes the size of a previously acquired storage area. The value of `ptr` points to the beginning of the storage area. The value of `size` is the new size requested. The contents of the storage area are unchanged up to the lesser of the new and old size.

If the `ptr` is a null pointer, `realloc` allocates the storage for the specified size. If `ptr` does not point to a previously acquired storage area, the behavior of the `realloc` is undefined.

- Return

The function returns either a null pointer or a pointer to the storage area. A null pointer is returned if the requested size is 0 or if there is insufficient space to honor the request. If a valid pointer is returned, this value may not be the same as the `ptr` argument passed to the `realloc` function.

remove—Delete a file.

```
#include <stdio.h>
int remove(const char *filename);
```

- Description

The `remove` function deletes a file. The name of the file is pointed to by `filename`.

- Return

    The function returns 0 if successful, non-zero if it fails.

rename—Rename a file.

    #include <stdio.h>

    int rename(const char *old, const char *new);

- Description

    The `rename` function changes the name of the file specified by `old` to the name specified by `new`. The value of `old` must point to a name of an existing file. The value of `new` should not point to the name of an existing file.

- Return

    The function returns a 0 value if the operation was successful. If an error occurs, a non-zero value is returned.

rewind—Set file position indicator.

    #include <stdio.h>

    void rewind(FILE *stream);

- Description

    The `rewind` function sets the file position indicator to the start of the file pointed to by `stream`. This function also clears the error indicator for the stream.

- Return

    This function does not return a value.

scanf—Formatted read data.

    #include <stdio.h>

    int scanf(const char *format,...);

- Description

    The `scanf` function reads input from the standard input stream, `stdin`, under the control of the format string pointed to by `format`. One or more pointers may be in the argument-list passed to this function. These pointers specify the locations where the input values will be stored.

    The format string may contain any of the following:

    - One or more white space characters.
    - Ordinary characters, excluding %.
    - Conversion specification.

    White space characters are those specified by the `isspace` function. The standard characters are space, form feed, new line, carriage return, horizontal tab, and vertical tab. A white space character causes `scanf` to read up to the first non–white space character or until no more characters can be read. These characters are not stored.

    Ordinary characters that are part of the format string cause `scanf` to read the next characters of the stream. If one of the characters differs from the format, `scanf` ends.

A conversion specification causes `scanf` to read characters from the input stream and convert them to the specified type. The converted values are stored at the locations specified by the pointers in the argument list.

The following describes the processing of the format string. Characters not within a conversion specification must match the sequence of characters in the input or else `scanf` ends. The matched characters are read, but not stored. Unmatched characters remain in the input stream.

When a conversion specification is found, the input item is converted accordingly and stored in the corresponding location. An input item is made up of all characters up to the first white space character, up to the first character that cannot be converted according to the specification, or until the maximum field width is reached, whichever comes first.

The following is the format of a conversion specification:

```
% * width x type
```

*	means that the input item will be converted accordingly, but its value will not be stored.
width	specifies the maximum number of characters read from the input and the maximum number of characters that may be converted and stored.
x	are the characters h, l, and L. The character h indicates that you use the short version of the type. The character l indicates that the long version should be used. The character L indicates that the long double version of the type is to be used.

Prefixes	Types
h	d,i,o,x,u
l	d,e,f,g,i,o,x,u
L	e,f,g

All of the above fields are optional. The simplest form of the conversion specification is `% type`.

Valid types	Meanings
d	Decimal integer. Corresponding location pointer in the argument list shall be a pointer to `int`.
i	Integer. Corresponding location pointer shall be a pointer to `int`.
o	Octal integer. Corresponding location pointer shall be a pointer to `unsigned int`.

Valid types	Meanings
u	Decimal integer. Corresponding location pointer shall be a pointer to unsigned int.
x,X	Hexadecimal integer. Corresponding location pointer shall be a pointer to unsigned int.
e,f,g E,G	Floating-point number. Corresponding location pointer shall be a pointer to float.
s	Non-white space characters. Corresponding location pointer shall be a pointer to a character array large enough to hold the entire input item plus a null character.
[...]	A character string with terminating null character automatically added. The input item is read up to the first character that does not appear in the string. If the first character in the string is circumflex (^), the input item is read up to the first character that does appear in the string. The corresponding location pointer shall be a pointer to a character array large enough to hold the input item plus the terminating null.
c	White space characters are read when this type is specified. The corresponding location pointer shall be a pointer to a character array large enough to hold the entire input item.
n	No input is read. The corresponding location pointer shall be a pointer to int that will contain the number of characters read so far by this execution of the scanf function.
p	Value of pointer converted to printable format. Corresponding location pointer shall be a pointer to void.

- Return

The function returns the number of input items assigned to locations. EOF is returned if an input failure occurs before any conversion. A value of 0 means that no items were assigned.

setbuf—Buffering control.

```
#include <stdio.h>

void setbuf(FILE *stream, char *buf);
```

- Description

The setbuf function allows you to control a stream's buffering. The pointer, stream, must point to an opened file that has not been read or written. If the pointer buf is a null pointer, the stream is unbuffered. If buf is not a null pointer, then full buffering is used for input and output. In the second case, buf must point to a character string array with a length of BUFSIZE. BUFSIZE is a macro defined in <stdio.h> include file and should be at least 256. The array is used for input and output buffering for the stream rather than the system-allocated buffer.

- Return

  This function does not return a value.

  Note: All input and output is buffered in S/370.

setjmp—Save calling environment.

```
#include <setjmp.h>

int setjmp(jmp_buf env);
```

- Description

  The setjmp function saves the current environment in env, an array of type set_jmp. The array is used by the longjmp function to restore the environment.

- Return

  A 0 value is returned from a direct invocation of the setjmp function. If the return is a result of a call from a longjmp function, a non-zero value is returned.

setlocale—Set current locale.

```
#include <locale.h>

char *setlocale(int category, const char *locale);
```

- Description

  The setlocale function returns or modifies a program's locale information. All or a portion of the locale information can be processed as specified by the category argument. The values and scope for *category* are as follows.

Category	Affects
LC_ALL	Names the program's entire locale.
LC_COLLATE	Affects behavior of the strcoll and strxfrm functions.
LC_CTYPE	Affects behavior of character handling functions.
LC_MONETARY	Affects monetary formatting information returned by the localeconv function.
LC_NUMERIC	Affects decimal-point character for formatted input/output functions, string conversion functions, and non-monetary formatting information returned by localeconv function.
LC_TIME	Affects behavior of the strftime function.

- Return

  If the value for locale is a null pointer, the setlocale function returns a string of the program's current locale information for the values specified by category. If the pointer is to a valid string, this function returns a string containing the new locale information for the specified categories. A null pointer is returned if the setlocale function cannot perform the requested update.

setvbuf—Buffering control.

    #include <stdio.h>

    int setvbuf(FILE *stream, char *buf, int mode, size_t size);

- Description

The `setvbuf` function allows you to control a stream's buffering. The pointer, `stream`, must point to an opened file, and this file must not have been previously read or written. The `mode` value determines how the stream will be buffered.

Mode	Meaning
_IOFBF	full buffering
_IOLBF	line buffering
_IONBF	unbuffered

If `buf` is not a null pointer, the array it points to is used for input/output buffering. The `size` value specifies the size of the array.

- Return

The function returns a zero value if successful. A non-zero value is returned if the `mode` value is invalid or if the request cannot be honored.

Note: All input and output is buffered in S/370.

signal—Signal handling.

    #include <signal.h>

    void (*signal(int sig, void (*func)(int)))(int);

- Description

The `signal` function allows you to choose the way the signal, `sig`, is to be handled when it is received. If the value of `func` is SIG_DFL, the system default action for that signal is performed. If the value is SIG_IGN, then the signal is ignored. In any other case, `func` points to a function to be called when the signal is received.

The signal values and their meanings are as follows.

Signal	Meaning
SIGABRT	Abnormal termination; may be initiated by the `abort` function.
SIGFPE	Invalid arithmetic operation—for example, divide by 0.
SIGILL	Invalid function image—for example, an illegal instruction.
SIGINT	Interactive attention signal; caused by attention (ATTN) or program attention 1 (PA1) key.
SIGSEGV	Invalid memory access.
SIGTERM	Termination request sent to program.

- Return

  The function returns the value SIG_ERR if the function call was unsuccessful.

sin—Trigonometric sine.

```
#include <math.h>

double sin(double x);
```

- Description

  The sin function computes the sine of x, where x is expressed in radians.

- Return

  The function returns the sine value.

sinh—Hyperbolic sine.

```
#include <math.h>

double sinh(double x);
```

- Description

  The sinh function computes the hyperbolic sine of x.

- Return

  The function returns the hyperbolic sine value. If the magnitude of x is too large, a range error occurs. x is too large when the result of a call to sinh cannot be represented as a double value.

sprintf—Formatted print to a buffer.

```
#include <stdio.h>

int sprintf (char *s, const char *format,…);
```

- Description

  The sprintf function converts each entry in the argument list and writes them to an array specified by s. The conversion is controlled by the string pointed to by format. Please refer to the description of fprintf function for a complete discussion of the format string.

  A null character is written to the end of the character array.

- Return

  The function returns the number of characters written to the array, not including the null character.

sqrt—Compute square root.

```
#include <math.h>

double sqrt(double x);
```

- Description

  The sqrt function computes the nonnegative square root of x.

- Return

  The function returns the square root value. If x is negative, a domain error occurs. In the error situation, the value returned is implementation-defined.

srand—Seed for random integer generation.

```
#include <stdlib.h>

void srand(unsigned int seed);
```

- Description

The srand function uses the argument value as a seed for a sequence of pseudo-random numbers generated by the rand function. If srand is not called or the rand function is called before srand, the default seed value is 1.

- Return

This function does not return a value.

sscanf—Read data from a string.

```
#include <stdio.h>

int sscanf(const char *s, const char *format,…);
```

- Description

The sscanf function reads data from the string specified by the s argument into the corresponding locations. Each location argument must be a pointer to a variable with a type corresponding to a type specified in the string pointed to by format. Please refer to the description of the fscanf function for a complete discussion of the format string.

- Return

The function returns the number of input items assigned to locations. EOF is returned if an input failure occurs before any conversion. A value of 0 means that no items were assigned.

strcat—Concatenate strings.

```
#include <string.h>

char *strcat(char *s1, const char *s2);
```

- Description

The strcat function appends or concatenates the string specified by s2 to the string specified by s1. The terminating null character of the copied string is included. The null character of the target string is overwritten by the initial character of the copied string.

- Return

The function returns the value of s1, a pointer to the string.

strchr—Find character within a string.

```
#include <string.h>

char *strchr(const char *s, int c);
```

- Description

The strchr function finds the first occurrence of c within the specified string. c is converted to a character.

- Return

The function returns a pointer to the character or a NULL pointer if the character is not found.

strcmp—Compare strings.

```
#include <string.h>

int strcmp(const char *s1, const char *s2);
```

- Description

The strcmp function compares the strings pointed to by s1 and s2.

- Return

The function returns a value indicating the result of the comparison. The values and their meanings are as follows.

Value	Meaning
< 0	s1 less than s2
= 0	s1 identical to s2
> 0	s1 greater than s2

strcpy—Copy strings.

```
#include <string.h>

char *strcpy(char *s1, const char *s2);
```

- Description

The strcpy function copies the string pointed to by s2 to the location specified by s1. The terminating null character of the copied string is included.

- Return

The function returns the value of s1, a pointer to the string.

strcspn—Find characters within a string.

```
#include <string.h>

size_t strcspn(const char *s1, const char *s2);
```

- Description

The strcspn function calculates the position of the first character in the string pointed to by s1 that belongs to the string pointed to by s2.

- Return

The function returns the position of the character in the s1 string. This is the length from the beginning of the string.

strcoll—Compare strings using collating sequence.

```
#include <string.h>

int strcoll(const char *s1, const char *s2);
```

- Description

The `strcoll` function compares the strings pointed to by s1 and s2 using the collating sequence specified by the LC_COLLATE category of the program's locale.

- Return

The function returns a value indicating the result of the comparison. The values and their meanings are as follows.

Value	Meaning
< 0	s1 less than s2
= 0	s1 equivalent to s2
> 0	s1 greater than s2

strerror—Get error message.

```
#include <string.h>
char *strerror(int errnum);
```

- Description

The `strerror` function maps the error number in errnum to an error message. The content of the message is implementation-defined.

- Return

The function returns a pointer to the message string.

strftime—Convert time to a string.

```
#include <time.h>
size_t strftime(char *s, size_t maxsize, const char *format,
        const struct tm *timeptr);
```

- Description

The `strftime` function converts a time value into a string, according to the specified format. The time value is a structure pointed to by timeptr. The destination is a character array pointed to by s. The conversion process is controlled by the string pointed to by format. The value specified by maxsize is the maximum number of characters placed in the destination string.

The conversion specifications for the format string follow. The behavior of these specifications depends on the program's locale.

%a	is replaced by the locale's abbreviated weekday name.
%A	is replaced by the locale's full weekday name.
%b	is replaced by the locale's abbreviated month name.
%B	is replaced by the locale's full month name.
%c	is replaced by the locale's data and time representation.
%d	is replaced by the day of the month as a decimal number from 01 to 31.

%H	is replaced by the hour as a decimal number from 00 to 23.
%I	is replaced by the hour as a decimal number from 01 to 12.
%j	is replaced by the day of the year as a decimal number from 001 to 366.
%m	is replaced by the month as a decimal number from 01 to 12.
%M	is replaced by the minute as a decimal number from 00 to 59.
%p	is replaced by the locale's equivalent of either AM or PM.
%S	is replaced by the second as a decimal number from 00 to 60.
%U	is replaced by the week number of the year as a decimal number from 00 to 53. Sunday is the first day of the week.
%w	is replaced by the weekday as a decimal number from 0 to 6. Sunday is day number 0.
%W	is replaced by the week number of the year as a decimal number from 00 to 53. Monday is the first day of the week.
%x	is replaced by the locale's date representation.
%X	is replaced by the locale's time representation.
%y	is replaced by the year without century as a decimal number from 00 to 99.
%Y	is replaced by the year with century as a decimal number.
%Z	is replaced by the time zone name or by no characters if a time zone cannot be determined.
%%	is replaced by %.

- Return

The function returns the number of characters placed in the string, excluding the terminating null character. If an error occurs, such as the conversion resulting in more than `maxsize` characters, 0 is returned and the contents of the destination buffer is indeterminate.

strlen—Compute string length.

```
#include <string.h>
size_t strlen(const char *s);
```

- Description

    The strlen function computes the length of the string pointed to by s.

- Return

    The function returns the number of characters in the specified string, excluding the terminating null character.

strncat—Append characters to a string.

```
#include <string.h>

char *strncat(char *s1, const char *s2, size_t n);
```

- Description

    The strncat function appends or concatenates, at most, n characters from the string pointed to by s2 to the string pointed to by s1. The first character of the s2 string overwrites the terminating null character of the s1 string. If a null character is detected in the s2 string before n characters have been appended, no further characters are concatenated. A terminating null character is always added to the end of the resulting string. The maximum number of characters in the target string, pointed to by s1, is the length of this string plus the number of characters added, n or less, plus the terminating null character.

- Return

    The function returns the value of s1, a pointer to the string.

strncmp—Compare characters in strings.

```
#include <string.h>

int strncmp(const char *s1, const char *s2, size_t n);
```

- Description

    The strncmp function compares, at most, n characters of the string pointed to by s1 to the string pointed to by s2.

- Return

    The function returns a value indicating the result of the comparison. The values and their meanings are as follows.

Value	Meaning
< 0	s1 less than s2
= 0	s1 equal to s2
> 0	s1 greater than s2

strncpy—Copy characters to a string.

```
#include <string.h>

char *strncpy(char *s1, const char *s2, size_t n);
```

- Description

    The strncpy function copies, at most, n characters from the string pointed to by s2 to the string pointed to by s1. If the s2 string is shorter than n characters, null characters are written to the s1 string until n characters have been written. If n is equal to or less than the length of the s2 string, excluding the terminating null character, then no terminating null character will be written to the string pointed to by s1.

- Return

The function returns the value of s1, a pointer to the string.

strpbrk—Find character within a string.

```
#include <string.h>

char *strpbrk(const char *s1, const char *s2);
```

- Description

The strpbrk function locates the first occurrence in the string pointed to by s1 of any character in the string pointed to by s2.

- Return

The function returns a pointer to the character or a NULL pointer if no characters from the s2 string are found in the s1 string.

strchr—Find last occurrence of a character within a string.

```
#include <string.h>

char *strchr(const char *s, int c);
```

- Description

The strchr function finds the last occurrence of c within the specified string. c is converted to a character.

- Return

The function returns a pointer to the character or a NULL pointer if the character is not found.

strspn—Find characters outside of a string.

```
#include <string.h>

size_t strspn(const char *s1, const char *s2);
```

- Description

The strspn function calculates the position of the first character in the string pointed to by s1 that is not in the character string pointed to by s2.

- Return

The function returns the position of the character in the s1 string. This is the length from the beginning of the string.

strstr—Find character string.

```
#include <string.h>

char *strstr(const char *s1, const char *s2);
```

- Description

The strstr function finds the first occurrence of the string pointed to by s2 in the string pointed to by s1. The terminating null character of the s2 string is excluded.

- Return

The function returns a pointer to the located string. If the s2 string is not found, a null pointer is returned.

strtod—Convert string to double.

```
#include <stdlib.h>

double strtod(const char *nptr, char **endptr);
```

- Description

The strtod function converts the character string pointed to by nptr to a double-precision value. This input string can be made up of white space characters, as specified by the isspace function, a plus or minus sign, digits, and a decimal point. It can also include the exponent indicator, e or E.

This function terminates when it detects the first character that is not part of the expected input. A pointer to the final string is stored in the object pointed to by endptr, unless endptr is a null pointer.

No conversion is performed if the input string is empty or does not have the expected form. In this case, the value of nptr is stored in the object pointed to by endptr, unless endptr is a null pointer.

- Return

The function returns the converted value. This value has the same sign as the input string. Zero is returned if a conversion could not be performed. If the converted value would cause overflow, plus or minus HUGE_VAL is returned, depending on the sign of the input string. Zero is returned if the value causes underflow. For both overflow and underflow, the value of the macro ERANGE is stored in errno.

strtol—Convert string to long.

```
#include <stdlib.h>

long int strtol(const char *nptr, char **endptr, int base);
```

- Description

The strtol function converts the character string pointed to by nptr to a long integer value. This input string can be made up of white space characters, as specified by the isspace function, a plus or minus sign, an octal or hexadecimal prefix, and digits.

The value of base determines the expected form of the input. If the value of base is 0, the prefix determines the base. A prefix of 0 means base 8 or octal. A prefix of 0x or 0X means base 16 or hexadecimal. A digit without a prefix means base 10 or decimal. If the value of base is between 2 and 36, it becomes the base of the number. This function terminates when it detects the first character that is not part of the expected input.

A pointer to the final string is stored in the object pointed to by endptr, unless endptr is a null pointer. No conversion is performed if the input string is empty or does not have the expected form. In this case, the value of nptr is stored in the object pointed to by endptr, unless endptr is a null pointer.

- Return

The function returns the converted value. This value has the same sign as the input value. Zero is returned if a conversion could not be performed. If the converted value would cause overflow, LONG_MAX or LONG_MIN is returned, according to the sign of the value. The value of the macro ERANGE is stored in errno.

strtok—Convert string to tokens.

```
#include <string.h>
char *strtok(char *s1, const char *s2);
```

- Description

The strtok function converts the string pointed to by s1 into a series of tokens delimited by a character pointed to by s2. This process is accomplished by a series of calls to strtok. The first invocation of the strtok function has s1 as its first argument. Subsequent calls use a null pointer as the first argument. The character pointed to by s2 may change from call to call. The initial call to strtok searches the s1 string for the first non-delimiting character and returns a pointer to it. If no such character is found, a null pointer is returned.

From there, the function searches for a character that is contained in the delimiting string. If one is found, it is replaced by a token-terminating null character. If no delimiting character is found, the current token extends to the end of the s1 string. A null pointer will be returned if strtok is invoked to process the same string.

Subsequent calls to strtok, with a null pointer as the first argument, starts the search for the delimiting character after the previous token's terminating null character. This continues until a null character is detected in the original string.

- Return

The function returns a pcinter to the first character of the delimited string or token. A null pointer is returned if there are no tokens.

strtoul—Convert a string to an unsigned long integer.

```
#include <stdlib.h>
unsigned long int strtoul(const char *nptr, char **endptr, int
                  base);
```

- Description

The strtoul function converts the character string pointed to by nptr to an unsigned long integer value. This input string can be made up of white space characters, as specified by the isspace function, a plus or minus sign, an octal or hexadecimal prefix, and digits.

The value of base determines the expected form of the input. If the value of base is 0, the prefix determines the base. A prefix of 0 means base 8 or octal. A prefix of 0x or 0X means base 16 or hexadecimal. A digit without a prefix means base 10 or decimal. If the value of base is between 2 and 36, it becomes the base of the number. This function terminates when it detects the first character that is not part of the expected input.

A pointer to the final string is stored in the object pointed to by endptr, unless endptr is a null pointer. No conversion is performed if the input string is empty or does not have the expected form. In this case, the value of nptr is stored in the object pointed to by endptr, unless endptr is a null pointer.

- Return

The function returns the converted value. Zero is returned if a conversion could not be performed. If the converted value would cause overflow, ULONG_MAX is returned. The value of the macro ERANGE is stored in errno.

strxfrm—Transform strings.

```
#include <string.h>
size_t strxfrm(char *s1, const char *s2, size_t n);
```

- Description

The strxfrm function transform the string pointed to by s2 and places the result in the string pointed to by s1. The transformation is determined by the program's locale, such that if the strcmp function is applied to the two transformed strings, the result would correspond to the result of the strcoll function applied to the original strings. Up to n characters are placed in the s1 string, including the terminating null character.

- Return

The function returns the length of the transformed string, excluding the terminating null character. If this value is equal to or greater than n, the contents of the s1 string are indeterminate.

system—Execute command.

```
#include <stdlib.h>
int system(const char *string);
```

- Description

The system function passes the string pointed to by string to a command processor.

- Return

If string is not a null pointer, this function returns an implementation-defined value. If the argument is a null pointer, a non-zero value is returned if a command processor is available.

tan—Trigonometric tangent.

```
#include <math.h>
double tan(double x);
```

- Description

The tan function computes the tangent of x, where x is expressed in radians. A large x value may produce a result with little or no significance.

- Result

  The function returns the tangent value.

tanh—Hyperbolic tangent.

```
#include <math.h>

double tanh(double x);
```

- Description

  The `tanh` function computes the hyperbolic tangent of x.

- Result

  The function returns the hyperbolic tangent value.

time—Determine current calendar time.

```
#include <time.h>

time_t time(time_t *timer);
```

- Description

  The `time` function determines the current calendar time.

- Return

  The function returns the value (`time_t`)-1 if the calendar time is unavailable. If `timer` is not a null pointer and the calendar time is available, the returned time value is stored in the location pointed to by `timer`.

tmpfile—Create a temporary file.

```
#include <stdio.h>

FILE *tmpfile(void);
```

- Description

  The `tmpfile` function creates a temporary binary file. This file is opened for update, `wb+` mode, by the function. The file is deleted when it is closed or the creating program ends.

- Return

  The function returns a stream pointer of structure FILE to the newly created file. A null pointer is returned if the file cannot be created.

tmpnam—Generate temporary file name.

```
#include <stdio.h>

char *tmpnam(char *s);
```

- Description

  The `tmpnam` function generates a string that is a valid file name. This function generates a different string each time it is called. It can be called up to TMP_MAX times. The value of TMP_MAX must be at least 25.

  Files created using the strings from the `tmpnam` function must be deleted by using the `remove` function when they are no longer needed and before the creating program ends.

- Return

If s points to an array of at least L_tmpnam characters, this function writes the generated string in that array and returns s as its value. If s is a null pointer, the generated string is left in an internal static buffer. Subsequent calls may modify the buffer.

tolower—Convert character to lower case.

```
#include <ctype.h>
int tolower(int c);
```

- Description

The tolower function converts an uppercase character, c, to the corresponding lower case character.

- Return

The function returns the corresponding lower case character if the argument is in uppercase; otherwise, the argument character is returned unchanged.

toupper—Convert character to uppercase.

```
#include <ctype.h>
int toupper(int c);
```

- Description

The toupper function converts a lower case character, c, to the corresponding uppercase character.

- Return

The function returns the corresponding uppercase character if the argument is in lower case; otherwise, the argument character is returned unchanged.

ungetc—Push character onto input stream.

```
#include <stdio.h>
int ungetc(int c, FILE *stream);
```

- Description

The ungetc function pushes the character, c, back onto the input stream pointed to by stream. Subsequent reads on the stream will return the pushed-back characters in the reverse order of their being pushed onto the stream. A call to a file positioning function, such as fseek, fsetpos, rewind, or an implementation-defined function, will cause pushed-back characters to be discarded.

The pushing back of one character is guaranteed. You cannot push back onto the stream a character equal to the EOF macro.

The end-of-file indicator is cleared by a successful call to the ungetc function. When you use this function, the value of the file position indicator will depend on the stream type. For a text stream, the value of the file position indicator is unspecified after a successful function call until all pushed-back characters are read or discarded. For a binary stream, the value of the file position indicator is decremented for each successful function call. If the file position indicator value was 0 prior to an `ungetc` function call, the value is indeterminate after the call.

- Return

The function returns the integer argument `c` converted to an unsigned character, if the call was successful. If the operation failed, then EOF is returned.

va_start—Initialize argument pointer.

```
#include <stdarg.h>

void va_start(va_list ap, parmN);
```

- Description

The `va_start` macro initializes `ap`, the argument pointer, for use by other variable argument list access macros. The value of `parmN` is the last of the named parameters in the function argument list. This macro must be invoked before any access is made to the unnamed arguments.

- Return

This macro does not return a value.

va_arg—Get next argument.

```
#include <stdarg.h>

v-type va_arg(va_list ap, v-type);
```

- Description

Every time the `va_arg` macro is invoked, it modifies `ap` so that the next argument in the list is returned. The argument pointer, `ap`, should be the same as that initialized by the `va_start` macro. The `v-type` value is the type of the returned argument and must be written in a form where `v-type*` is the type of a pointer to an object of that type. For example, `int` would be a valid type because `int*` is the type of a pointer to an integer.

- Return

The `va_arg` macro returns the next argument in the argument list.

va_end—End argument processing.

```
#include <stdarg.h>

void va_end(va_list ap);
```

- Description

The `va_end` macro completes the processing of the variable argument list. The argument pointer, `ap`, should be the same as that initialized by the `va_start` macro. If a function is processing a variable argument list and the `va_end` macro is not issued before this function ends, the return behavior is implementation-defined.

- Return

This macro does not return a value.

vfprintf—Write formatted argument to a file.

```
#include <stdarg.h>
#include <stdio.h>
int vfprintf(FILE *stream, const char *format, va_list ap);
```

- Description

The vfprintf function formats and writes the argument pointed to by ap to the output stream pointed to by stream under control of the format string pointed to by format. This function is equivalent to the fprintf function. The argument pointer, ap, must be initialized by the va_start macro, and may be modified by successive invocations of the va_arg macro.

- Return

The function returns the number of characters written to the output stream, if successful. A negative value is returned if an error occurs.

vprintf—Write formatted argument to stdout.

```
#include <stdarg.h>
#include <stdio.h>
int vprintf(const char *format, va_list ap);
```

- Description

The vprintf function formats and writes the argument pointed to by ap to the standard output stream under control of the format string pointed to by format. This function is equivalent to the printf function. The argument pointer, ap, must have been initialized by the va_start macro, and may be modified by successive invocations of the va_arg macro.

- Return

The function returns the number of characters written to the standard output stream, if successful. A negative value is returned if an error occurs.

vsprintf—Write formatted argument to a string.

```
#include <stdarg.h>
#include <stdio.h>
int vsprintf(char *s, const char *format, va_list ap);
```

- Description

The vsprintf function formats and writes the argument pointed to by ap to the array pointed to by s under control of the format string pointed to by format. This function is equivalent to the sprintf function. The argument pointer, ap, must have been initialized by the va_start macro, and may be modified by successive invocations of the va_arg macro.

- Return

The function returns the number of characters written to the array, excluding the terminating null character.

wcstombs—Convert a wide character string.

```
#include <stdlib.h>
size_t wcstombs(char *s, const wchar_t *pwcs, size_t n);
```

- Description

The wcstombs function converts the wide character string pointed to by pwcs to a series of multibyte characters and stores them in the array pointed to by s. The conversion stops if more than n bytes are filled or if a null character is stored. If n is equal to the size of the array pointed to by s, there will not be a terminating null character.

- Return

The function returns the number of bytes of the destination array that were modified, excluding the terminating null character. If the sequence of characters in the input string is invalid, (size_t)-1 is returned.

wctomb—Convert a wide character.

```
#include <stdlib.h>
int wctomb(char *s, wchar_t wchar);
```

- Description

The wctomb function determines how many bytes are needed to represent the wide character whose value is whcar. This converted value is stored in the array pointed to by s. The maximum number of characters that can be stored is limited by the MB_CUR_MAX macro. This macro is defined in the <stdlib.h> header. The wctomb function is left in its initial shift state if the value of wchar is 0 (see following note).

- Return

If s is not a null pointer, the number of bytes that make up the multibyte character corresponding to the value of wchar is returned. If wchar is an invalid multibyte character, -1 is returned.

If s is a null pointer, a non-zero value is returned if the multibyte character encodings have state-dependent encodings or a zero value is returned if the multibyte character encodings do not have state-dependent encodings.

Note: According to the ANSI standard for C, a multibyte character may have *state-dependent encoding*. Each sequence of multibyte characters begin in an *initial shift state* where all single characters have their usual meaning. When specific multibyte characters are encountered, an implementation-defined *shift state* is entered. The characters following are interpreted based on the *shift state*. In an MVS environment, you encounter these *shift states* when dealing with languages that contain more symbols than can be represented by 256 codes. Japanese and Chinese are two such languages and are represented using the Double_Byte Character Set(DBCS).

Glossary

access method A way of transferring data to and from storage devices from and to main storage. In MVS there are a number of access methods. This refers to how record access is managed—sequentially or randomly.

addressing mode (AMODE) A program attribute that indicates the address length used during program execution.

alternate index Key sequenced data set (KSDS) that provides another means of accessing records in a base VSAM file. Its entries are values in a record other than the prime key.

American National Standards Institute (ANSI) A U.S. standards body.

AMODE *See* addressing mode.

ANSI *See* American National Standards Institute.

ASCII American National Standard Code for Information.

batch processing Program execution with little or no user interaction.

binary stream A series of bytes, each representing the full range of the binary numbers. Unlike text stream, during input or output the data is not altered. There is one-to-one correspondence between the characters read or written and the actual data in the external device.

byte A unit of storage consisting of a string of 8 bits.

call-by-reference When calling a function, the address of a variable is passed as an argument. It is possible for the called function to manipulate the content of the variable.

call-by-value When calling a function, the value of a variable is passed as an argument. The content of the variable is not changed by this call.

catalogued procedure A series of JCL statements in a library that can be retrieved by name. It is used to store a commonly used set of job control language (JCL) statements instead of each user creating their own.

CICS *See* Customer Information Control System.

CLIST *See* command list.

command list (CLIST) A series of TSO commands contained in a data set that can be executed via the EXEC command.

compiler A program to translate a program written in a computer language into another program, namely object or assembly. If the conversion is to object program, a linkage editor produces an executable code.

Customer Information Control System (CICS) A general purpose online transaction processing system providing a complete execution environment for programs.

data base management system (DBMS) Software that manages access, creation, deletion, modification, and organization of data.

data component The portion of a VSAM data set that contains the data records.

DATABASE 2 (DB2) A relation data base management system.

DB2 *See* DATABASE 2.

DBMS *See* data base management system.

DD A data definition statement in JCL.

DDNAME A data definition name.

doubleword A memory space comprising of two contiguous words or 8 bytes. Each doubleword addresses as one unit.

dynamic allocation Acquiring a data set by data set name or a volume by volume-serial number instead of using JCL.

EBCDIC Extended binary-coded decimal interchange code. It is a code using 8 bits to represent a charater in IBM mainframe computers.

entry sequenced data set (ESDS) A VSAM data set whose records are stored in the order they are presented. Records are added to the end of the data set.

escape sequence It is a series of characters to represent a control character. In C, it starts with a single quote, followed by a backslash (\) and a character (a,b,f,n,r,t,v,',", or \) and closed with a single quote. For example, escape sequence '\n' represents a cariage return.

ESDS *See* entry sequenced data set.

extended addressing An addressing mode that can access up to 2 gigabytes of data.

fixed-data set A format in which all of the records are of the same length.

floating-point register A register that is 64 bits long and is used to hold data in floating-point format.

fullword *See* word.

function A part of a program, possibly with declarations and statements. It is given a name by which it is invoked. A function may receive parameters, from none to many in numbers, and it can also return a value or pointer.

function prototype A declaration of a function, consisting of storage class, type, identifier, and parameter-list. The identifier and any parameter-list must be included, while the others specifiers are optional.

GDDM *See* Graphical Data Display Manager.

general-purpose register A register that is 32 bits long and can be used for a number of purposes—for example, an index, an accumulator, or a fast data store.

Graphical Data Display Manager (GDDM) A product that mediates the communication between application programs and devices, such as plotters, printers, and terminals.

identifier The name of a data object or function. It can be made of letters, digits, and underscores.

IMS *See* Information Management System.

include file A file to contain a portion of a program that can be included in another program using the preprocessor *#include* directive. There two kinds of include files ones that come with the C compiler and the others that are created by the user.

include library A file to store a system of user include files.

index component The portion of a VSAM data set that establishes the order of the data records. It is used to access records in the data component.

Information Management System (IMS) A hierarchical data base management system.

interactive processing A way of processing data in which the user interacts while the programs are executed.

JCL *See* job control language.

job control language (JCL) A language used to perform the following task enter a job into the system, control the job processing, and request resources.

key sequenced data set (KSDS) A VSAM data set whose records are stored in ascending, collating sequence by key. New records are inserted in key sequence.

KSDS *See* key sequenced data set.

linkage editor A program that creates load modules from object modules or load modules.

load module An executable form of a program.

macro A macro is defined with a preprocessor directive *#define*, followed by an identifier and parameters. When it is used, the preprocessor replaces the arguments with the parameters found in the definition.

memory file A file that resides in memory rather than an external device. Operations can be performed on it, like any other file.

memory allocation To reserve memory space.

memory deallocation To free memory previously allocated.

multitasking When two or more tasks can execute concurrently.

null statement A C statement with a semicolon (;).

null character A binary zero value. It is used as an end-of-string terminator.

NULL pointer A pointer variable that is pointing to no data. It's value is 0.

object module The output of a compiler or an assembler produced by processing a source program.

partitioned data set (PDS) A data set that is made up of a directory and members or partitions.

PDS *See* partitioned data set.

pointer A variable to hold the memory address of another variable.

preprocessor A program that looks for preprocessor directives in a source program, and changes the program if necessary.

prime key A field of more than one character within a record that uniquely identifies that record.

prime index The index component of a key sequenced data set (KSDS).

RBA *See* relative byte address.

reentrancy A program attribute that allows a program to be used by more than one task concurrently.

relative record number (RRN) A number that identifies a slot or record in a relative record data set (RRDS). It is used for record access.

relative byte address (RBA) The offset of a data record from the beginning of a data set. The first byte of the data set is byte 0.

residence mode (RMODE) A program attribute that determines where a program will reside in virtual storage.

RMODE *See* residence mode.

RRDS *See* relative record data set.

RRN *See* relative record number.

run-time library A file or PDS that contains executable programs.

segment The smallest piece of data that can be transferred by a call to IMS.

segment search argument (SSA) The identifier of a segment or group of segments in a call to IMS.

serially reusable A program attribute that allows a program to be used by tasks one at a time.

source library A file or PDS that contains all source programs.

SSA *See* segment search argument.

standard error stream This stream is opened automatically at the start of a C program. It is an output device, associated with stream *stderr*, to direct error messages for certain library functions used in a C program.

standard input stream This stream is opened automatically at the start of a C program. It is an input device, associated with the stream *stdin*, to accept input data for certain library functions used in a C program.

standard output stream This stream is opened automatically at the start of a C program. It is an output device, associated with stream *stdout*, to direct output data for certain library functions used in a C program.

string A sequence of characters terminated with a null character.

string constant Between two double quotes, zero or more characters are enclosed.

supervisor call (SVC) An instruction that stops program execution in order to pass control to a component of the operating system so that it can perform the service specified in the supervisor call.

SVC *See* supervisor call.

task The smallest piece of work that can be managed by the operating system.

text stream A series of characters that form a line. Each line can have zero or more characters terminated with a newline character. During input or output operations on the text stream, library functions may add, alter, or delete some of the special characters. Therefore, there may not be a one-to-one correspondence between the characters read or written and the actual data in the device.

Time Sharing Option (TSO) This product provides an interactive time sharing environment for remote terminal users.

trigraph Some of the characters used in C language are not available in all keyboards. Such characters can be represented by a sequence of three characters entered, called a trigraph. The trigraph is entered in a program where such characters are needed. The following is a list of all trigraph sequences.

??=	#
??(	[
??)	]
??<	{
??>	}
??/	\
??!	|
??-	~

TSO *See* Time Sharing Option.

undefined data set A format in which lengths of data blocks are unknown.

UNIX A multitasking and multi-user operating system developed by AT&T's Bell Laboratories. UNIX was written using the C language. It is used in various computer systems, from micro to mainframe.

variable data set A format in which lengths of records vary. If blocked, the lengths of the blocks may vary. Both records and blocks are preceded by a length field. This length field is included in the length of the record or block.

virtual storage access method (VSAM) A method for accessing fixed-length or variable-length records in an indexed or sequential manner. These records can be organized by physical sequence (ESDS), by a key field (KSDS), or by a relative record number (RRDS).

VSAM *See* virtual storage access method.

word A memory space that is comprised of 4 bytes. Each word must be addressable as one unit.

Bibliography

Dictionary of Computing, Information Processing, Personal Computing, Telecommunications, Office Systems, IBM-specific Terms. 1987. International Business Machines Corporation, 8th Edition. Poughkeepsie, N.Y.

Freedman, Alan. 1989. *The Computer Glossary*, 4th Edition. Point Pleasant, PA: AMACOM.

Hosier, Jeff (Compiler). 1990. *The Handbook of IBM Terminology*. Berkshire, England: Xephon Technology Transfer.

Compilers

Kelly, A.L., and Ira Pohl. 1990. *A Book on C*. Redwood City, CA: The Benjamin/Cummings Publishing Company, Inc.

Kernighan, Brian, and Dennis Ritchie. 1978. *The C Programming Language*. Englewood Cliffs, NJ: Prentice Hall, Inc.

Microsoft. 1990. *Microsoft C Reference*. Redwood, WA: Microsoft Corporation.

Borland. 1987. *Turbo C, User's Guide*. Scotts Valley, CA: Borland International, Inc.

The American National Standards Institute. 1988. *Programming Language C*, Doc. No. X3J11/88-090. Washington, DC.

IBM C/370 User's Guide SC09-1264. Systems Application Architecture Common Programming Interface C Reference—Level 2 SC09-1308.

Whitesmiths, Ltd. *C Compiler User's Guide for MVS, MVS/XA*. Version 3.13. May 1989.

Carmody, M.J., D.W. Mulholland, E.M. Ruest, and G.L. Simmons. February 1, 1989. *Waterloo C Development System Version 3.2 for OS, MVS and MVS/XA User's Guide*. Waterloo, Canada: WATCOM Products Inc.

Carmody, M.J., and D.W. Mulholland. February 1, 1989. *Waterloo C Development System Version 3.2 for OS, MVS and MVS/XA Run-time Library Reference.* Waterloo, Canada: WATCOM Products Inc.

Simmons, G.L. February 1, 1989. *Waterloo C Development System Version 3.2 for OS, MVS and MVS/XA Panel Library Reference.* Waterloo, Canada: WATCOM Products Inc.

SAS Institute Inc. 1989. *SAS/C Compiler and Library User's Guide,* 2nd Edition. Release 4.50. Cari, North Carolina: SAS Institute Inc.

SAS Institute Inc. 1989. *SAS/C Library Reference,* 2nd Edition, Volume 1, Release 4.50. Cari, North Carolina: SAS Institute Inc.

SAS Institute Inc. 1989. *SAS/C Library Reference,* 2nd Edition, Volume 2. Release 4.50. Cari, North Carolina: SAS Institute Inc.

SAS Institute Inc. 1988. *SAS/C Full-Screen Support Library User's Guide.* Release 4.00. Cari, North Carolina: SAS Institute Inc.

VS COBOL II Application Programming Guide for MVS and CMS SC26-4045.
VS COBOL II Application Programming: Sample Programs SC26-4046.
VS COBOL II Application Programming: Language Reference GC26-4047.
Assembler H Version 2 Programming Guide Release 1 SC26-4036.
Assembler H Version 2 Language Reference Release 1 GC26-4037.

Customer Information Control System (CICS)

CICS/ESA 3.1.1 Application Programmer's Reference SC33-0676.
CICS/ESA 3.1.1 Application Programming Guide.

DATABASE 2

DATABASE 2 General Information Manual GC26-4073.
DATABASE 2 Application Programming Guide SC26-4293.
DATABASE 2 SQL Learner's Guide SC26-4082.
DATABASE 2 SQL Reference SC26-4346.

Information Management System (IMS)

IMS/ESA 3.1 Application Programming: Design Guide SC26-4279.
IMS/ESA 3.1 Application Programming: DL/I Calls SC26-4274.
IMS/ESA 3.1 Data Communication Administration Guide SC26-4286.
IMS/ESA 3.1 Application Programming: Data Communication SC26-4283.
IMS/VS 2.2 Application Programming SC26-4178.
IMS/VS 2.2 Data Base Administration Guide SC26-4179.
IMS/VS 2.2 Message Format Service User's Guide SC26-4181.

Interactive System Productivity Facility (ISPF)

ISPF Dialog Management Guide and Reference Version 3 Release 2 for MVS SC34-4266.
ISPF and ISPF PDF Primer Version 3 Release 2 for MVS SC34-4256.
ISPF Dialog Management Examples Version 3 Release 2 for MVS and VM SC34-4265.

Time Sharing Option (TSO)

TSO Extensions 2.2 Command Reference SC28-1881.
TSO Extensions 2.2 User's Guide SC28-1880.

Screen Definition Facility II

SDF II General Information SH19-6457.
SDF II General Introduction Part I SH19-8128.
SDF II General Introduction Part II SH19-8129.
SDF II Reference Information SH19-6454.
SDF II Primer CICS/BMS Programs SH19-6118.
SDF II Primer for ISPF Programs SH19-6119.
SDF II Primer for IMS/MFS Programs SH19-6453.
SDF II Primer for GDDM-IMD SH19-6459.

Graphical Data Display Manager

GDDM Application Programming Guide SC33-0337.
GDDM Base Programming Reference SC33-0332.

Miscellaneous

MVS/DFP 3.3 Linkage Editor and Loader SC26-4564.
MVS/DFP 3.3 Using Data Sets SC26-4749.
MVS/DFP 3.3 Access Method Services for VSAM Catalogs SC26-4570.
MVS/DFP 3.3 Access Method Services for the Integrated Catalog Facility SC26-4562.
MVS/ESA JCL Reference GC28-1654.
MVS/ESA Application Development Guide GC28-1821.
MVS/ESA System Programming Library: Application Development 31-Bit Addressing GC28-1820.

MVS/ESA System Programming Library: Application Development Guide GC28-1852.

MVS/ESA Principles of Operation SA22-7200.

MVS/XA System Programming Library: System Macros and Facilities, Volume 1 GC28-1150 and *Volume 2* GC28-1151.

MVS/XA Data Administration Guide GC26-4140.

MVS/XA VSAM Administration Guide GC26-4151.

MVS/XA Linkage Editor and Loader User's Guide V2R4 GC26-4143.

Index

abort, terminate program abnormally, 259
abs, calculate absolute value, 260
Absolute value
  calculation of, 260, 278
  converting floating-point value to, 266
Access direction, VSAM files, 177
Accessing files
  fixed-length records, 183–185
  variable-length records, 185–186
  VSAM files, 186–190
Access Method Services commands, VSAM file creation, 180–181
Access mode, VSAM files, 176
acos, calculate arc cosine, 260
Addition
  addition operator
    example of use, 118–119
    use of, 55
  example in program, 120
  increment operator, 118–119
Address
  address operator, use of, 53
  errors
    and MVS, different addressing modes, 152
    passing, 148
Addressing mode, program attributes, 164–165
ALLOCATE, 171–172, 180, 183
Alphabetic character, test for, 276
Alphanumeric character, test for, 275–276
Alternate index, and VSAM files, 175
AMODE, 152, 164–165
AND operator, 59, 150
  & operator, 150
  && operators, 150
  errors related to, 150
ANSI
  C standard, 1

functions and ANSI C, 89
Arc cosine, calculation of, 260
Arc sine, calculation of, asin, 261
Arc tangent
  calculation of x, atan, 261
  calculation of y/x, atan2, 261
argc, 82–83
Arguments
  end processing of, 306
  of function call, 90
  get next argument, 306
  initialize argument pointer, 306
  passing
    call-by-value, 90
    reference, 90
  pointers as function arguments, 123–124
    example in program, 124
  of printf function, 90
  write to file, 307
  write to stdout, 307
  write to string, 307
argv, 82–83
Arithmetic conversions, nature of, 63
Arithmetic operations
  and pointers
    comparison and assignment, 122–123
    decrement and subtraction, 120–122
    increment and addition, 118–120
Array element specification, nature of, 49
Arrays, 23–27
  accessing, 25
  allocate memory for, 263
  character array, 24
  compilation of, 24–25
  declaration of, 23–27
    array of characters, 19–20
  indexing, errors in, 147
  initialization of, 26–27

integer array, 23–24
multidimensional array, 25–26
nature of, 23
of pointers, 128–129
  programming errors, 146
single dimensional array, 23–24
storage specifier, 23
type specifier, 23
variable name, 23
ASA files, 96
  escape sequences and control characters of, 96
asctime, convert time to string, 260
asin, calculate arc sine, 260
assert, print diagnostic message, 260
Assignment
  assignment conversions, nature of, 63
  of pointers, 122–123
Assignment operator, 60–61
  compound assignment, 61
  examples of, 61
  simple assignment, 61
Associativity, direction of operation, 45, 46
atan, calculate arc tangent of x, 261
atan 2, calculate arc tangent of y/x, 261
atexit, register program termination function, 262
atof, convert character string to floating-point value, 262
atoi, convert character string to integer value, 262
atol, convert character string to long integer value, 262
ATTACH, 209
ATTRIB, 180
auto, 37, 43, 85
  class specifier, 37
Automatic local variables, 37

INDEX

Basic Mapping Support, CICS, full-screen application development, 228
Batch mode
  compiling program, 14–16
  file creation, non-VSAM files, 180
Binary operators, 54–59
  addition operator, 55
  bitwise AND operator, 57–58
  bitwise exclusive OR operator, 58
  bitwise inclusive OR operator, 58
  division operator, 55
  equality operators, 57
  logical AND operator, 59
  logical OR operator, 59
  multiplication operator, 54–55
  precedence, 54
  relational operators, 57
  remainder operator, 55
  shift operators, 56–57
  subtraction operator, 56
Binary stream, 96
  nature of, 96
Bitfield, 32–33
  example in program, 33
  nature of, 32
  reasons for use of, 32
Bitwise operators
  | operator, 150
  bitwise AND operator, use of, 57–58, 150
  bitwise exclusive OR operator, use of, 58
  bitwise inclusive OR operator, use of, 58
  bitwise negation operator, use of, 52
Blksize, 99, 100, 101
Block of data, read from file, 270–271
Block statement, 64
break statement, 70, 71, 77–78
  example of, 77–78
  form for, 77
  use of, 77
bsearch, search an array, 262–263
Buffers
  buffering control, 291–292, 293
  clear data buffer, 267
  compare two buffers, 282
  copy buffer, 283
  formatted print to buffer, 294
  initialize buffers, 283
  search for in buffer, 282

C/370 compiler, 155–156
  features of, 155–156
  MultiTasking Facility, 165
  See also Interlanguage communication
Call-by-reference, 124
Call-by-value, 90
Calling environment
  restoration of, 280
  saving, 292
calloc, 206
  allocate memory for array, 263
  nature of, 111
Case, 70, 71–72
  case label, 65
  case sensitivity, internal and external names, 9
convert character to uppercase, 305
test for lower case character, 276–277
test for upper case character, 277
Cast operator, use of, 53
CC, 16
ceil, get integer greater than or equal to floating-point value, 263
C for System/370, 156
  features of, 156
char, 19, 20, 24, 41, 42, 84
Character array, 24
Character constant, 11
  examples of, 11
Character handling, library function, 247
Characters, 19–20
  appending to string, 299
  comparing in string, 299
  convert multibyte character, 281–282
  copy to string, 299–300
  declaring array of characters, 19–20
  finding characters in, 300
  finding character within, 295–296
  finding last occurrence in string, 300
  finding outside string, 300
  get character, 267
  get character from file, 274
  get character from standard stream, 274
  initializing character variable, 19–20
  print character, 186–287
  pushing onto input stream, 305
  recognized by C language, 6–7
  search for in buffer, 282
  similarity to integer variable, 19
  for string variables, 20
  test for printable character, 276, 277
  types of data types, 19
  write character to file, 270
Character strings
  convert multibyte character string, 281
  convert to floating-point value, 262
  convert to integer value, 262
  convert to long integer value, 262
  convert wide character string, 308
  finding, 300–301
  get length of multibyte string, 281
CICS and C, 218–223
  accessing CICS resources and facilities, 222
  exception handling, 219–220
  EXEC CICS ADDRESS command, 219
  file access, 220–221
  full-screen application development, 228–230
    Basic Mapping Support, 228
    conversational programming, 228–229
  preparation of C programs for CICS execution, 222
  program termination, 221
  run-time options, 222
  special considerations, 222
  storage management, 220
  unavailable C functions, 221
version for C programming, 218
C language
  benefits of, 1–2
  development of, 1
  elements of
    characters, 6–7
    comments, 8–9
    constants, 10–11
    escape sequences, 7
    identifiers, 9
    language keywords, 9–10
    tokens, 7
    trigraphs, 7
  and portability, 2–3
  programming of, 3
  traditional C, 1
  See also C programming
Class specifier
  auto, 37
  extern, 39–40
  register, 41
  static, 37–38
clearerr, clear error indicators, 263–264
CLIST, 16, 82
  compiling, 158–159
clock, get elapsed time, 264
Close file, 101
  and failure, 101
  form for, 101
  function for, 101
CMOD, 16
COBOL. See Interlanguage communication
Command, execution of, 303
Comma operator, 62
  example in program, 62
  use of, 62
Comments
  example of, 8–9
  nature of, 8
Communication. See Interlanguage communication
Comparison
  double equal sign for, 149
  of pointers, 123
Compilers
  and arrays, 24–25
  C/370, 155–156
  C for System/370, 156
  and precedence, 45
  run-time libraries, 154
  SAS/C compiler, 156–157
  Waterloo C, 154–155
Compiling program
  batch mode, 14–16
  interactive compilation, 16
  with Job Control Language, 159
  with TSO, 158–159
Complex data types, 18
  types of, 18
COMPLINK, 15
Compound assignment, 61
  listing of operators, 61
Concatenation
  of data sets, 214–215
  of strings, 295
Conditional compilation, 136–141
  conditional directives, 136

INDEX

#elif, 139–140
#else, 137–139
#endif, 137–139
#if, 137–139
#ifdef, 140
#ifndef, 140–141
example in program, 137–138
nature of, 135–136
Conditional operator, 59–60
example of use, 60
form for, 60
rules for use, 60
use of, 59–60
const, 42–43
Constant expression, 139
nature of, 46–47
situations for use, 47
Constants
character constant, 11
enumeration constant, 11
floating point constant, 11
integer constant, 10
nature of, 10
string constant, 11
continue statement, 78–79
example in program, 79
form for, 78
use of, 78–79
Control characters, 7
of ASA files, 96
test for, 276
Control statements
block statement, 64
functions of, 64
Null statement, 65
single statement, 64
types of, 65
Conversational programming
CICS
full-screen application development, 228–229
pseudo-conversational application, 229
Conversions, 62–63
arithmetic conversions, 63
assignment conversions, 63
function conversions, 63
type conversions, 63
Copying, reserving storage before, 146
cos, calculate cosine, 264
cosh, calculate hyperbolic cosine, 264
cosine
calculate cosine, 260, 264
hyperbolic cosine, 264
Counter, 40
C programming
advanced
dynamic file allocation, 213–217
multitasking, 205–213
reentrancy, 203–205
compiling program
batch mode, 14–16
interactive compilation, 16
data declaration, 17–18
errors made. See Programming errors
example of basic program, 12–13
source module, 39
testing program, 16

ctime, convert time to a string, 264
ctype.h, macros in, 136

Database 2 and C, 226, 243–245
accessing DBS2, 226, 243
example of use, 243–245
preparation of C programs to access DB2, 226
Structured Query Language (SQL) statements, 243
structure of, 243
Databases
Database, 2, 243–245
Information Management System, 240–243
Data buffer, 113
Data declaration, 17–18
data types, 18–37
declarators, 42–43
form for, 18
initializers, 43
nature of, 17–18
purposes of, 17
storage specifier, 18, 37–41
type specifier, 18
variable list, 18
Data definition name, 98
redirection of streams, 170–171
Data exchange. See Interlanguage communication
Data object, nature of, 46
Data passing, multitasking, 207
Data representation, 4
Data sets
concatenation of, 214–215
name, 98
releasing, 214
Data types, 18–37
arrays, 23–27
characters, 19–20
complex data types, 18
enumerations, 28–29
floating-point variables, 21
integers, 21–23
pointers, 29–30
scalar data types, 18
structures, 30–33
typedef-name, 35–37
unions, 33–35
void type, 23
DATE, 135
library function, 257–258
Decimal constant, 10
examples of, 10
Declarators, 42–43
example in program, 42
form for, 42
function of, 42
Deconcatenation, data sets, 215
Decrement operator, 120–122
and subtraction, 120–122
use of, 51
Default, 70
default label, 65
#define, 133–134
advantages to use, 133
form for, 133
stopping operation of, 133
Delete file, 104

failure, reasons for, 104
remove, 104, 288–289
Diagnostics
library function, 247
print diagnostic message, assert, 261
difftime, calculate time difference, 265
Direct records, 173
div, division, 265
Division
div, 265
division operator, use of, 55
of long integer, 278
double, 21
do/while statement, 76–77
example in program, 76–77
form for, 76
use of, 76
Dynamic file allocation, 182–183, 213–217
allocate/acquire file, 214
concatenation, 214–215
deconcatenation, 215
example of, 215–217
file information retrieval, 215
unallocate/release file, 214
Dynamic memory allocation, 111–117
example in program, 114–117
heap storage, 112
library functions, 111–112
memory file, 112–117

Elements, 30
nature of, 23
#elif, 139–140
#else, 137–139
example in program, 138–139
else statement, 65–66, 67
errors related to, 150–151
dangling else in example program, 151
#endif, 137–139
example in program, 138–139
End of file, test for, 266
Enterprise System Architecture, 164
enum, 28
Enumerations, 28–29
assignment of values, 29
enumeration constant, 11
examples in program, 28–29
examples of, 11
form for, 28
function of, 28
Environment variables, get environment variables, 274
Equality operators, use of, 57
= and ==, 43
and programming errors, 149
#error, 143
Error handling, 171–172
activation of, 171–172
examples of, 172
raise function, 172
signal function, 171–172
termination of, 172
Error messages
getting, 297
printing, 284

INDEX

Errors
  clear error indicators, 263
  library function, 248
Escape characters, of ASA files, 96
Escape sequences, listing of, 7
ESDS, and VSAM files, 175
Exception handling
  CICS and C, 219-220
  Information Management System and C, 224-225
  multitasking, 207
EXEC CICS ADDRESS command, 219
EXEC statement, 15
  JCL, 163
Execution of program
  error handling, 171-172
    examples of, 172
    raise function, 172
    signal function, 171-172
  and Job Control Language, 169
  preparation of programs
    linking, 160-164
    module replacement, 165-166
    program attributes, 164-165
  redirection of standard streams, 169-171
    data definition name association, 170-171
    freopen function, 169-170
    redirection symbols, 170
  run-time options, 167-168
  and TSO, 168-169
exit, terminate program, 265
exp, exponential function, 265-266
Exponential function, exp, 265-266
Expressions
  classes of, 44
  constant expression, 46-47
  lvalue expression, 46
  nature of, 44
  primary expression, 48-49
Extended addressing, 164
extern, 37, 39-40, 83, 84
  class specifier, 39-40

fabs, convert floating-point value to absolute value, 266
fclose, 101
  close a stream, 266
  form for, 101
fdelrec, 178
feof, test for end of file, 266
ferror, test read/write error, 266-267
fflush, 95
  clear data buffer, 267
fgetc, get character, 267
fgetpos, 95
  get file position, 267
fgets, get string, 267-268
Field, 30
FILE, 97, 135, 142
File access
  CICS and C, 220-221
  in MVS, 4
File access functions, 97-104
  close file, 101
  memory file, 103-104
  open file, 97-101

  read and write file, 102-103
File allocation, 182-183
  dynamic allocation, 182-183
  Job Control Language, 182
  TSO, 183
  See also Dynamic file allocation
File handle, 97-98
  function of, 97-98
File information retrieval, 215
File I/O, 106-108
  example in program, 107
  fprintf, 106-108
  fscanf, 106-108
Filename
  forms of, 98-99, 104
  renaming file, 105, 289
  temporary, 304-305
File operations, 104-105
  delete file, 104
  rename file, 105
  temporary file, 105
File positioning
  file-position indicator, 97
    setting, 273
  get file position, 267, 273
  VSAM files, 177-178
File processing, VSAM files, 186-190
Files, 96-97
  and stream, 96-97
First, 40, 43
Fixed-length files
  accessing, 183-185
  non-VSAM files, 174
Float, 21, 24, 41, 84
Floating-point constant, 11
  examples of, 11
Floating-point limits, library function, 248
Floating-point remainder, 268
Floating-point value
  break down of, 284
  conversion from absolute value, 266
  decompose floating-point value, 271
  get integer less than or equal to floating-point value, 268
Floating-point variables, 21
  declaration of, 21
  example in program, 21
floor, get integer less than or equal to floating-point value, 268
fmod, floating-point remainder, 268
fopen, 97-101, 102
  and file handle, 97-98
  filename of, 98-99
  form for, 97
  mode of, 99
  in MVS, 97-101
  open file, 268-269
for statement
  example in programs, 73, 74
  form for, 72
  use of, 72-74
fprintf, 106-108
  write formatted string to file, 269-270
fputc, write character to file, 270
fputs, write string to file, 270
fread, 102-103
  read block of data from file, 270-271

free, 171
  nature of, 112
  release memory, 271
freopen, redirection of streams, 169-170, 271
frewind, 95
frexp, decompose floating-point value, 271
fscanf, 106-108
  read formatted data from file, 272
fseek, 95
  move file pointer, 272
fsetpos, 95
  set file-position indicator, 273
ftell, 95
Full-screen application development
  Customer Information Control System, 228-230
  Interactive System Productivity Facility, 234-237
  SAS/C, 239
  Waterloo C Panel Library, 237-239
Function call, nature of, 48-49
Function conversions, nature of, 63
Function definition, 83-88
  example in program, 83-84, 86-87
  form for, 83
  function name, 84-85
  header, 88
  parameter declaration list, 87-88
  parameter list, 85-86
  storage class, 83-84
Function name, function definition, 84-85
Function pointers, 125-127
  declaration of, 125
  example in program, 126
Function prototype, 88-89
  examples of, 89
  form for, 88
Functions
  and ANSI C, 89
  beginning of execution of, 89
  function call
    as argument, 90
    example in program, 89-90
  functions of, 81
  guidelines for use of, 81
  and include file, 89
  main function, 81-83
  and pointers
    as function arguments, 123-124
    function returning pointers, 124-125
    pointer to a function, 125-127
  recursion, 92-93
  return statement, 91
  termination of, 91
fwrite, 102-103
  write data to file, 273-274

getc, get character from file, 274
getchar, get character from standard stream, 274
getenv, get environment variables, 274
gets, get line from standard stream, 275
global initializers, 43
gmtime, convert calendar time, 275
goto statement, 79-80

example in program, 80
form for, 79
use of, 79

Header
  function definition, 88
  See also #include
HEAP, 112
  at run-time, 167
Heap storage, 112
  controlling size of, 112
  Initial Storage Area, 206
Hexadecimal character, test for, 277
Hexadecimal constant, 10
  examples of, 10
Hyperbolic cosine, calculation of, 264
Hyperbolic sine, 294

Identifiers
  length limitations, 9
  nature of, 9
#if, 137–139
  example in program, 138–139
#ifdef, 140
If-else-if-ladder, 68–69
  example in program, 69
  form for, 68
  use of, 68
#ifndef, 140–141
if statement, 65–69
  example in program, 66, 67
  form for, 65
  if-else-if-ladder, 68–69
  nested ifs, 67–68
  use of, 65–67
#include, 130–133
  for character handling, 247
  for commonly used definitions, 252
  contents of include file, 131
  for diagnostics, 247
  double quotation marks with, 132
  for errors, 248
  example in program, 131–132
  for floating-point limits, 248
  form for, 130
  for input and output, 252–254
  for integer limits, 248
  for localization, 249
  for mathematics, 249–251
  and MVS naming conventions, 132
  for nonlocal jump, 251
  for signal handling, 251
  single quotation marks with, 132
  for strings, 256–257
  for time and date, 257–258
  for utilities, 254–256
  for variable arguments, 252
Include library, nature of, 6
Increment operator, 118–119
  and addition, 118–119
  use of, 50
Indexing
  alternate index, 175
  arrays, 147
Indirection operator, 119
  use of, 53, 119
Information about file, retrieval of, 215
Information Management System and C, 223–226, 240–243

accessing database, 223–224, 242
exception handling, 224–225
extended addressing, 224
full-screen application development
  example program, 231–234
  Message Format Services, 230–31
program communication block, 241–242
program termination, 225
segments of, 241
structure of, 240–241
Structure Query Language (SQL)
  statements, 230–234
types of databases, 242
Initializers, 43
  example in program, 43
  function of, 43
  global initializers, 43
  local initializers, 43
Initial Storage Area, 206
Input and output
  ASA file, 96
  binary stream, 96
  buffering for stream processing, 95
  direct I/O, 178
  file access functions, 97–104
  file operations, 104–105
  files, 96–97
  formatted
    file I/O, 106–108
    standard I/O streams, 105–106
  library function, 252–254
  multitasking, 207
  and portability, 94, 95
  and standard library, 94
  streams, 95–96
  text stream, 95–96
  unformatted
    example in program, 108–109
    functions for, 108
INSPECT, testing program, 16
Instance memory, 113
int, 17–18, 32, 41, 84, 85
Integer constants, 10
  decimal constant, 10
  hexadecimal constant, 10
  octal constant, 10
Integer limits, library function, 248
Integers, 21–23
  conversion from character strings, 262
  declaration of, 21–22
  example in program, 22–23
  get integer greater than or equal to floating-point value, 263
  integer array, 23–24
  listing of type/storage size/range of data types, 22
  random
    generation of, 288
    seed for generation, 295
Interactive compilation, compiling program, 16
Interactive System Productivity Facility, 186
  full-screen application development, 234–237
  elements of dialog, 234–235
  example of program, 236–237

Interlanguage communication
  C/370 compiler, 192–196
    compatible data types, 193
    examples of, 193–196
    management of C environment, 193
    registers at routine entry, 182
    registers at routine exit, 193
    special considerations, 196
  COBOL, 196–199
    COBOL to C, 197–198
    compatible data types, 197
    creation of COBOL environment, 196–197
    special considerations, 198–199
  data exchange, 191
  FORTRAN, 200–202
    compatible data types, 201–202
    creation of FORTRAN environment, 201
    special considerations, 202
  linkage pragma, 192
  PL/I, 199–200
    compatible data types, 200, 201
    creation of PL/I environment, 200
    special considerations, 200
ISAINC, at run-time, 168
isalnum, test for alphanumeric character, 136, 275–276
isalpha, test for alphabetic character, 136, 276
ISASIZE, at run-time, 168
iscntrl, test for control character, 136, 276
isdigit, test for numeric character, 136, 276
isgraph, test for printable character, 136, 276
islower, test for lower case character, 136, 276–277
isprint, test for printable character (including space), 136, 277
ispunct, test for punctuation character, 136, 277
isspace, test for white space character, 136, 277
isupper, test for upper case character, 136, 277
isxdigit, test for hexadecimal character, 136, 277

Job Control Language
  compiling with, 159
  example of, 14–15
  execution of program, 169
  file allocation, 182
  file creation, VSAM files, 181–182
  linking with, 162–164
  program execution under, 169
  statements
    EXEC statement, 163
    SYSLIN DD statement, 163
    SYSLMOD DD statement, 163
    SYSPRINT DD statement, 163
    SYSUT1 DD statement, 163
JOB statement, 15

Keywords, 9–10
  listing of, 9

INDEX

KSDS, 178, 181, 186
  and VSAM files, 175

Labels
  case label, 65
  default label, 65
  nature of, 65
  plain label, 65
labs, calculate long absolute value, 278
Last, 43
ldexp, multiply value by power of 2, 278
ldiv, division of long integer, 278
Libraries
  file
    include library, 6
    load library, 6
    object library, 6
    run-time library, 6
    source library, 5–6
Library functions, 4, 111–112
  calloc function, 111
  free function, 112
  malloc function, 111
  notation conventions of functions, 246
  realloc function, 111–112
  returning pointers, 125
  tasks
    character handling, 247
    commonly used functions, 252
    diagnostics, 247
    errors, 248
    floating-point limits, 248
    input and output, 252–254
    integer limits, 248
    localization, 249
    mathematics, 249–251
    nonlocal jump, 251
    signal handling, 251
    strings, 256–257
    time and date, 257–258
    utilities, 254–256
    variable arguments, 252
  See also Run-time library functions
#line, 142–143
LINE, 135, 142
#line, 142–143
LINE, 135, 142
Line renumbering, 142–143
  example in program, 142–143
Linkage editor, 160–161
  functions of, 160–161
Link-edit, 16, 39
Linking
  with Job Control Language, 162–164
  with TSO, 161–162
Load library, nature of, 6
Load module
  program attributes, 164–165
  subtask load module, 208
localeconv, get locale settings, 278–279
Locale settings
  getting, 278–279
  set current locale, 292
Local initializers, 43
Localization, library function, 249
localtime, convert time, 279–280
Local variable
  automatic local variables, 37

  declaration of, 37
  static local variables, 37–38
log, calculate natural log, 280
log10, calculate log base 10, 280
Logical operators
  || operator, 150
  AND operator, use of, 59, 150
  negation operator, use of, 52
  OR operator, use of, 59
long double, 21
longjmp, restore calling environment, 280
lrecl, 99, 100, 101
lvalue expression, nature of, 46

Macros, 134–136
  in ctype.h, 136
  example in program, 134
  form for, 134
  predefined macros, 135–136
  usefulness of, 135
main function, 40, 81–83, 111
  example in program, 82
  and function call, 89
  parameters of, 82
  rules related to, 82
malloc, 146, 206
  nature of, 111
  reserve memory, 280–281
Mathematics, library function, 249–251
mblem, get length of multibyte character string, 281
mbstowcs, convert multibyte character string, 281
mbtowx, convert multibyte character, 281–282
Members, 30
memchr, search for character in buffer, 282
memcmp, compare two buffers, 282–283
memcpy, copy buffer, 283
memmove, copy buffer, 283
Memory
  reserve memory, 280–281
  See also Dynamic memory allocation
Memory file, 103–104, 112–117
  example of use, 113–114
  fopen, 103–104
  form for, 103
  functions of, 112–113
  guidelines for use, 104
  instance memory, 113–114
memset, initialize buffer, 283
Message Format Services, Information Management System, full-screen application development, 230–31
mfist, 124
mfp, 104
mktime, convert to local time, 283
mode, 99
modf, break down floating-point value, 284
Modularity, of C, 2
Module replacement, example of, 165–166
Multiply
  multiplication operator, use of, 54–55
  value by power of 2, 278

Multitasking, 205–213
  data passing, 207
  example of, 210–213
  exceptional condition handling, 207
  input and output, 207
  Multitasking Facility, 205
    task attach function, 209
    task detach function, 210
    task scheduling function, 209–210
    task synchronization function, 210
  redirection of streams, 207
  special considerations, 208–209
  storage allocation, 206
  structure of, 205–206
  subtask load module, 208
  use of, 205
MVS, 3, 4
  accessing files
    fixed-length files, 183–185
    variable-length files, 185–186
    VSAM files, 186–190
  addressing modes, and different versions, 152
  compiling with Job Control Language, 159
  file access in, 4
  file allocation, 182–183
  open file, 101
  virtual storage access method (VSAM files), 174–178, 180–181

Nested ifs, 67–68
  form for, 67
  use of, 67
Nonlocal jump, library function, 251
Non-VSAM files
  file creation, 179–180
    batch file creation, 179
    TSO file creation, 180
  organization of, 173–174
  record formats, 174
    fixed-length files, 174
    undefined files, 174
    variable-length files, 174
Not editable attribute, 165
NULL, 20, 96
NULL directive, 141
Null statement, 65
Number, 37

Object library, nature of, 6
Octal constants, 10
  examples of, 10
oldname, 105
Open file, 97–101
  function options, 97, 100
  legal values of open status, 99
  in MVS, 101
  redirect, 271
  VSAM files, 177
Operating system
  multi-tasking vs. single tasking, 3–4
  See also MVS
Operators
  assignment operators, 60–61
  binary operators, 54–59
  classes of, 44
  comma operator, 62
  conditional operators, 59–60

INDEX

conversions, 62–63
nature of, 44
unary operators, 49–54
OR operator, 59

Parameter declaration list, function definition, 87–88
Parameter list, function definition, 85–86
Parenthesized expression, nature of, 48
Partitioned data set, 4, 6
Partitioned records, 173
perror, print error message, 284
Plain label, 65
PL/I. *See* Interlanguage communication
Pointers, 29–30, 84
  arithmetic operations, 118–123
    comparison and assignment, 122–123
    decrement and subtraction, 120–122
    increment and addition, 118–120
  and arrays, 25, 128–129
  and C programming, 29
  declaration of, 29–30
  dynamic memory allocation, 111–117
  example in program, 120
  function of, 29
  and functions
    as function arguments, 123–124
    function returning pointers, 124–125
    pointer to a function, 125–127
  move file pointer, 272–273
  programming errors, 144–146
    pointer and array, 146
    pointer and string, 146
    uninitialized pointer, 144–145
  and strings, 127–128
  uninitialized, 144–145
    example in program, 145
Portability
  advantages of, 2–3
  examples of, 2
  and input and output, 94, 95
  # operator, 141–142
  ## operator, 142
pow, calculate power, 284
Power, calculation of, 284
#pragma, 141
  and reentrancy, 204–205
Precedence, 45–46
  changing, 45, 48
  order of operations, 45, 46
Predefined macros, 135–136
  example in program, 135–136
  listing of, 135
Preprocessor
  benefits of use, 130
  conditional compilation, 136–141
  macros, 134–136
Preprocessor directives
  #define, 133–134
  #error, 143
  #include, 130–133
  #line, 142–143
  NULL directive, 141
  operator #, 141–142
  operator ##, 142

#pragma, 141
#undef, 134
Primary expression
  array element specification, 49
  function call, 48–49
  nature of, 48–49
  parenthesized expression, 48
  structure and union specifications, 49
printf, 18, 28, 31, 89, 127
  arguments of, 90
  failure of, 147
  print formatted data, 285–286
  for standard output stream, 105–106
Program attributes, 164–165
  addressing mode, 164–165
  not editable attribute, 165
  residency mode, 164–165
  reusability attributes, 165
Programming
  aspects of
    database, 4
    data representation, 4
    file access, 4
    operating systems, 3–4
    processing speed, 4
    user interfaces, 4
  See also C programming
Programming errors
  addressing mode errors, 152
  array indexing, 147
  case sensitivity, 148–149
  misuse of & and |, 150
  misuse of else, 150–151
  misuse of equal sign, 149
  passing address, 148
  with pointers, 144–146
    pointer and array, 146
    pointer and string, 146
    uninitialized pointer, 144–145
  string and characters, 147–148
Programming languages. *See* Interlanguage communication
Pseudo-conversational application, conversational programming, CICS, 229
Punctuation character, test for, 277
putc, print character, 286–287
putchar, print character to standard output, 287
puts, print string, 287

qsort, sort array, 287
Quotes
  double quotation marks, 132
  double quotes, 19
  single quotation marks, 132
  single quotes, 19

raise
  error handling, 172
  send signal, 288
rand, generate random integer, 288
Random integer
  generation of, 288
  seed for, 295
Read and write file, 102–103
  example in program, 102–103
  form for, 102

fread, 102–103
functions for, 102–103
fwrite, 102–103
guidelines for use, 103
Read/write error, test for, 266
realloc, 206
  change storage size, 288
  nature of, 111–112
recfm, 100, 101
Record format, VSAM files, 177
recp, 85
Recursion, 92–93
  example in program, 92
  nature of, 92
  reason for use, 93
  use of, 92–93
Redirection of streams, 169–171
  data definition name association, 170–171
  freopen function, 169–170
  multitasking, 207
  redirection symbols, 170
Reentrancy, 203–205
  creating reentrant program, 204
  pragma, use of, 204–205
Reference, argument passing, 90
register, 37, 85
  class specifier, 41
Relational operators, use of, 57
Remainder operator, use of, 55
remove, 104
  delete file, 288–289
rename file, 105
  form for, 105
  newname, 105
  oldname, 105
  rename, 105, 289
REPORT, 112
  at run-time, 168
Residency mode, program attributes, 164–165
return statement, 91
  examples of, 91
  form for, 91
  and function, 91
Reusability attributes, 165
  reenterable attribute, 165
  serially reusable attribute, 165
rewind, set file position indicator, 289
RMODE, 164–165
RRDS, 178
  and VSAM files, 175
Run-time libraries
  compilers, 154
  nature of, 6
Run-time library functions
  abort, terminate program abnormally, 259
  abs, calculate absolute value, 260
  acos, calculate arc cosine, 260
  asctime, convert time to string, 260
  asin, calculate arc sine, 260
  assert, print diagnostic message, 260
  atan, calculate arc tangent of x, 261
  atan 2, calculate arc tangent of y/x, 261
  atexit, register program termination function, 262
  atof, convert character string to

INDEX

Run-time library functions *(continued)*
  floating-point value, 262
  atoi, convert character string to integer value, 262
  atol, convert character string to long integer value, 262
  bsearch, search an array, 262–263
  calloc, allocate memory for array, 263
  ceil, get integer greater than or equal to floating-point value, 263
  clearerr, clear error indicators, 263–264
  clock, get elapsed time, 264
  cos, calculate cosine, 264
  cosh, calculate hyperbolic cosine, 264
  ctime, convert time to a string, 264
  difftime, calculate time difference, 265
  div, division, 265
  exit, terminate program, 265
  exp, exponential function, 265–266
  fabs, convert floating-point value to absolute value, 266
  fclose, close a stream, 266
  feof, test for end of file, 266
  ferror, test read/write error, 266–267
  fflush, clear data buffer, 267
  fgetc, get character, 267
  fgetpos, get file position, 267
  fgets, get string, 267–268
  floor, get integer less than or equal to floating-point value, 268
  fmod, floating-point remainder, 268
  fopen, open file, 268–269
  fprintf, write formatted string to file, 269–270
  fputc, write character to file, 270
  fputs, write string to file, 270
  fread, read block of data from file, 270–271
  free, release memory, 271
  freopen, redirect open file, 271
  frexp, decompose floating-point value, 271
  fscanf, read formatted data from file, 272
  fseek, move file pointer, 272
  fsetpos, set file-position indicator, 273
  fwrite, write data to file, 273–274
  getc, get character from file, 274
  getchar, get character from standard stream, 274
  getenv, get environment variables, 274
  gets, get line from standard stream, 275
  gmtime, convert calendar time, 275
  isalnum, test for alphanumeric character, 275–276
  isalpha, test for alphabetic character, 276
  iscntrl, test for control character, 276
  isdigit, test for numeric character, 276
  isgraph, test for printable character (excluding space), 276
  islower, test for lower case character, 276–277
  isprint, test for printable character (including space), 277
  ispunct, test for punctuation character, 277
  isspace, test for white space character, 277
  isupper, test for upper case character, 277
  isxdigit, test for hexadecimal character, 277
  labs, calculate long absolute value, 278
  ldexp, multiply value by power of 2, 278
  ldiv, division of long integer, 278
  localeconv, get locale settings, 278–279
  localtime, convert time, 279–280
  log10, calculate log base 10, 280
  log, calculate natural log, 280
  longjmp, restore calling environment, 280
  malloc, reserve memory, 280–281
  mblem, get length of multibyte character string, 281
  mbstowcs, convert multibyte character string, 281
  mbtowx, convert multibyte character, 281–282
  memchr, search for character in buffer, 282
  memcmp, compare two buffers, 282–283
  memcpy, copy buffer, 283
  memmove, copy buffer, 283
  memset, initialize buffer, 283
  mktime, convert to local time, 283
  modf, break down floating-point value, 284
  perror, print error message, 284
  pow, calculate power, 284
  printf, print formatted data, 285–286
  putc, print character, 286–287
  putchar, print character to standard output, 287
  puts, print string, 287
  qsort, sort array, 287
  raise, send signal, 288
  rand, generate random integer, 288
  realloc, change storage size, 288
  remove, delete file, 288–289
  rename, rename file, 289
  rewind, set file position indicator, 289
  scanf, formatted read data, 289–291
  setbuf, buffering control, 291–292
  setjmp, save calling environment, 292
  setlocal, set current locale, 292
  setvbuf, buffering control, 293
  signal, signal handling, 293–294
  sin, trigonometric sine, 294
  sinh, hyperbolic sine, 294
  sprintf, formatted print to buffer, 294
  sqrt, compute square root, 294
  srand, seed for random integer generation, 295
  sscanf, read data from string, 295
  strcat, concatenate strings, 295
  strchr
    find character within string, 295–296
    find last occurrence of character in string, 300
  strcmp, compare strings, 296
  strcoll, compare strings using collating sequence, 296–297
  strcpy, copy strings, 296
  strcspn, find characters within string, 296
  strerror, get error message, 297
  strftime, convert time to string, 297–298
  strlen, compute string length, 298–299
  strncat, append characters to string, 299
  strncmp, compare characters in strings, 299
  strncpy, copy characters to string, 299–300
  strpbrk, find character within string, 300
  strspn, find characters outside string, 300
  strstr, find character string, 300–301
  strtod, convert string to double, 301
  strtok, convert string to tokens, 302
  strtol, convert string to long, 301–302
  strtoul, convert string to unsigned long integer, 302–303
  strxfrm, transform strings, 303
  system, execute command, 303
  tan, trigonometric tangent, 303–304
  tanh, hyperbolic tangent, 304
  time, determine current calendar time, 304
  tmpfile, create temporary file, 304
  tmpnam, generate temporary file name, 304–305
  tolower, convert character to lower case, 305
  toupper, convert character to upper case, 305
  ungetc, push character onto input stream, 305–306
  va_arg, get next argument, 306
  va_end, end argument processing, 306
  va_start, initialize argument pointer, 306
  vfprintf, write formatted argument to file, 307
  vprintf, write formatted argument to stdout, 307
  vsprintf, write formatted argument to string, 307
  wcstombs, convert wide character string, 308
  wctomb, convert wide character, 308
Run-time options, 167–168
  CICS and C, 222
  HEAP, 167
  ISAINC, 168
  ISASIZE, 168
  REPORT, 168

SPIE, 168
STAE, 168

SAS/C compiler, 156–157
  features of, 157
  full-screen application development, 239
Scalar data types, 18
  types of, 18
scanf, 66
  formatted read data, 289–291
Sequential file, 4
Sequential records, 173
setbuf, buffering control, 291–292
setjmp, save calling environment, 292
setlocal, set current locale, 292
setvbuf, buffering control, 293
Shift operators, use of, 56–57
SIGABRT, 171
SIGFPE, 171
SIGILL, 171
SIGINT, 171
Signal function, 171–172
  ANSI defined signal values, 171
  sending signal, 288
  signal handling, 251, 293–294
Signed, 32
signed char, 19
SIGSEGV, 171
SIGTERM, 171
Simple assignment, 61
sine
  calculation of, 261
  hyperbolic sine, 294
  trigonometric sine, 294
Single statement, 64
sinh, hyperbolic sine, 294
sizeof operator
  example in program, 54
  use of, 53–54
Sorting, arrays, 287
Source library, nature of, 6
Source module, 39
Speed of processing, 4
SPIE, at run-time, 168
sprintf, formatted print to buffer, 294
sqrt, compute square root, 294
square root, computation of, 294
srand, seed for random integer generation, 295
sscanf, read data from string, 295
STAE, at run-time, 168
Standard library, and input and output, 94
Standard output stream
  example in program, 106
  printf, 105–106
Statements, 72–74
  break statement, 77–78
  continue statement, 78–79
  do/while statement, 76–77
  goto statement, 79–80
  if statement, 65–69
  for statement, 72–74
  switch statement, 69–72
  while statement, 75–76
static, 37–38, 42, 83, 84
  class specifier, 37–38
Static local variables, 37–38

STDC, 135
stderr, 97, 108
stdin, 97, 108
stdout, 97, 108
Storage allocation, multitasking, 206
Storage class, function definition, 83–84
Storage size, changing, 288
Storage specifier, 18, 37–41
  arrays, 23
  class specifier
    auto, 37
    extern, 39–40
    register, 41
    static, 37–38
strcat, concatenate strings, 295
strchr
  find character within string, 295–296
  find last occurrence of character in string, 300
strcmp, compare strings, 127, 296
strcoll, compare strings using collating sequence, 296–297
strcpy, 127, 128, 146
  copy strings, 296
strcspn, find characters within string, 296
Streams, 95–96
  ASA files, 96
  binary streams, 96
  close stream, 266
  get line from standard stream, 275
  redirection of
    data definition name association, 170–171
    freopen function, 169–170
    and multitasking, 207
    redirection symbols, 170
  standard I/O streams, 105–106
  text streams, 95–96
strerror, get error message, 297
strftime, convert time to string, 297–298
strlen, compute string length, 298–299
String constants, 11
  examples of, 11
Strings
  appending characters to, 299
  comparing characters in, 299
  comparison of, 296
  compute string length, 298–299
  concatenation of, 295
  converting to double, 301
  converting to long, 301–302
  converting to long unsigned integer, 302
  converting to tokens, 302
  copy characters to, 299–300
  finding characters in, 300
  finding characters outside of string, 300
  finding character within, 295–296
  finding last occurrence of character in, 300
  get string, 267
  library function, 256–257
  and pointers, 127–128
    programming errors, 146
  printing, 287
  read data from string, 295
  transforming strings, 303

write string to file, 270
strncat, append characters to string, 299
strncmp, compare characters in strings, 299
strncpy, copy characters to string, 299–300
strpbrk, find character within string, 300
strspn, find characters outside string, 300
strstr, find character string, 300–301
strtod, convert string to double, 301
strtok, convert string to tokens, 302
strtol, convert string to long, 301–302
strtoul, convert string to unsigned long integer, 302–303
struct, 30–32
Structure and union specifications, nature of, 49
Structured Query Language (SQL) statements, 226
  Database 2, 243
  Information Management System, 230–234
Structures, 30–33
  bitfield, 32–33
  declaration of, 30–31
  example in program, 31–32
  and members, 30
strxfrm, transform strings, 303
Subtraction
  decrement operator, 120–122
  example in program, 122
  subtraction operator, use of, 56
sum function, 89
Supervisor call, 213
swap, 144–145
switch statement, 69–72, 76, 148–149
  example in program, 70–71
  form for, 70
  use of, 69–72
SYSLIN DD statement, JCL, 163
SYSLMOD DD statement, JCL, 163
SYSPRINT DD statement, JCL, 163
System, execute command, 303
Systems Application Architecture
  nature of, 3
  and software development, 3
SYSUT1 DD statement, JCL, 163

Tangent
  tan, trigonometric tangent, 303–304
  tanh, hyperbolic tangent, 304
tanh, hyperbolic tangent, 304
Task attach, 209
Task detach, 210
Task scheduling, 209–210
Task synchronization, 210
Temporary file, 105
  creating, 105, 304
  tmpfile, 105
  tmpnam, 105
Temporary filename, 304–305
Terminate program
  abort, 259
  register program termination function, atexit, 262
Testing program, INSPECT, 16
Text stream, 95–96

nature of, 95–96
TIME, 135
  calculation of time difference, 265, 2651339
  convert calendar time, 275
  convert time, 279
  convert to local time, 283–284
  convert to string, 260, 264, 297
  determine current calendar time, 304
  get elapsed time, 264
Time and date, library function, 257–258
tinit function, 209
tmpfile, create temporary file, 105, 304
tmpnam, generate temporary file name, 105, 304–305
Tokens, converting strings to, 302
tolower, convert character to lower case, 136, 305
toupper, convert character to upper case, 136, 305
Trigraphs, listing of trigraph sequences, 7
tsched function, 209–210
TSO
  compiling, 158–159
  execution of program, 168–169
  file allocation, 183
  linking with, 161–162
  non-VSAM file creation, 180
  program execution under, 168–169
tsyncro function, 210
tterm function, 210
Type conversions, 63
Typedef-name, 35–37
  example in program, 36
  form for, 35
  function of, 35–36
Type specifier, 18, 30
  arrays, 23

Unary minus operator, use of, 51–52
Unary operators, 49–54
  address operator, 53
  bitwise negation operator, 52
  cast operator, 53
  decrement operator, 51
  increment operator, 50
  indirection operator, 53
  logical negation operator, 52
  nature of, 49
  sizeof operator, 53–54
  unary minus operator, 51–52
  unary plus operator, 51
Unary plus operator, use of, 51
#undef, 134
  use of, 134
Undefined files, non-VSAM files, 174
Unformatted I/O, 108–109
  example in program, 108–109
  functions for, 108
ungetc, push character onto input stream, 305–306
union keyword, 34
Unions, 33–35
  declaration of, 34
  example in program, 35
  form for, 33
  function of, 33
unsigned, 32
unsigned char, 19
Utilities, library function, 254–256

va_arg, get next argument, 306
va_end, end argument processing, 306
Variable arguments, library function, 252
Variable-length files
  accessing, 185–186
  non-VSAM files, 174
Variable-list, 18, 30
  function of, 28
Variable name, arrays, 23
Variables
  storage specifier, 37–41
  See also Local variables
va_start, initialize argument pointer, 306
vfprintf, write formatted argument to file, 307

Virtual storage access method (VSAM files), 174–178, 180–181
  accessing, 186–190
  alternate index, 175
  direct input and output, 178
  file access, 176–177
    access direction, 177
    access mode, 176
    OPEN example, 177
    record format, 177
  file creation, 180–182
    Access Method Services commands, 180–181
    Job Control Language, 181–182
  file positioning, 177–178
  file processing, 186–190
  record management
    ESDS, 175
    KSDS, 175
    RRDS, 175
  selection of file type, 176
  See also Non-VSAM files
void, 23, 84, 91
void type, 23
vprintf, write formatted argument to stdout, 307
VSAM, 4
vsprintf, write formatted argument to string, 307

Waterloo C, 154–155
  features of, 154–155
  Waterloo C Panel Library, full-screen application development, 237–239
wcstombs, convert wide character string, 308
wctomb, convert wide character, 308
while statement, 75–76
  example in program, 75
  form for, 75
  use of, 75
White space, test for, 277
Writable static, 204, 206
Write data to file, 273–274